HOW
DO YOU KNOW
HE'S REAL?

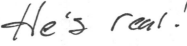

To John & Kim –
He's real!

To John + Kim,

He's real!

[signature]

HOW
DO YOU KNOW
HE'S REAL?

Celebrity Reflections on Christ

AMY HAMMOND HAGBERG

Author's photograph on the back cover courtesy of Jackie Vaughan

Destiny Image® Publishers, Inc.

P.O. Box 310
Shippensburg, PA 17257-0310

"Speaking to the Purposes of God for This Generation
and for the Generations to Come"

For Worldwide Distribution, Printed in the U.S.A.

ISBN 10: 0-7684-2332-5

ISBN 13: 978-0-7684-2332-7

This book and all other Destiny Image, Revival Press, MercyPlace, Fresh Bread, Destiny Image Fiction, and Treasure House books are available at Christian bookstores and distributors worldwide.

For a U.S. bookstore nearest you, call
1-800-722-6774.

For more information on foreign distributors, call
717-532-3040.

Or reach us on the Internet:
www.destinyimage.com

1 2 3 4 5 6 7 8 9 10 11 / 09 08 07 06

Acknowledgments

THIS book is dedicated to my Lord and Savior Jesus Christ, with whom all things are possible. This has been an incredible journey.

To my husband Craig—I am overwhelmed with gratitude for your love, support, and encouragement during this long and sometimes daunting project. Your unwavering faith and sacrificial spirit are a constant source of inspiration for me. I'm crazy about you.

To our children, Kaia and Connor—thanks for hanging in there with joyful hearts. I know it hasn't always been easy. I couldn't have asked for better cheerleaders.

To the participants—I offer a special thank you to my brothers and sisters in Christ who shared their stories with me, resulting in the book you are about to experience. Together we laughed, we cried, and we marveled at our wondrous Creator. May your lives continue to be richly blessed.

And to those on the sidelines—managers, publicists, friends, family—who made this project come to life...thank you.

And finally, this book is dedicated to you, the reader. It's no accident that you hold this book in your hands.

Table of Contents

Quick Topic Finder

Abortion
Gloria Gaynor
Kabeer Gbaja-Biamila

Abstinence
Tara Dawn Christensen
Kabeer Gbaja-Biamila
Zoro

Accomplishment
David Carr
Tara Dawn Christensen
Ken Hensley
Kerry Livgren
Charlotte Smith-Taylor
Nancy Stafford
David Wheaton
Jacklyn Zeman
Zoro

Accountability
David Carr

Ken Hensley
Bethel Johnson
Jonny Lang
Ricky Skaggs

Addiction
Clay Crosse
Gloria Gaynor
Jonny Lang
Heather Powers

Anxiety
Kabeer Gbaja-Biamila
Jason Hanson
Al Kasha
Corey Koskie
Zoro

Attitude
Laurie Boschman
Clay Crosse
Luther Elliss

Gloria Gaynor
Kabeer Gbaja-Biamila
Rudy Sarzo
Jacklyn Zeman
Zoro

Beauty
Nancy Stafford

Behavior
Andrew DeClercq
Ken Hensley
Bethel Johnson
David Wheaton

Blessings
David Carr
Charlie Daniels
Luther Elliss
Ken Hensley
Bethel Johnson
Corey Koskie
Rudy Sarzo
Zoro

Character
Clay Crosse
Andrew DeClercq
Kabeer Gbaja-Biamila
Bethel Johnson
Nancy Stafford
David Wheaton

Competition
Laurie Boschman
Jenny Boucek
David Wheaton

Confession
Laurie Boschman
Bethel Johnson
Jonny Lang
Noel Paul Stookey

Contentment
Laurie Boschman
Jenny Boucek
David Wheaton

Creation
Gary Burghoff
Ricky Skaggs
David Wheaton

Death
Billy Ray Cyrus
Kabeer Gbaja-Biamila
Jonny Lang
Rudy Sarzo
Charlotte Smith-Taylor
T-Bone
Jacklyn Zeman

Decisions
Laurie Boschman
Jenny Boucek
Tara Dawn Christensen
Clay Crosse
Andrew DeClercq
Jason Hanson
Ricky Skaggs
T-Bone
Jacklyn Zeman
Zoro

Deliverance
Gloria Gaynor
Al Kasha
Jonny Lang
Heather Powers

Desperation
Bonnie Bramlett
Billy Ray Cyrus
Heather Powers

Discipline
Clay Crosse
Kabeer Gbaja-Biamila
John Schneider
David Wheaton
Zoro

Discouragement
Billy Ray Cyrus
Heather Powers
Rudy Sarzo
Nancy Stafford
Zoro

Doubt
Andrew DeClercq
Jonny Lang
Kerry Livgren
Ricky Skaggs

Drinking and Drugs
Bonnie Bramlett
Andrew DeClercq
Gloria Gaynor
Jonny Lang
Heather Powers

Eternal Life
Tara Dawn Christensen
Billy Ray Cyrus
Ken Hensley
T-Bone
Zoro

Fear
Al Kasha
Corey Koskie
Noel Paul Stookey
T-Bone

Forgiveness
Laurie Boschman
Bonnie Bramlett
Kirk Cameron
Clay Crosse
Gloria Gaynor
Kabeer Gbaja-Biamila
Ken Hensley

Frustration
Gary Burghoff
Luther Elliss
Kabeer Gbaja-Biamila
John Schneider

God's Plan
David Carr
Tara Dawn Christensen
Luther Elliss
Jason Hanson
Bethel Johnson
Corey Koskie
Leon Patillo
Rudy Sarzo

John Schneider
Jacklyn Zeman
Zoro

Good Works
Luther Elliss
Jason Hanson
Steve Stevens
Zoro

Gospel
Jenny Boucek
Kirk Cameron
Charlie Daniels
Kerry Livgren
David Wheaton

Grace
Charlie Daniels
Gloria Gaynor
Ken Hensley
Heather Powers
Ricky Skaggs
Steve Stevens
Zoro

Grief
Kabeer Gbaja-Biamila
Charlotte Smith-Taylor
Jackie Zeman

Guidance
Laurie Boschman
Luther Elliss
Charlotte Smith-Taylor
Jacklyn Zeman

Guilt
Kirk Cameron
Gloria Gaynor
Heather Powers
Rudy Sarzo
Charlotte Smith-Taylor
Noel Paul Stookey

Healing
Tara Dawn Christensen
Clay Crosse
Charlie Daniels
Al Kasha
Corey Koskie
Jonny Lang
Heather Powers
Zoro

Holy Spirit
Laurie Boschman
Gloria Gaynor
Ricky Skaggs
Charlotte Smith-Taylor
David Wheaton

Hope
Kirk Cameron
Clay Crosse
Jason Hanson
Corey Koskie
Ricky Skaggs
Zoro

Humility
Jenny Boucek
Kirk Cameron

Kabeer Gbaja-Biamila
Noel Paul Stookey

Hypocrisy
Kabeer Gbaja-Biamila
Jonny Lang
Kerry Livgren

Joy
Kirk Cameron
Kerry Livgren
Ricky Skaggs
Steve Stevens
Noel Paul Stookey
David Wheaton
Zoro

Legalism
Rudy Sarzo

Loneliness
Jenny Boucek
Billy Ray Cyrus
Gloria Gaynor
Kabeer Gbaja-Biamila
Charlotte Smith-Taylor

Love
Bonnie Bramlett
Tara Dawn Christensen
Kirk Cameron
Clay Crosse
Billy Ray Cyrus
Charlie Daniels
Kabeer Gbaja-Biamila
Ken Hensley
Al Kasha
Jonny Lang

John Schneider
Ricky Skaggs
T-Bone
Zoro

Marriage
Kabeer Gbaja-Biamila
Ken Hensley
Al Kasha
Heather Powers
Zoro

Miracles
Gary Burghoff
David Carr
Luther Elliss
Gloria Gaynor
Corey Koskie
Jonny Lang
Heather Powers
Ricky Skaggs
Noel Paul Stookey
T-Bone
Jacklyn Zeman

Money/Giving
David Carr
Steve Stevens
Zoro

Obedience
Kirk Cameron
Heather Powers
David Wheaton
Zoro

Occult
Jonny Lang

Peace
Charlie Daniels
Luther Elliss
Jason Hanson
Al Kasha
Corey Koskie
Jonny Lang
Rudy Sarzo
John Schneider
Charlotte Smith-Taylor
Nancy Stafford
Zoro

Persecution
Laurie Boschman
Jenny Boucek
T-Bone

**Personal Relationship
with Christ**
Laurie Boschman
Jenny Boucek
Luther Elliss
Jason Hanson
Ken Hensley
Rudy Sarzo
John Schneider

Pornography
Clay Crosse
Kabeer Gbaja-Biamila

Praise
Gloria Gaynor
Leon Patillo
Charlotte Smith-Taylor
Nancy Stafford

T-Bone
Zoro

Prayer
Bonnie Bramlett
Charlie Daniels
Kabeer Gbaja-Biamila
Bethel Johnson
Leon Patillo
Rudy Sarzo
Ricky Skaggs
Steve Stevens
Noel Paul Stookey
T-Bone
Jacklyn Zeman
Zoro

Pride
Jenny Boucek
Kabeer Gbaja-Biamila
Bethel Johnson
Charlotte Smith-Taylor
Nancy Stafford
Noel Paul Stookey
David Wheaton

Priorities
Kirk Cameron
Clay Crosse
Billy Ray Cyrus
Charlie Daniels
Nancy Stafford

Protection
David Carr
Charlie Daniels
Andrew DeClercq

Luther Elliss
Bethel Johnson
Corey Koskie
Steve Stevens
T-Bone
Zoro

Purity
Tara Dawn Christensen
Kabeer Gbaja-Biamila
Zoro

Purpose
David Carr
Billy Ray Cyrus
Gloria Gaynor
Jason Hanson
Bethel Johnson
John Schneider
Zoro

Rejecting God/Rebellion
Kirk Cameron
Kabeer Gbaja-Biamila
Jonny Lang
Kerry Livgren
Heather Powers
Nancy Stafford

Repentance
Kirk Cameron
Andrew DeClercq
Heather Powers
Noel Paul Stookey
David Wheaton

Salvation
Laurie Boschman

Jenny Boucek
Charlie Daniels
Luther Elliss
Gloria Gaynor
Ken Hensley
Bethel Johnson
Kerry Livgren
Leon Patillo
Ricky Skaggs

Satan
Clay Crosse
Billy Ray Cyrus
Charlie Daniels
Andrew DeClercq
Luther Elliss
Kabeer Gbaja-Biamila
Bethel Johnson
Corey Koskie
Jonny Lang
Heather Powers
John Schneider
Ricky Skaggs
T-Bone

Self-Control
Kabeer Gbaja-Biamila
Heather Powers

Self-Esteem
Nancy Stafford

Self-Reliance
David Wheaton

Service
John Schneider
Steve Stevens

Sex
Tara Dawn Christensen
Clay Crosse
Gloria Gaynor
Kabeer Gbaja-Biamila
Heather Powers
Zoro

Sin
Jenny Boucek
Kirk Cameron
Charlie Daniels
Andrew DeClercq
Kabeer Gbaja-Biamila
Heather Powers
David Wheaton

Spiritual Gifts
Rudy Sarzo
Charlotte Smith-Taylor

Struggles
Bonnie Bramlett
David Carr
Heather Powers
Charlotte Smith-Taylor
T-Bone
Zoro

Success
Gary Burghoff
David Carr
Tara Dawn Christensen
Gloria Gaynor
Jason Hanson
Al Kasha
Leon Patillo

Nancy Stafford
T-Bone
David Wheaton
Zoro

Talent
Al Kasha
Leon Patillo
Rudy Sarzo
Zoro

Temptation
Andrew DeClercq
Kabeer Gbaja-Biamila

Thankfulness
Jenny Boucek
Gary Burghoff
Kirk Cameron
David Carr
Billy Ray Cyrus
Luther Elliss
Gloria Gaynor
Ken Hensley
Bethel Johnson
Jonny Lang
Kerry Livgren
Leon Patillo
Heather Powers
Charlotte Smith-Taylor
T-Bone
Jacklyn Zeman
Zoro

Trust
Gary Burghoff
Kirk Cameron

Clay Crosse
Charlie Daniels
Luther Elliss
Kabeer Gbaja-Biamila
Jason Hanson
Bethel Johnson
Corey Koskie
Heather Powers
Charlotte Smith-Taylor
T-Bone
David Wheaton
Zoro

Truth
Tara Dawn Christensen
Billy Ray Cyrus
Kabeer Gbaja-Biamila
Jason Hanson
Bethel Johnson
Jonny Lang
Kerry Livgren

Victory
Gloria Gaynor
Kabeer Gbaja-Biamila
Al Kasha
Heather Powers
David Wheaton

Witnessing
Jenny Boucek
Luther Elliss
Ken Hensley
Al Kasha
Leon Patillo
Charlotte Smith-Taylor

Noel Paul Stookey
T-Bone

World Religions
Gary Burghoff
Gloria Gaynor
Kabeer Gbaja-Biamila
Al Kasha
Kerry Livgren
Nancy Stafford

Worldliness
Bonnie Bramlett
Clay Crosse
Gloria Gaynor
Jason Hanson
Jonny Lang
Kerry Livgren
Leon Patillo
Nancy Stafford
Steve Stevens
Noel Paul Stookey

Worry
Kabeer Gbaja-Biamila
Corey Koskie

How Do I Know He's Real?

YOU hold in your hands a true miracle. This book is a piece of God's handiwork—no human being could have possibly orchestrated such an incredible adventure. I knew He was real before I wrote this book—but this...this has been unbelievable.

My husband, Craig, and I have been married for over 21 years—very happily for about half that time. Like many other couples have experienced, our beginning was rocky, especially the first few years. Living in the same household enlightened us to each other's idiosyncrasies—the way he matched his socks, for example, just about sent me over the edge.

As the years went by, we focused more and more on our growing family and careers, and less and less on one another. We were certainly *not* focused on God. So in His infinite wisdom, God found a way to change that.

Craig went through a serious bout of clinical depression following a disappointing business venture. He medicated himself with drugs and alcohol to ease the pain, only to become more and more depressed. Many of my friends and coworkers encouraged me to leave him and get a divorce. But even though I wasn't a Christian at the time, I took my vows seriously. I'd meant it when I'd said, "...for better or for worse, in sickness and in health." So I worked hard on encouraging him and maintaining the facade of a happy home.

Gradually the prescribed antidepressant worsened his symptoms. He spent much of the daytime sleeping, and it was hard to hold the family together without him. One day it all came to a head.

We had an English au pair, Christine, living with us to assist in the care of our two children. (I'm sure this period of time was no picnic for her either.) In Minnesota, the winters are harsh—so bitter cold that special engine block heaters are installed to make sure cars will start if exposed to the elements. One such winter day, Christine was unable to get her car started; it sat frozen and lifeless in the driveway. The battery needed to be jump-started, and Craig was the only one who knew how to do it. But he was in bed sleeping....again. At my wit's end, I screamed at him to get up and do something! He got out of bed, went outside to start the car, and promptly disappeared.

Several hours later there was still no sign of him, and I was starting to panic. I regretted the harsh way I'd spoken to him and was terribly worried about what kind of shape he was in, mentally and physically, at this point.

Finally, he walked through the front door. He'd been crying—that was obvious. As I learned what he'd been through that day, I understood his anguish. When Craig had left our home, he'd headed down to a nearby river. He'd sat in his SUV along the riverbank sobbing, contemplating the unthinkable—suicide. He figured we were better off without him, and a determined plunge into the frigid water would end his pain quickly and decisively. Sitting there he said a prayer asking God to send an angel, a visible sign that He is real, before he made the final, irreversible decision to end his own life.

As soon as he opened his eyes, he saw a strange sight. A beat-up, late-model Chevy Impala was lumbering straight for him towing a trailer and snowmobile. It was amazing to see this awkward vehicle fishtailing through the impassable snow of the boat landing where Craig's Jeep had barely made it through. The car pulled up alongside him. Behind the wheel, Craig said, was a scruffy man who looked like he was down on his luck. The man rolled down his window and asked, "Are you alright?"

Craig wiped away his tears and said, "Yeah, I'm okay." Without another word, the stranger turned around and drove away. That was it.

A coincidence? I don't think so. I believe God answered Craig's prayer and sent him an angel that day. That man saved Craig's life along a frozen riverbank in rural Minnesota. There is no reasonable explanation how that man found Craig hidden off a beaten path.

That experience was life-changing for both Craig and me. Not long afterward, Craig gave His life to Christ and asked the Lord to heal his brokenness and pain. And God was faithful. Craig's cravings stopped—even his long-term addiction to chewing tobacco. He had tried unsuccessfully to quit chewing many times, only to be defeated. But on the day he gave control to God, both the addictions and the depression were gone.

I witnessed a miracle happen right before my very eyes—a miracle accomplished through the sheer power of faith. The peace that emanated out of him was palpable; it was a peace that I too longed for. But I was carrying around a burden of guilt, a guilt that came from past regrets and nearly driving him to the point of suicide. More importantly, I was a control freak—I couldn't possibly imagine handing over the reins of my life to God.

But one evening, while sitting in the bathtub, I did just that. As I soaked in the tepid water, the weight of my misery came crashing down upon me. I said my own version of the "Sinner's Prayer" and asked Jesus Christ to come into my life.

Now, there was no bolt of lightning or crack of thunder in the bathroom that night, but I did sense a huge weight being lifted off my shoulders. I felt a peace that I'd never before experienced, and life hasn't been the same since.

As we learned to live completely for Him, Jesus Christ began to have a tremendous impact on our marriage and our family—even our kids. One day in the summer of 2003, our 15-year-old daughter, Kaia, was talking with a boy who lives across the lake from us. Kaia is very involved in her church youth group, and she was bound and determined to bring Justin to a meeting. But he wasn't interested. Instead, he looked at her square in the face and asked, "But how do you know He's real?"

That is the universal question, isn't it? How *do* we know Christ is real? I just couldn't let go of that question; it haunted me for months. Many of my friends and family members aren't believers, and I worry about what eternity might look like for them. What would convince people like them that Jesus is worth a try? The thought came to me that the American culture worships celebrity...maybe if an admired celebrity talked about Jesus, they would listen. It was worth a try.

So I took Justin's challenge and embarked on a journey to prove that Christ is real. I was going to write a book—no, a series of books—that shared the testimonies of celebrities. In November of that year I started emailing; sending letters; and calling actors, professional and Olympic athletes, and musicians—people whom my research revealed were fired-up Christians. Pretty gutsy move, really. Although I'd earned a minor in English in college, I'd spent the last 20 years as a sales executive. Writing had been my passion, but not my career. What made me think that any of these people would give me the time of day?

But they did, and in vast numbers. It amazes me to think how many of them have shared their personal stories—oftentimes private things they had never shared before. Why? Because I believe God led them to. From the very beginning of this project, I put it all in God's hands. *He* would put the right people in the book; *He* would find the right publisher; and *He* would put it in the hands of those people who needed to read it. And He has been so faithful. Whether I was speaking with an Academy Award winner or a country music legend, they all treated me like a sister in Christ. What an awesome God we have!

This has been a huge, life-changing project. In the beginning, I had precious little time to devote to it while working full-time in a pressure-intensive job that involved a great deal of travel. But then, in April 2004, the Lord saw fit to free me from that job. I remember driving home the day I got laid off, wondering how I was going to take care of my family without the income. I knew I didn't want to go to work for another greedy corporation, but I had bills to pay!

When I walked through the front door of our home that morning, the phone was ringing. It was my dad calling, which was strange for two reasons. First of all, he rarely called me during the day. Secondly, he never called me in the middle of the day on my home phone; it would normally be on my cell phone. His reason for calling was to let me know that he wanted to give me some money.

I started to cry on the phone because Daddy had no idea that I had just lost my job. Completely out of the blue, he called to offer me financial support. God found an immediate way to encourage and sustain me. From that point on, I vowed to concentrate on this project.

The Lord started opening doors the very next day. I received an offer for a lucrative consulting job a couple days a week that would afford me the freedom to write and still keep us on solid financial ground. And many celebrities I'd been trying to connect with for months started calling back. It was like magic!

It would be disingenuous to say that writing this book has been a piece of cake. It has been a true labor of love and a colossal leap of faith. Even though I knew this was what God called me to do, there were many times I felt dispirited and overwhelmed by the task before me. Yet every time, the Lord came through with flying colors.

One such time was in December, 2004. I'd had a gut-wrenching conversation with one of my biggest champions, Amy Peterson. We commiserated about her broken heart and my discouragement. The next day, she forwarded the regular email devotion she'd received in her inbox—and it gave me chills. It was from Galatians 6:9-10: *"Let us not become weary in doing good, for at the proper time we will reap a harvest if we do not give up. Therefore, as we have opportunity, let us do good to all people, especially to those who belong to the family of believers."* The devotion went on to say, *"God has a harvest of blessing in mind for you. Don't let the devil steal it away from you by discouraging you into giving up. Trust in God.* That's exactly what I needed to hear at that moment in my life, and I moved on with renewed resolve.

I kept at it, working nights and weekends in order to finish the book. Although my agent had received a great deal of interest from several publishers, none of them was stepping to the plate with a contract. I couldn't imagine that God had brought me to this point without having a publishing partner in mind. I was frustrated and disillusioned—I was honestly losing my faith.

Then in March 2005, while on a business trip in San Francisco, I met a woman who told me about a spiritual retreat center she frequented in Minnesota. She would go there annually to restore her soul and spend quiet time with God. Pacem in Terris offers "hermitages," simple one-room cabins nestled among 240 heavily wooded acres.

Now, for an overachieving, working mother with a "Type A" personality and a tendency toward anxiety, the concept of being "still" was more than a little frightening. Like so many Christians, I can be silent and listen to God for, oh, about 15 seconds, before the noise of my overstimulated mind breaks in. So imagine putting me in a place for 36 hours where true silence and isolation are observed. Then consider that this bona fide city girl would have no electricity or indoor plumbing, and you'll get an idea of how daunting the whole idea was for me.

However, God put it on my heart to go, and I fought Him—big time. My husband pestered me because he knew I was at the breaking point. I settled on the only available weekend I had for the foreseeable future; and finally, on Thursday of that week, I made a phone call to see if they had any hermitages available. I figured my procrastination would pay off, and they wouldn't be able to accommodate me on such short notice. As I expected, the woman who answered the phone told me they were booked, but she put me on hold when another caller beeped in. When she returned to my line, she told me that they'd just had a cancellation. A coincidence? I don't think so.

I have to tell you, that once I was delivered to my hermitage by the loving directors, I didn't know quite what to do with myself. I unpacked my belongings, took out my Bible and the books I'd brought along to study, and settled myself on the screened porch. I prayed, "Father, I just lift up this weekend to You. Help me sense Your presence and understand Your will. Teach me to be silent so that I might hear You."

Almost immediately, I felt a warm sensation throughout my entire body. And I heard His voice in my heart—just as clearly as if He were sitting next to me. What an awesome feeling that was, to know the Creator of the universe had filled my soul! Who was I to deserve that?

The first book I took out was *Success God's Way* by Charles Stanley, and the first thing I read screamed out to me: *"It [success] is refusing to become discouraged, disheartened, or dissuaded from God's goals."*[1] God was speaking to me already, and we continued our conversation throughout the weekend. It was as if nobody else existed in the world; it was just God and me.

All day Saturday I studied a book entitled *Let Go*, and it was as if this 17th-century bishop, Francois Fenelon, had written it just for me for that precise moment in time.

In one particular passage, the author referred me to a Scripture passage. On my way to look it up in my Bible, *The TouchPoint Bible*[2] a sidebar caught my attention. It was titled "Perseverance" and read in part: *"Trophies in life are bestowed according to the measure of accomplishment, not the measure of intent. Trophies and medals are the rewards of a job well done, not a job well begun...what are some of the "races" in your life that began well but in which you now need to make a renewed push to propel you toward the finish line?"* I had definitely been slowing down in my charge toward the finish line.

Then, when I looked at the referenced Scripture—Second Corinthians 8:10-11 (NLT), I stopped dead in my tracks. I couldn't believe what I was reading.

> *I suggest that you finish what you started a year ago, for you were the first to propose this idea, and you were the first to begin doing something about it. Now you should carry this project through to completion just as enthusiastically as you began it.*

It had been almost exactly one year since I'd been laid off and committed myself to writing this book. Obviously, I needed to see it through to completion; it couldn't have been more clear. The rest of my reading struck similar chords—in particular these statements:

> *You know what God requires of you. The question is, will you do it?*
>
> *Live in quiet peace, my dear young lady, without any thought for the future. Keep on with the good things you are doing, since you are leaning in these directions, and certainly you will be able to get them done.*

And finally,

> *Deep down in your heart, I believe you know what God demands of you but you are resisting Him. And this is the cause of all of your distress. You are beginning to think that it is impossible for you to do what God requires. Recognize this for what it is, a temptation to lose hope. Never give up hope in God! He will give you whatever you need according to your faith.*

The time I spent alone with God in the woods that weekend answered my questions and gave me the impetus to carry on. With a renewed sense of surrender, I once again gave the project to God and vowed to see it through.

The next day, I had an offer from a publisher. Yes—I know God is real; He has shown Himself over and over again.

On the pages to follow, you will read inspiring stories of how people from the worlds of sports and entertainment also know God is real. You'll read accounts of miraculous healings, redemption, and salvation; and I pray they are an inspiration to you. If you have questions about what you read, the Bible passages at the end of each chapter will provide insight and answers. You'll also find a topical index at the beginning of the book that may help you if you are struggling with a particular issue.

If you have questions, ask them; consult a trusted Christian friend or a clergy member. As you progress through the pages of this book, be open to what God is telling you. Your life will never be the same.

ENDNOTES

1. Charles Stanley, *Achieving True Contentment and Purpose... Success God's Way.* (Nashville, Tennessee: Thomas Nelson Publishers, 2000), 7.

2. *The Touchpoint Bible.* Wheaton, Illinois: Tyndale House Publishers, 1996.

Laurie Boschman

Retired National Hockey
League Player

WHO would think that a boy named Laurie would wind up being a household name in the rough-and-tumble world of professional hockey? Growing up on the frozen prairie of Saskatchewan, Canada, retired pro hockey player Laurie Boschman had plenty of opportunities to skate.

As a young man, Boschman was selected by the Toronto Maple Leafs in the first round (number 9 overall) of the 1979 NHL Entry Draft. Over the course of his 14-year pro career (1979-1993), Boschman played for Toronto, Edmonton, Winnipeg, New Jersey, and Ottawa. This 6-foot, 185-pound forward scored 229 goals, had 348 assists in 1009 regular season games, and 57 playoff appearances.

During his early days, Boschman suffered some professional setbacks due to his faith. Compared with other sports, there are few professing Christians among the ranks of pro hockey players; perhaps because players fear management would question their aggressivenes if they knew they were believers. Boschman is now in full-time ministry with Hockey Ministries International, an organization that provides support to these players and introduces amateurs and pros alike to the love of Christ.

As a pro in the National Hockey League, I was an aggressive player and took lots of penalties. People would sometimes ask me how I could reconcile the violence of the sport with my Christian faith. But hockey is very physical and I wasn't afraid to get in there and work hard. Sometimes if somebody would push at me, I would push back. And many times I dropped my gloves and fought. If I crossed the line, I spent time in the penalty box. In life, if you break the rules or break the laws, you have a penalty to pay. It's the same in hockey. But I didn't have a problem with that. It was just a game.

I grew up in the central part of Canada where hockey was and is very, very popular. I played a lot of sports, but really gravitated to hockey. And I played a lot of hockey! I played it outdoors and I played it indoors. I played it in the fall and the winter and the spring and the summer. I played street hockey and ball hockey and regular old ice hockey. I guess you could say I was a hockey nut. Like so many other kids, my dream as a youngster was to one day play at the highest level—the National Hockey League.

My family moved to Brandon, Manitoba. Brandon had a major junior hockey team called the Brandon Wheat Kings. In Canada, playing major junior hockey is like playing for a large American university. As a 17 year old, I was asked to try out for the Wheat Kings and I made it! So there I was going to high school and playing the equivalent of college hockey. It was a great thrill for me.

My final year of junior hockey was 1979. That year our team went to the Memorial Cup Championship, the Canadian version of the Final Four. At this tournament, the top teams from the three leagues compete: the Western Hockey League, the Quebec Hockey League, and the Ontario Hockey League. My team made it to the final game but lost in overtime; it was a huge disappointment. But there were a lot of pro scouts there, and for the first time I heard that there was a good chance I was going to be a first-round pick in the draft.

I went home that summer to get ready for the NHL draft. 1979 was also the year that the hockey countries were having training camps in the summer to get ready for the 1980 Olympics that were to be held in Lake Placid. The Canadian National Team asked me to come to their training camp in Calgary with the expectation that I would represent my country at the Olympics. One day I took off practice with the National team and went downstairs in the arena so I could listen in on the NHL draft conference call. Sure enough the phone rang and I was told that Toronto had picked me up in the first round—9th overall! I was thrilled, not only because I was going to play professional hockey, but I was going to play for the Toronto Maple Leafs, the team I had grown up watching on TV.

Now I had a decision to make. The National team was getting ready to head to Europe to play some exhibition games prior to the February Lake Placid Olympics. Was I going to continue on with the Olympic program or join the Leafs at training camp? I decided to head out to my first professional training camp and was never disappointed. I was totally in awe of being on the same ice as the players I had watched on television. I was literally skating with guys like Darryl Sittler, Borje Salming, and Ronnie Ellis.

After training camp, the coach told me that I had made the club. It was so cool to call my parents and share the joy with them. As a youngster I never, ever, thought I'd actually make it to the NHL.—it was just an impossible dream I'd had. I always thought when I made it to the NHL I would have everything I ever wanted in life.

But about a quarter of the way through the season, I distinctly remember waking up one morning thinking that there had to be more to life than what I was experiencing. I'd played about 25 games, and had been to a lot of cities and played against the players I'd grown up idolizing. I finally recognized that all these players were just normal people—regular guys who happened to play professional hockey. That was so surprising to me. Was this all there was to playing in the National Hockey League? I had this real emptiness in my heart. I guess I was under the impression that if I made the NHL, I would be truly happy. But it didn't bring me the satisfaction I thought it would.

I had a teammate during this time named Ron Ellis. He was 35 years old, married, and had two kids. I was just 19 and unattached. I thought he was a fossil because he was so old! Obviously, we didn't have much in common. But despite the age difference, I found myself watching him—this quiet individual in the locker room. What impressed me the most about him was that his language was different, and he treated his wife and kids with respect. And the way he handled adversity was really something. Like so many other vocations, hockey has its ups and downs, but unlike other careers, everybody knows if you aren't successful...it's all over the TV and newspapers.

One thing I noticed through all of that pressure was that Ron was always on an even keel. He had a real peace about the way he conducted himself whether we were winning or losing. I was really attracted to that. As a result, one day I asked him, "Ron, you know I've been watching you for a good part of the season. What makes you tick?" And what he said to me I'd never heard before, "Laurie, I'm a born-again Christian. I try to use the Bible to guide my life."

I'd never heard that term before—"born-again." When I was a kid, my family actually went to church on a regular basis, but I always thought the Bible was for the priest to read and interpret and then tell us how to live. I didn't think the Bible was something I could understand myself. And I certainly didn't think there was anything in there that was relevant for me! When Ron told me he tried to use the Bible to guide his life, I was really interested. But more importantly, I was interested in what Ron had—and that was peace. It was definitely something I didn't have.

That conversation began my process of spiritual discovery. Ron conducted a team chapel service on Sundays during the season. We'd get together for about 15 minutes before games and listen to a guest speaker who would talk about biblical principles. I ended up going to the last chapel of the year in Quebec City. That day the speaker talked about Bible prophecy and the things that were predicted in the Bible that have come true. I had never heard any of that stuff before.

I was very much intrigued and went back to speak with Ron and the chaplain after our pre-game meal about what I'd heard that day. I knew that I had done some things in my life that were wrong and that I had a problem called sin. I believed in God, and I believed that He had sent His Son Jesus to live on this earth. And I believed that He died and rose again three days later. I knew those things intellectually, but I heard for the first time in that hotel room in Quebec City that I could have a personal relationship with Him. But my sin separated me from God and prevented me from having that close relationship. I learned that if I confessed my sin and asked Christ to come into my heart and give me forgiveness that He would restore that broken relationship.

So that day I prayed a simple prayer, "Lord, forgive me for being a sinner. Come into my life and make me a new person." Afterward, I knew I had done something that was right—I knew I'd made a decision that would have impact on my life. Even still, when I left that hotel room, I said to Ron Ellis, "Ron, no matter what you do, don't tell anybody about this." I didn't want my teammates to know because I didn't want them to change the way they might look at me. I was a little worried about how they'd perceive me after this.

Shortly thereafter, the season ended and the chaplain gave me a Living Bible to study in the off-season. During my downtime over the summer, I found myself reaching for that Bible and reading it for the first time. As I was growing up, my family had a big King James Bible in our house, but I'd never once opened that thing up. I moved it when I did some dusting, but I never opened it up to see what it had to say. And now the words in that book were starting to make sense to me!

When I made the decision to follow Christ, the Holy Spirit came to dwell within me. He slowly started to work in me and change my life. When my buddies came to visit me at my cottage up north, to go out and party and do some of the things I used to do, I found myself not wanting to participate. I found myself making excuses not to go. That showed me there was something going on in my heart.

At the start of the second season, my teammates recognized that I was a different person. I quietly let them know that I'd become a Christian. Once I let them know, and showed them consistency in my life and a desire to move forward, my teammates were terrific. I got a lot of teasing and ribbing, but overall they were very respectful.

But not everyone on the team respected my decision for Christ. By the third year, my game wasn't going very well. Harold Ballard, the owner of the team, came out publicly on television after a game in New York City and said that he was going to trade me or send me to the minors because I had too much religion. He felt my faith was a distraction and that I wasn't playing as aggressively as I should be. He even sent me to a psychiatrist to see if I had been "brainwashed."

The real cause for my performance was a bout of mononucleosis. Nonetheless, Ballard's comments were a lightning rod for discussion across Canada. And because Toronto was and is one of the preeminent hockey cities in North America, the national media picked up on the story. For several months there was quite a debate on what it means to be a born-again Christian. Could a born-again Christian play a physical sport like hockey? I became known as "Born-again Boschman."

In the end, I was traded to Edmonton. Switching teams is part of the game, but it was particularly difficult because I knew I had been traded, in large part, because of my faith. This was just a small taste of what it feels like to be persecuted. It was a very challenging time professionally, but yet very rewarding spiritually; I was growing very much in my young faith. And no matter which team I played for, my relationship with Christ was always at the center of my career. I have a lot of wonderful memories of people in the NHL whom I played with and have had a lot of great experiences. I feel so privileged to have been able to play hockey and make a living at it. I just feel very fortunate. For whatever reason, God allowed all this to happen.

There are a lot of questions we have on our journey of faith. Sometimes, things don't make sense. But I truly do believe that God is in control. When I made the decision to ask Christ into my heart and to change my life, I knew without a doubt He is real. Making that decision wasn't easy, but I know He's real as a result of the change that He brought about in my heart and attitude and my view of the world. The prayer I said in the hotel room in Quebec City resulted in what I sought the most—peace.

GOD'S ROAD MAP

The Holy Bible is a guide to help you live a happy and satisfying life. To learn more about the concepts presented in the chapter you've just read, take a look at these passages:

PERSECUTION

In many countries around the world, religious oppression is a fact of life. Right here in North America, such persecution can take the form of simple prejudice and impact a person's career and earning potential. But it should come as no surprise—Christian persecution is foretold in the Bible.

John 15:18-21

If the world hates you, keep in mind that it hated Me first. If you belonged to the world, it would love you as its own. As it is, you do not belong to the world, but I have chosen you out of the world. That is why the world hates you. Remember the words I spoke to you: "No servant is greater than his master." If they persecuted Me, they will persecute you also. If they obeyed My teaching, they will obey yours also. They will treat you this way because of My name, for they do not know the One who sent Me.

Matthew 5:11

Blessed are you when people insult you, persecute you and falsely say all kinds of evil against you because of Me.

CONTENTMENT

Peggy Lee sang a great song, "Is That All There Is?" which summarizes the outcome that can result from fame and fortune. That theme is repeated throughout this book—that despite achievement, true happiness is elusive without God.

Philippians 4:12-13

I know what it is to be in need, and I know what it is to have plenty. I have learned the secret of being content in any and every situation, whether well fed or hungry, whether living in plenty or in want. I can do everything through Him who gives me strength.

1 Timothy 6:6-7

But godliness with contentment is great gain. For we brought nothing into the world, and we can take nothing out of it.

Jenny Boucek

Assistant Coach, Seattle Storm,
WNBA; Former WNBA Player

JENNY Boucek was a four-year starter on the basketball team at the University of Virginia from 1992-1996. She helped her team earn four regular-season ACC championships and three NCAA Elite Eight appearances. While at UV, she was a two-time GTE Academic All-America team member and two-time ACC selection. Boucek finished her career at Virginia as a member of the 1,000-point club. She started her professional WNBA career with the Cleveland Rockers in 1997. She even played in Iceland in 1998 and was voted the country's best player after averaging 23 points, 7 rebounds, and 6 assists per game. She returned to Cleveland for the 1998 season but was forced to retire after a career-ending back injury.

Boucek has been an assistant coach in the WNBA for six seasons. She began her career in 1999 with the Washington Mystics. Her next three years were spent with the Miami Sol before moving to her current home with the Seattle Storm—2004 WNBA Champions.

My mission as a coach with the WNBA is about more than winning games—it's about winning souls. To me, once we get saved, we are all ambassadors for Christ; we are just disguised as other things. So whether you are a student or a doctor or a fireman or a coach, if you are a believer, you are an ambassador for Christ. That's my job too; I'm just disguised as a professional basketball coach.

I was raised in a home with no talk of God or Jesus, so I didn't know anything. I never read one word of the Bible growing up and seriously didn't know the difference between Jesus Christ and the Easter Bunny.

In Nashville everybody goes to church, but it was more like a social thing. Everybody would dress up and go see their friends—almost like going to the country club. That was my perception of it. And there was no difference between the church-goers and everybody else as to how they were living. My family was a very moral family; my dad was a doctor and my mom was a social worker and guidance counselor. They were just honest, good, serving people. So in my mind, my family was better because they weren't hypocritical like those Christians who went to church on Sunday but didn't live a "Christian" life the rest of the week. I had a pretty negative perception of church.

I grew up a tomboy and played everything—all sports. I played high school basketball and then went on to play college ball at the University of Virginia. When I lost my last game in college during my senior year, there was no WNBA yet; so I thought my basketball career was over. Basketball had become my god really. I was a very good student and focused a lot on basketball. So when that ended, I had a huge void in my life—a really big hole.

One day I was eating in the cafeteria at school, and this girl came up to me and asked me if I wanted to go to a Bible study. She came up to me totally out of the blue; I didn't even know her! And I never would have done that—gone to a Bible study—if I hadn't been so broken. Usually, a Bible study would have been totally intimidating to me. I was just against those kinds of things. But for some reason I went. And I went for a while until it was a bit too much for me. It seemed like they were pushing me too much. I dated a few Christian guys during college and I asked them a lot of questions. But they were more adversarial questions. I didn't agree with them, but it sparked a lot of dialogue and curiosity.

Then I got a Bible and started reading some on my own for my own comfort. But it meant nothing to me. It gave me comfort during that time but it was just like words on a paper. I would read it every now and then but had no idea what it was saying or even how to read it.

The next year I went to play professional basketball for Cleveland. The WNBA is such a lonely, cutthroat environment. You really don't know anybody and you can't trust anybody. And it was the first year the league was in existence so it was even more cutthroat because nobody knew what was going on. You're on the road a lot; it's a very lonely profession. They had a chapel service before every game; it was just these little 10-15 minute sessions right before the game and the chaplain would give you a little nugget from the Word and apply it to sports. That's really the first time I truly heard the Bible. Before then I didn't consume anything from it other than that it felt comforting. But this was like the first time I'd actually read it and every single thing that she read from that Bible felt like I'd heard it a million times over in my life. That's how I knew He was real. It was like I had written it myself. I realized that this Book was exactly what I believed—but how could that be? These were all the things that I believed in my heart but I didn't understand God.

I'd always been a person who was very in tune with my heart—very introspective. And I do believe that's how God speaks to us—through our hearts. But most people are so confused with all the clutter that they don't really introspect very well and can't really hear God. So the Bible helps us to hear God tangibly. Even people who are stranded on a desert island could still hear from God, even if they didn't have a Bible there. I experienced that. It was very profound for me to learn the Word of God and know that it'd been on my heart all along. That can't be a coincidence. It was almost like I knew God, but I didn't know His name!

Becoming a Christian was a process. The concept of God and the biblical principles were easy for me. But Jesus Christ and the concept of us being sinners were not. My mom was a psychologist and had raised me to think I was perfect and that all people were good. In her mind everybody is good and they do things for a reason so we don't judge them; we understand why they're doing what they're doing. They've either been hurt in their lives or they've got mental problems or chemical imbalances that cause them to act a certain way. But everybody has a good heart. People are never bad; they are just doing bad things.

That's the exact opposite of the Gospel message. According to the Bible, we are all born into a fallen world as sinners. Without God in our lives, our flesh is going to lead us down a sinful life. Until you know that you are a sinner, you don't see the need for Jesus dying for you; you don't understand the significance of that. So that was really a major process for me. When people would talk about Jesus coming to die for my sins, it was hard because I didn't think I was a sinner. That understanding was something that came along years later.

But God started revealing Himself through answering prayers and speaking through other people. It was a huge revelation for me to see myself as a bad person. And it was painful, very painful. He allowed me to fall in some things just to break me and let me know that I needed Jesus. I had to surrender. It wasn't an overnight thing. A lot of my changes were heart changes because I was living a good life. I was a prime candidate for never being saved because I was just so subtly off. When people saw how I lived they would have guessed that I was a Christian; I heard that before. But I had no clue; I was just living close to alignment. I had always been a very goal-oriented person. I had a goal of making straight A's, playing basketball in college, then playing in the WNBA, and then being a starter in the WNBA. I would always raise the bar, and I reached them all. I had everything—a great family, money, friends, boyfriends, success in the classroom. And yet, I always felt like there was something missing, something more.

And it wasn't until I got to the peak as a starter in the WNBA that I just knew there must be more to this life thing—there had to be more. I was achieving everything I wanted to achieve; I had everything, but I was so unfulfilled. That's before God started breaking me; that's when He was calling me to Him. He was wooing me and He was getting me sold on Him and how real He was. There was a bigger picture because I needed to learn about Him. My relationship with Him came first—the wooing. Then it was the brokenness and the need for Jesus. God will call people either when they hit rock bottom or by giving them a ton of everything and they realize they're still not satisfied. It's one extreme or the other. He's still vague to people who are in between those two extremes.

I ended up retiring from playing professional ball after just two seasons because of a back injury. I fractured my sacrum in my lower back. If you injure that, you're done; your career is over because it never really heals.

I got a job coaching in Miami. When I moved there, I didn't know anybody. I wasn't a Christian yet, but I was talking to God in my own way. And He was putting it on my heart that I needed to find a church there. In my prayer time, I specifically asked Him to help me find the right church.

I played beach volleyball nearly every day where there was this gorgeous guy playing, and I was totally digging him. One day after one of the games, we got to talking, and out of the blue he asked me if I wanted to go to church. This was just one day after I'd asked God to help find me a church, and there He was answering my prayer with this great-looking guy! I knew He was real that day. It wasn't long before I made the greatest decision of my life—the decision to accept Christ as my personal Lord and Savior.

Moving around the WNBA has been difficult and lonely sometimes. In a way it's also been good because I've never gotten comfortable. I've had to lean on the Lord and draw Him close. When you move frequently, you don't have friends or family comforting you and can more dramatically feel His comfort. It made my relationship with Him that much more real because I could feel Him. When I moved to Seattle, I didn't know anybody else in the whole entire city or even that whole entire half of the country, but I knew God was with me and I could feel Him.

It's our nature to be independent and self-sufficient to the point where we think we don't need anybody or anything. That's pride—one of the biggest sins there is. It's definitely one of my biggest sins. So I pray regularly for humility. And I'm always thankful for those humbling moments when I get back my perspective and my dependence on Him. It's a hard thing to do when things are going great.

Being a Christian coach in a professional sports setting has its challenges. I've been in a situation where my boss has pulled me into his office and said, "What's all this God stuff? I see you sign your letters 'God Bless' and stuff like that. You know I care about you; but there's no place for that, and it's going to hurt you professionally. You are not to talk to the players about God." He point-blank told me that I was not to talk to the players about my faith. So I just had to be more strategic about it. For three years I was working for him and stuff was happening right and left, every day for the Lord. God has never used me more than He did in that place.

This can be an intense, stressful job at times. I keep my focus on Jesus, representing Him and being a light. It's a challenge, but that's my goal. Our walk is a lot more powerful than our talk, so I'm just trying to say the right thing, do the right things, and be different—to let seekers get curious and be drawn to the light.

GOD'S ROAD MAP

The Holy Bible is a guide to help you live a happy and satisfying life. To learn more about the concepts presented in the chapter you've just read, take a look at these passages:

THE BIBLE

God uses His Word, the Bible to communicate with us and teach us. Over several hundred years, God inspired a select group of people to write down His Word for us to read and study centuries later. Isn't that amazing? The Bible isn't just a collection of stories and legends; it is the divinely inspired Word of God—the ultimate owner's manual.

2 Timothy 3:16

All Scripture is God-breathed and is useful for teaching, rebuking, correcting and training in righteousness.

Joshua 1:8

Do not let this Book of the Law depart from your mouth; meditate on it day and night, so that you may be careful to do everything written in it. Then you will be prosperous and successful.

John 8:32

Then you will know the truth, and the truth will set you free.

COMPETITION

Jenny Boucek experienced firsthand the cutthroat world of professional basketball. Our world is driven by competition—in school, in love, at work, and in sports. Competition can be healthy and beneficial, or it can take control of our lives. Remember where your ultimate victory is— in Heaven.

1 Corinthians 9:24-27

Do you not know that in a race all the runners run, but only one gets the prize? Run in such a way as to get the prize. Everyone who competes in the games goes into strict training. They do it to get a crown that will not last; but we do it to get a crown that will last forever. Therefore I do not run like a man running aimlessly; I do not fight like a man beating the air. No, I beat my body and make it my slave so that after I have preached to others, I myself will not be disqualified for the prize.

Colossians 3:23-24

Whatever you do, work at it with all your heart, as working for the Lord, not for men, since you know that you will receive an inheritance from the Lord as a reward. It is the Lord Christ you are serving.

Bonnie Bramlett

Rock, Pop, R&B Musician

BONNIE Bramlett is a rock star, blues singer, and rhythm & blues legend all rolled into one. Her beautiful vocals are smooth as liquid velvet, her soulful lyrics profound and sometimes gut-wrenching. This hard-hitting singer/songwriter's list of collaborations reads like a who's who of rock and roll. Over the years she has worked with such well-known performers as Ike and Tina Turner, Jimi Hendrix, Rita Coolidge, Leon Russell, Eric Clapton, George Harrison, Joe Cocker, John Lennon, Dave Mason, Carly Simon, Stephen Stills, Gregg Allman, Jimmy Buffett, Dwight Yoakam, Delbert McClinton, and the Average White Band. Her influence as a performer and as a songwriter has left an indelible mark on the face of modern music.

One of her biggest accomplishments is writing mega-hit "Superstar," alongside Leon Russell. It has since been recorded by The Carpenters, Bette Midler, Cher, Luther Vandross, The Boston Pops, and most recently received a Grammy nomination for Ruben Studdard's performance on "American Idol." But nobody can sing it like Bonnie. Bramlett also appeared in the film, *The Doors* and on the hit TV series, "Roseanne." Bonnie Bramlett is a national treasure, aptly called, "The First Lady of Rock and Roll."

I'm a Christian who is a sinner still. I'm a tough Christian—one of those beat-up ones. I know that God is real because I'm still standing here. And the only reason I'm not dead is because He isn't finished with me yet.

I didn't become a Christian—I've always been one. I spent the first two years of my life with my great grandmother who was a minister. After my grandfather died, she would take her four kids to people's houses and do Bible teaching. She would offer all kinds of advice to people and pray for them. That's how she would earn her living. Sometimes they would give her money, or sometimes they would just feed them. She would call these love offerings her "smiles from Heaven."

As a kid coming up in church I never felt good enough. I thought everybody else was really perfect and were without sin, unlike me. As a child I believed in Jesus, like a child believes in a fairy godmother. That kind of blind faith is the same kind of faith that God would have for me. As adults, our faith should be like that of a child. But somewhere along the line we lose that innocence.

I grew up singing my brains out in church. I come from a long line of gospel singers—my mom, my uncle Paul—generations of gospel singers. I was blessed, truly anointed with musical talent at a very young age. Anointing is when you can master something that nobody has ever taught you. I've been anointed with the gift of song my whole life.

When I was about 14, I started going out of the house with my friends and sneaking into adult rhythm-and-blues clubs in the Gaslight Square district of St. Louis. We were underage, of course, but somehow we managed to get in. Somebody heard me sing there—somebody with some influence. Before you knew it, he called my mom and asked if he could hire me to sing. So there I was, only 14 years old, singing the blues and getting paid for it!

My career grew from there, and I ended up moving out to California. I was one of the "kids" of rock and roll at the time. Nobody started out being a big superstar; we were all just as green as could be. And I was pretty innocent. I'd never even heard of cocaine—it was running show business at that time. Before I got to California, I'd never done a drug in my life. But to fit in with the other musicians I started partying too. You see, the difference between me and most everybody out there that was using at that period of time was that they didn't think they were doing anything wrong. I knew darn good and well that I was doing something very bad; I was taught better than that. If I hadn't known that, I probably would have been dead. I never had to shoot heroin in my veins because I knew I was wrong just smoking that joint. I could barely live in my own skin. The Lord has always been with me, but I never realized when I was doing all this that I was taking the Lord with me. I was taking Him to the nightclubs. It wasn't fun for me, and I was able to do something about it.

In 1979 I began living again. I was really messed up, depressed and sick of it all. The partying had taken its toll on me. One day I was sitting out on the patio in the backyard of my home with a 12-gauge shotgun in my mouth. It was time for me to put an end to my misery—I was finished. I prayed and asked God to reveal Himself to me because I couldn't take it anymore. He needed to reveal Himself so that I knew He was real. I looked at my reflection in the sliding glass door holding that gun. And I saw my children standing there. I saw myself pull the trigger and my head being blown off. And I saw the blood slap my children across the face as they were screaming, "Mom!"

And then, poof, it was gone. I took the shotgun out of my mouth and shot it into the air because I didn't know how to uncock it. Then I checked myself into the hospital for help.

That day, I asked God to reveal Himself because I was ready to kill myself, and God did just that. I didn't see God; I just saw what would happen if I had made that choice. I know He's real because I'm still here. He saved my life.

And He has revealed Himself to me so many times since then. Years after this incident, I was living in Idaho and going through a horrible divorce. My life was filled with problems. I was an open wound; I felt forsaken. I was praying for God to send me a nice Christian man.

One day I called my daughter at her friend's house to chat, but when the answering machine came on it wasn't his usual message. I left a message anyway, leaving my name and phone number and asked them to call me back if I had the wrong number. About an hour and a half later my phone rang, and the guy on the other end of the line was country musician

Ricky Skaggs. I had left a message on his answering machine by mistake. I told Ricky that I had prayed the night before to be in touch with a Christian man because I was desperate for direction. As Ricky said, there are no accidents.

For a year and a half he called me up every month or so just to see how I was doing. And I wasn't doing well all the time. But Ricky and his wife continued to pray for me. And do you know what? I didn't even know him. He was that special Christian man in my life that God sent to help me. Ricky sent me the most beautiful book on worship...that's when I really started worshiping God. Ricky stuck with me for a couple of years; it wasn't until I moved to Nashville that I finally met him.

There's another reason I know He's real. My daughter and her husband were married for 12 years and they were trying desperately to have children. She would cry every month when she found out she wasn't pregnant. I have the most incredible prayer circle out behind my house. It's a grove of trees in a meadow that is formed in a perfect circle. So when I want to communicate with God I stand in the center of that circle and talk to Him. I pray for what I want or need, but at the end I finish the prayer with "Thy will be done. And if the answer is no, please give me the strength to take it." I prayed hard for my daughter to conceive, but left it up to God's will. After over a decade of trying, my grandson was born.

At the end of the day, we all have the same story. We've lost our way and need to get back to Him. God goes out and looks for us lost little sheep. God works for me. I love the Lord in my own special way. You see, God is a friend of mine. Jesus is my Savior and my teacher and my path to God. He is an inside job. You shouldn't look out there for God; look inside yourself.

If you can believe in Feng Shui and all those other cosmic, supernatural things like Tarot cards and everything else that is really hip, slick, and cool in Hollywood, how can you not believe in the power of prayer? My life has been a little rocky, but I've always known the Lord was right there next to me. And I have faith that everything happens for a reason. The lessons are in the storm.

GOD'S ROAD MAP

The Holy Bible is a guide to help you live a happy and satisfying life. To learn more about the concepts presented in the chapter you've just read, take a look at these passages:

SIN

Christians are not perfect. Because we were born into sin, it will be with us throughout our lives. But by His death on the cross, Jesus created a way to rescue us from our sin and bridge the gap that separates us from God. Daily time with God and reading His Word give us victory over sin.

Romans 6:12-13

Therefore do not let sin reign in your mortal body so that you obey its evil desires. Do not offer the parts of your body to sin, as instruments of wickedness, but rather offer yourselves to God, as those who have been brought from death to life; and offer the parts of your body to Him as instruments of righteousness.

Romans 7:21-25

...When I want to do good, evil is right there with me. For in my inner being I delight in God's law; but I see another law at work in the members of my body, waging war against the law of my mind and making me a prisoner of the law of sin at work within my members. What a wretched man I am! Who will rescue me from this body of death? Thanks be to God—through Jesus Christ our Lord!....

FORGIVENESS

Every day is a new beginning, a chance to wipe the slate clean and start a new chapter in your life. Life can be one big do-over when we give our lives to Christ. There is no hierarchy for sin—all sin is equal in the eyes of God whether it is lying or killing. No matter what you've done, it can be forgiven.

Colossians 1:21-23

Once you were alienated from God and were enemies in your minds because of your evil behavior. But now He has reconciled you by Christ's physical body through death to present you holy in His sight, without blemish and free from accusation— if you continue in your faith, established and firm, not moved from the hope held out in the gospel....

Lamentations 3:21-23

Yet this I call to mind and therefore I have hope: because of the Lord's great love we are not consumed, for His compassions never fail. They are new every morning; great is Your faithfulness.

Gary Burghoff

Actor, "Radar" O'Reilly, Hit TV Series
"M*A*S*H"/Painter
(Photo credit: Scott Stander & Associates, Inc.)

GARY Burghoff, a veteran of Broadway, got his big break in the lead role of the original off-Broadway production, *You're a Good Man, Charlie Brown*. Over the course of three years he performed the part of Charlie Brown over 1,000 times. Burghoff is probably best known for his role as Corporal Walter "Radar" O'Reilly in the hit movie and subsequent TV series "M*A*S*H." He received seven Emmy nominations for his work and won the coveted award for Best Supporting Actor in a Comedy Series in 1977. After leaving the show, he created the All-Star Dixieland Jazz Band and toured jazz clubs around the country. He is still active directing and acting in regional theater, most recently in Neil Simon's *Last of the Red Hot Lovers*.

But Burghoff is more than a great actor. Since 1992 he has also been recognized for his talent as a wildlife painter. He started painting wildlife in his 50's as a way of leaving a legacy for his children. It's his way of honoring God for life and for all the beautiful things he's seen in his life.

There's no such thing as a tunnel without a light at the end of it, now. There used to be a tunnel in total darkness. Life had a different perspective.

As a kid, I always felt a religious urge and had a belief, but I turned agnostic when I went to New York as a young man. And the ways of the world and the ideas of the world became more dominant than my home life. So I began to change and liberalize myself.

I was a struggling actor in New York City, and after six years I returned to Wisconsin to think about my future. One night I picked up a Bible and prayed to God for an answer. When I opened it, this is what I found: "Young men in youth, be true to your hearts." I hopped the next train back to New York. The next day a producer called me to see if I would play Charlie Brown. One of the performances was seen by the director of "M*A*S*H," Robert Altman. I did the television series from 1972-1979.

The year 1979 was my rebirth. It was a time period when there was a lot going on in my life and about the time when I was leaving "M*A*S*H." I had just gone through 15 years of being passionately devoted to career, and it blinded me to everything else in life.

That was also the year that my father died. He used to say that without the Bible you don't have a foundation. I remembered one specific thing in Scripture—"Honor your father and mother." I loved my father so much that I went out and bought a Bible and started reading it. I'd read it many other times throughout my life, but I didn't understand it. My heart wasn't open; I was an empty vessel.

I started searching all kinds of different religions for answers and for guidance. The odd thing was that they started coming to me, not even knowing that I was searching. It was by mail, knocking at the door—it was incredible! I received letters from fans who said they had been receiving very strong impressions of me even though I hadn't been saying anything publicly at all; this was all very private. As these experiences continued to happen, I started opening the door to everyone—Jehovah's Witnesses, Hindus, Baptists, Buddhists—everyone. A lot of unusual stuff was going on.

I started to understand that I had an obligation to read God's words rather than just accepting them on blind faith. That approach made studying the Scriptures more of a scientific approach. I learned that God had respect for my intellect—the intellect that He created. One day I finally understood and gave my life to Christ.

Miracles suddenly became conscious in my mind. I had a very good friend and neighbor who owned a health food store with his wife. It was going broke and they had almost no money left. With what money they had, they hired a Mexican crew to build a new store in a different location. One day he noticed a young Mexican man of about 16 who was new on the job, and had obviously just come across the border. The other workers weren't treating him very well; they were bossing him around and being cold to him.

At lunchtime, the boy was eating a very small sandwich while reading his Bible in Spanish. My friend noticed this and went over to talk to the boy. My friend had a $100 bill in his pocket—all he had left to his name. He gave the boy that $100 knowing that he probably had an even greater need.

When my friend went home that night, he found very little food in the house. Knowing that they needed to at least get some milk for the kids, his wife found some change they kept in a jar. He and I went to the supermarket together to buy a gallon of milk. As he opened the door to the store, he looked down and found a $100 bill on the pavement right at his feet. God never gives you what you want when you want it; He gives you what you need when you need it. This is one of hundreds of little miracles I've seen since I gave myself over.

In 1979 I also got divorced. I was given the honor of caring for my four-year-old daughter for the first year. I had not been a very involved father up until that point, so it was a big adjustment for both of us. The agreement was that I would keep her for a year until her mother got established in another state and then I would turn her over and have her only on vacations.

My ex-wife was living in a very mountainous area in another state, a vacation area of sorts, comprised of over 40,000 condominiums. Two days before Christmas, I drove the 1,800-mile journey from California to pick up my daughter so that she could spend the holidays with me. I arrived at about 9:00 one night, later than expected, because the directions I had been given were either erroneous or I had taken a wrong turn.

When I finally arrived, I called my ex-wife. She was very angry with me because I hadn't arrived on time and my daughter had gone to bed. She hung up on me without even giving me her address.

It had been a long drive and I was beat. I asked the motel manager if there was someplace to eat close by. He said there was a bar across the street and they could make me a sandwich. Now, I was a new Christian at this point, and I didn't drink; but I went across to that bar for a bite anyway. I walked in, and there were about a half dozen people inside. And for some reason, I was very drawn to a young couple sitting at one of the tables. I went over and asked them if they minded if I joined them—I didn't want to eat alone. They turned out to be born-again Christians too! What were the odds of finding two other Christians sitting in a bar having a sandwich?

After we ate, they invited me over to their parent's condo which they were using for the weekend. I went over and we had some dessert. I was so propped up in my faith, so renewed after having talked with them that I suddenly got braver and said, "You know, I'm not going to take this. I need to be there first thing in the morning to see my kid, and I'm going to call her even though it's 10:00 at night. I'm going to call her and get that address." So I went over to the phone next to the window and dialed the number. As the phone rang, I saw a woman directly across the street—no more than 50 yards from me—pick up the phone. It was my ex-wife. The Lord had brought me right across the street from her condominium—one out of over 40,000 units. Is that a miracle or what?

And those miracles just keep on happening. I did a job for a company that was doing a series of vacation videos. The filming was taking place at the same mountain lodge where *The Shining* had been filmed, a hotel in Rocky Mountain National Park, Colorado. The altitude was over 11,000 feet, and I didn't realize that I was not acclimated to that altitude. I was only there for four days and it takes you about five days to get used to the thinner air. I had a terrible time staying awake during the shooting, and I was disoriented. I felt truly ill.

After the shooting was complete, I drove back down the mountain in my Ford Explorer. I was crossing the Nevada desert on Route 80 with my cruise control set at 70 mph, and I fell asleep at the wheel. I was in the speed lane, and the only thing that woke me up was hitting a 2-inch wide reflector—just two inches. These reflectors were at least 100 feet apart, and in between them there was nothing. Had I gone in between them, I would have been airborne and fallen into a 40-foot trench due to the road construction being done.

When I hit the reflector, it went off like a gunshot and woke me up. I over-corrected the car and went clear across, at a 90-degree angle, into the slow lane, and then back again into the fast lane, before I could bring the car under control. Now, I'm no mathematician, but the odds of hitting that 2-inch reflector rather than going through the 100-foot gap have to be something like a million to one. So to me, that's what it feels like to be in God's hands—it was no coincidence. Although it was frightening, it was a faith-renewing moment.

Over the years, I have tried my best to share my faith with my children. One day I picked up my son from school when he was about five. When I saw him, he had a real frown on his face. When I asked him if something was bothering him, he said, "I was just wondering if there is or isn't a God."

At this point on the drive home, we were passing through a wooded area. I pulled over and got as far away from the public roads and traffic as I could. It was real quiet there; and squirrels, blue jays, bugs, and butterflies were all around. I asked my sons to look around and name all the man-made things they could see. Of course, they couldn't find any. Mankind cannot make a tree or an insect or an animal or any of the natural things. These things were created before people were here. When people finally came, they became aware of the wonders around them and began to understand that there was a Creator. Some of the greatest scientists, including Albert Einstein, understood that it would be impossible for the order of nature to happen haphazardly. That's what I've asked my kids to remember all of their lives—that no man has ever made a tree.

The world and my life have been filled with tiny miracles all adding up to a very strong faith. Life is very good. If you were to ask me if life is always "peachy creamy," the answer would be "no." Life has its ups and downs, and we all have to deal with it. But now I deal with it from a different perspective. Remember, God never gives you what you want because you want it; He gives you what you need when you need it. I'm in good hands now.

GOD'S ROAD MAP

The Holy Bible is a guide to help you live a happy and satisfying life. To learn more about the concepts presented in the chapter you've just read, take a look at these passages:

CREATION

Try taking a walk into the woods like Gary did with his sons. Look around and identify all those things that are man-made and you'll come up empty-handed. Even if you see a building that was constructed by the hands of man, you must realize that the materials came from God—the wood, the stone, even the steel came from God-inspired ingredients. In the following verses, you will see God's careful and deliberate creation—not a big bang in the cosmos where all of a sudden, life existed. And when Jesus comes again, the Earth will once again be a new creation.

Genesis 1:1,9-13,20-26

In the beginning God created the heavens and the earth. ... And God said, "Let the water under the sky be gathered to one place, and let dry ground appear." And it was so. God called the dry ground "land," and the gathered waters He called "seas." And God saw that it was good.

Then God said, "Let the land produce vegetation: seed-bearing plants and trees on the land that bear fruit with seed in it, according to their various kinds." And it was so. The land produced vegetation: plants bearing seed according to their kinds and trees bearing fruit with seed in it according to their kinds. And God saw that it was good. And there was evening, and there was morning— the third day. ... And God said, "Let the water teem with living creatures, and let birds fly above the earth across the expanse of the sky." So God created the great creatures of the sea and every living and moving thing with which the water teems, according to their kinds, and every winged bird according to its kind. And God saw that it was good. God blessed them and said, "Be fruitful and increase in number and fill the water in the seas, and let the birds increase on the earth." And there was evening, and there was morning—the fifth day.

And God said, "Let the land produce living creatures according to their kinds: livestock, creatures that move along the ground, and wild animals, each according to its kind." And it was so. God made the wild animals according to their kinds, the livestock according to their kinds, and all the creatures that move along the ground according to their kinds. And God saw that it was good.

Then God said, "Let Us make man in Our image, in Our likeness, and let them rule over the fish of the sea and the birds of the air, over the livestock, over all the earth, and over all the creatures that move along the ground."

Kirk Cameron

Actor, Hit TV Series
"Growing Pains"

AT the tender young age of 14, Kirk Cameron became one of the biggest teenage heartthrobs in the world of entertainment. From 1985-1992 he played the role of Mike Seaver on the wildly successful television sitcom "Growing Pains." At the height of the show he was making $50,000 an episode, was nominated for two Golden Glove awards, and was gracing the covers of magazines like *16*, *Tiger Beat*, and *Teen Beat*.

His conversion to Christianity in the early '90s sent his career in a different direction. To many Christians he is well-known as journalist Buck Williams on the film versions of the best-selling *Left Behind* novels by Tim LaHaye and Jerry Jenkins.

Cameron, along with evangelist and author Ray Comfort, created The Way of the Master, an organization designed to teach Christians how to more effectively share the Gospel with others. More information can be found at www.wayofthemaster.com.

For me in my life, the biggest celebrity, the biggest star, the one who is famous in my mind—not just here on earth, but throughout the universe—is Jesus Christ. He's the One who I applaud and thank.

I'll be honest with you—I was not always a good Christian guy. I grew up in a home where we didn't go to church. I didn't believe in God. I was a staunch atheist for most of my life. I thought I was just too smart to believe in a fairy tale like that.

When I was about 14 years old, I had been working in the entertainment industry for a few years, and I got the part of Mike Seaver on "Growing Pains." Within a few years, it was a hit show. I had everything that I wanted. I had as much money as I wanted to spend. I was traveling around the world meeting famous people. I was a famous person. I had everything that I wanted.

But I met a man, who was the father of a girl that I liked, and I got to talking to this man, and he said, "There's still something that you don't have, though, Kirk. You have a lot, but you don't have the Lord." I'm thinking to myself, *Okay, what's your point? I don't believe in God, and that's really not something I'm interested in.* But I thought, *Well, I better not turn down his invitation to go to church. After all, this is the girl I like's father."*

So, I went to church with them, and I heard the Gospel for the very first time. And I listened because it wasn't what I thought it was. This man stood up front and he opened up a Bible, which I thought was just this big, thick, dusty book full of rules designed to suck all the fun out of your life. The man at the front said it was the Word of God. He explained that there is a God who made me and you, and everyone on this planet, and everything in this universe; and He sustains our life, moment by moment. He is a holy God. He is a pure God. He is a good, amazing, wonderful God.

He went on to explain that we were designed by God to know Him, and to love Him, and obey Him with all of our heart, to be in a right relationship with Him. But that kind of right relationship does not naturally exist between us and God because of something that separates us from God, and that something he called *sin.* I didn't understand what sin was, and he explained it to me very simply. He said, "Sin is this stubborn, selfish streak that runs deep through the heart of every person. It shows up in many different kinds of ways in your life. It shows up when you lie. It shows up when you steal. It shows up when you dishonor your mother and father. It shows up when you think you're better than other people. And one of the clearest ways it shows up is when you put other things in your life in a more important position than God, who gave you those things."

As I was listening to him, I was feeling really guilty, because if that was true, I was in big trouble. I was guilty of all those things. My dirty socks were more important to me than God, because in my mind, God didn't even exist. He said that God hates sin. God is pure and holy, and He hates sin, not only because it separates us from Him, but because it's wrong, and that God will punish sin and those who commit sin in a place called hell. I'm thinking, *Wow, that's really harsh.*

But he went on to explain the character of God as also being loving and compassionate and merciful, and that He has provided a way for each and every person who has sinned against God to be forgiven. He did that through sending His Son, Jesus Christ, who died on a cross and then rose from the grave; and if we will humble ourselves before God, repent of our sin, and trust in Jesus Christ who died to pay the price for our sins, God would grant us forgiveness and everlasting life. He did that to demonstrate His great love for us.

Now I'm sitting at the back of this church feeling two things: one, very guilty because I knew that I had sinned, if anyone had ever sinned against God; and two, I felt this incredible sense of hope. My heart was swelling with hope that this story of an amazing God who sees my sinful heart would be compassionate enough to actually take my punishment for me, forgive me, and welcome me back into a right relationship with Him.

So I went home not knowing what to say to my friend's father, but I sure had lots of questions. I asked him about evolution. I asked him about all kinds of religions. I asked him about the Bible, and I asked him for answers. He gave me lots of intelligent answers to these questions, but he said, "Kirk, there's one question you need to ask God Himself. I can't answer it for you. And that's whether or not He's real." I thought, *Well, how am I supposed to do that?*

Well, about a month later, I was sitting in my car all by myself on the side of the road, and the thought occurred to me, *Kirk, if you get in a car accident and die today, will you be going to Heaven?* I knew the answer was no. I knew that I had ignored God my whole life, put everything in a more important position than He was, and I had sinned against Him. Even though I knew the things I was doing were wrong, I did them anyway, because I could get away with it. But God saw all of that, and I knew that there was no reason He should let me into Heaven, especially in light of what He had done by sending His Son, Jesus Christ, to die on a cross for me.

And so, I knew it was time for me to do something about that. I decided I would pray. I didn't know how to do it. I had never done it before, but I closed my eyes and I prayed the clumsiest prayer ever prayed in the history of prayer praying. I just said, "God, if You're there, I need to know. God, if You're real, would You please show me? And would You please forgive me? And would You please change me into the person that You want me to be?"

I opened my eyes, and it wasn't like a gust of wind blew through my window or I saw visions of Jesus on my windshield, but I had a very real sense that God heard me. I felt He was listening to me, that He was real. And it felt so good.

I went back home and told a friend who was a Christian. He gave me a Bible, and I started reading my Bible. And I started learning about this amazing God who is not this big bad cop up in the sky just waiting to punish people because He somehow gets His kicks by doing that. He is a holy, just, righteous God who desires for us to turn from our sin so that we can be forgiven of our sin. It's an amazing story of love that's spelled out in the Bible, and that's the God that I have fallen in love with and that I live for.

I can honestly tell you today that of all the places I've ever been, of all the people I've ever met, of all the fun and exciting things I've ever done, absolutely nothing compares to the joy of knowing Jesus Christ, of knowing that my sins are forgiven and that I'm in a right relationship with God.

GOD'S ROAD MAP

The Holy Bible is a guide to help you live a happy and satisfying life. To learn more about the concepts presented in the chapter you've just read, take a look at these passages:

GOD'S LOVE

God loves you more than you can possibly imagine. And He loves you unconditionally; His love is not based on what you do or who you are. He loves every man, woman, and child on the planet—even those who turn away from Him. Once you experience that love personally, you'll never turn away again.

First John 4:7-12

Dear friends, let us love one another, for love comes from God. Everyone who loves has been born of God and knows God. Whoever does not love does not know God, because God is love. This is how God showed His love among us: He sent His one and only Son into the world that we might live through Him. This is love: not that we loved God, but that He loved us and sent His Son as an atoning sacrifice for our sins. Dear friends, since God so loved us, we also ought to love one another. No one has ever seen God; but if we love one another, God lives in us and His love is made complete in us.

Romans 8:35-39

Who shall separate us from the love of Christ? Shall trouble or hardship or persecution or famine or nakedness or danger or sword? As it is written: "For Your sake we face death all day long; we are considered as sheep to be slaughtered." No, in all these things we are more than conquerors through Him who loved us. For I am convinced that neither death nor life, neither angels nor demons, neither the present nor the future, nor any powers, neither height nor depth, nor anything else in all creation, will be able to separate us from the love of God that is in Christ Jesus our Lord.

First Corinthians 2:9

However, as it is written: "No eye has seen, no ear has heard, no mind has conceived what God has prepared for those who love Him."

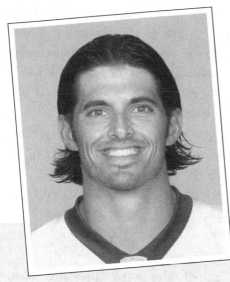

David Carr

NFL Quarterback, Houston Texans
(Photo, courtesy of the Houston Texans)

I N 2002, quarterback David Carr was the first overall pick of the NFL draft. He was chosen by the new expansion team, the Houston Texans, and has been their starter ever since.

A California native, Carr earned all-league honors at Stockdale High School in Bakersfield. He was recruited by Fresno State where he went on to be one of the most successful athletes in the school's history. As a Bulldog senior, he led the nation in both passing yards and touchdown passes. Carr was a first-team All-Western Athletic Conference selection and WAC Offensive Player as a senior. He is the recipient of the Johnny Unitas Golden Arm award, given to the country's most outstanding college senior. Carr also won the Sammy Baugh Award, presented annually to the nation's top quarterback.

Now starting his fourth year in the NFL, Carr is one of the league's rising young quarterbacks. He has thrown for 8,136 yards with 34 touchdowns in 44 career games, despite getting sacked 140 times. He is one of the league's top rushing quarterbacks with 732 career yards and five touchdowns. One of five finalists for the 2002 NFL Rookie of the Year honors, Carr set an NFL record for consecutive starts for an expansion team.

I was raised in the church my entire life. I first received Christ at Wagon Train Camp when I was in fourth grade. My cousin and I both dedicated our lives to Him the same day, and we've been best friends ever since. As I grew older, I was very involved with my youth group. The friends I made in that group are still my friends today—even more so than the friends I made in high school and college.

Going away to college was hard at first, mostly because I had to leave my family. Anytime you go out on your own, it's human nature to explore everything. A lot of my friends chose to get mixed up in bad crowds, but I never fell into that. The thing that always brought me back into focus was my family. I had such a good support system around me that I was never able—as much as I tried—to veer off track. My family always slapped me back in line. It was nice to have them around.

High school and college were a time of intense peer pressure. Being involved in sports, especially football, helped me stay focused on God. It's amazing how many football players find a way to believe in God or at least believe there's someone out there helping them. There are a lot of things that can go wrong in the game. I've seen some very serious injuries. And I've seen some guys who are just as talented as I am who just didn't happen to make it because of some freak accident.

Football is a serious contact sport as everyone knows, and there's a lot of violent action that goes on. That's especially true when you're the quarterback. When you drop back in the pocket, you've got five guys fighting for you and five guys coming to get you. You're at the mercy of whatever they do. But you really can't worry about it because you have a job to do—you need to throw the ball out on the field and complete passes. It involves a lot of faith. I've been playing football since I was in fifth grade, and to think that I've gotten this far without any serious injuries is really remarkable. And to think I've done that all on my own would be foolish.

There's no doubt I've been blessed. Every day I count my blessings and realize that I'm not here just by accident. It's tempting for professional athletes to take credit for their own accomplishments and let their celebrity impact their egos. My grandparents always used to tell me that I was never going to get too big for anything I did in life. They told me that God had a reason for putting me in these prominent positions...never forget it.

I've tried very hard not to take advantage of my success. I've played ball with so many friends who have fallen fast. At any time this can all be taken away. In just one play, an entire career can be over. So you can go out there and get a big head and think it's all because of you; but to me, that just doesn't make sense. I don't have to try very hard to believe that God's protecting me and He's got His hand on my life.

I remember one time in particular when I knew Christ was real. We played the Tampa Bay Buccaneers in the last pre-season game before my official NFL debut in 2002. I was scheduled for only five plays in that game. After that, they were going to take the starters out and rest them for the season opener the following week. We were basically going to go in, get a couple of snaps, and get back out.

It just so happened we got a couple of first downs, and they decided to leave us in and keep the drive going. On a pass rush, a guy came around and came free, and as I threw the ball, I got hit hard in my left leg. My cleat stuck in the turf and my knee hit the ground before the rest of my body. I heard it "pop" and thought to myself, *This is not good.*

As I lay on the ground waiting for the trainers to check me out, so many things went through my mind. I refused to believe that I'd gone through all those years of training to have my career end before my very first game. Right at that second, in a very quiet voice inside my heart, I heard, *Get up, you're not done yet.*

To the surprise of the coaches, I stood up, tested out my leg, and walked off the field under my own power. The doctors did x-rays but found there was nothing at all wrong with my knee. It was obviously a miracle, because I've seen it on film—your knee is not supposed to bend that way. I knew that I'd been protected. At that moment, I just knew that God had brought me there for a bigger purpose. It was about more than just a football game. That sort of divine intervention has happened many times over the course of my football career.

About six months ago, my 5-year-old son, Austin, was diagnosed with juvenile diabetes. My wife, Melody, and I were shocked when we heard the diagnosis. We kept asking, "Why did this happen to him? Why do we have to go through this right now?" But at the same time, I knew God gave me peace me in the midst of this struggle. I knew that the peace I felt could have only come from God alone, because my normal fatherly instinct would have caused me to respond very differently. I would have been a mess knowing that my firstborn son had a disease that would affect him for the rest of his life. But God helped me realize we could turn this into something good; it wasn't just all about me.

I knew everything was going to be okay and it was happening for a good reason. Since then, we've been able to help so many other kids who have diabetes. When we first found out about Austin, we went to a class to learn how to give insulin shots and check his blood sugar. Many of the parents of stricken children, even kids as young as six or seven months, weren't able to be there because they had to work. I knew right there that we had to do something. We had to go out and try to raise awareness, and raise money—do something to cure this disease. And because of my platform, we're able to raise so much more money to help out these kids.

Football has always been just a game for me. It just so happens that I get paid way too much money to play it. And I'm thankful every day for the opportunities I have been given. I'm doing something I love, and more importantly, I believe God has called me to do it. Being in the NFL, especially being a quarterback, can bring with it a lot of pressure. But I know that God wouldn't have me here in this position if it wasn't for a purpose. Even if bad things happen and we lose a couple of games, it's all part of God's plan. If I didn't believe that, I'd just as soon be a normal, everyday person who doesn't believe in God at all. Because without faith, I wouldn't have anything.

GOD'S ROAD MAP

The Holy Bible provides a road map to help you live a happy and satisfying life. To learn more about the concepts presented in the chapter you've just read, take a look at these passages:

ACCOUNTABILITY

Once you become a Christian, it is critical to surround yourself with other believers. God puts these people in our lives to help keep us accountable and walking on the straight and narrow path. God, of course, also holds us accountable. The Bible says that one day we all will account for what we've done in our lives.

Proverbs 27:5-6

Better is open rebuke than hidden love. Wounds from a friend can be trusted, but an enemy multiplies kisses.

Proverbs 12:15

The way of a fool seems right to him, but a wise man listens to advice.

Ecclesiastes 11:9

Be happy, young man, while you are young, and let your heart give you joy in the days of your youth. Follow the ways of your heart and whatever your eyes see, but know that for all these things God will bring you to judgment.

ACCOMPLISHMENTS

David Carr has had an incredible amount of success in his young life. But he understands that everything he has done comes from God, which keeps him grounded. In all ways we should acknowledge where true success comes from.

Isaiah 25:1

O Lord, You are my God; I will exalt You and praise Your name, for in perfect faithfulness You have done marvelous things, things planned long ago.

First Corinthians 4:7

For who makes you different from anyone else? What do you have that you did not receive? And if you did receive it, why do you boast as though you did not?

Matthew 23:12

For whoever exalts himself will be humbled, and whoever humbles himself will be exalted.

Tara Dawn Christensen

Miss America 1997
(Photo, courtesy of Tim Tew)

O N September 14, 1996, Tara Dawn Christensen was crowned Miss America 1997. It was only after she laid her ambitions at the foot of the cross that God blessed her with the title. Tara earned a Bachelor's degree in Music Education from Florida State University and a Master's degree from the University of Missouri, Kansas City. Well-known for her spectacular voice, Tara has had the honor of performing for countless high-profile events, including President George W. Bush's Inaugural Ball, the Ronald Reagan Awards Dinner, and Macy's Thanksgiving Day parade. She has been interviewed on the "Tonight Show" with Jay Leno, "Today," "Live with Regis and Kathie Lee," "Entertainment Tonight," and in publications such as *People Magazine, Reader's Digest,* and *TV Guide.* During her reign, she was named the 1997 Kansan of the Year and was the National Spokesperson for the Library of Congress "Building a Nation of Readers" campaign.

Well-known for her focus on literacy, Tara is probably even more recognized for her position on abstinence. In junior high school, Tara made a decision to abstain from drugs, alcohol, and premarital sex. When she married U.S. Congressman Jon Christensen at the age of 26, she was still a virgin. She now tours the country speaking to young people in schools and churches on the importance of abstaining from premarital sex. Her website is www.taradawnchristensen.com.

✦❖❖❖❖✦

Let me save you some time—you can't find assurance in the world; you can't find it in riches or success; it's not found in an address like Hollywood, Broadway, Wall Street, or Washington DC. The road to success and personal happiness is littered with those who have tried that route and failed. Just examine the lives of Elvis Presley, Marilyn Monroe, or Nirvana's lead singer, Curt Cobain. Personal happiness is attainable only when you turn your life over to the One who loves you the most—Jesus Christ.

My mom and dad were living in Mobile, Alabama when I was born. By the age of five, I had moved six times because of my dad's work. When I was young, moving wasn't really hard on me because on the playground you'd say, "Hi. What's your name? Let's play ring-around-the-rosy." And you're done—instant friend. When I was older and we moved, it was a little more difficult. However, I had one constant and steadying force with me during the rest of those moves. When I was five years old, I accepted Christ as my Lord and Savior in my bedroom, as Mom and Daddy prayed with me. Since that night, I've always tried to live for Him.

In the seventh grade, I was given an assignment to read an autobiography and present a book report. I had always been interested in the Miss America Pageant, so I decided to read *A Bright Shining Place* by Cheryl Prewitt, Miss America 1980. The requirement for this report was that we had to come into the classroom and present ourselves as if we were the person about whom we had read. Now, at that time, you couldn't just go to a party shop and buy a crown like you can today. So, I made one out of cardboard and put foil and glitter on top. I wore my best clothes to school and took a fake rose on the bus to complete the look. On that day in the seventh grade, I stood in front of my peers and said, "Good morning, I'm

Miss America." Who would have thought that I would be saying that same thing for real, 12 years later?

Several things happened for me through reading this book. I found out that a normal, average girl who was raised in the South could become Miss America. Cheryl Prewitt said herself that she's not the smartest, the most talented, or the prettiest girl in the world, but that with God and perseverance anything is possible. Secondly, I knew then that I wanted to be Miss America and do pageants in the name of the Lord.

When I was a senior in high school I started competing. I did my high school pageant and the Junior Miss program, which was just for seniors in high school. Then I started in the Miss America system. When I was 17, I won my third local pageant and went to the Miss Florida Pageant. There were 47 contestants and I came in 1st runner-up, which really blew me away. It actually scared me somewhat because I knew I wasn't ready to be Miss Florida and certainly not Miss America. At that time the age span for competing in the Miss America system was 17-26, so at 17, I was the youngest possible competitor. There is a big difference between a 26-year-old professional woman and a 17-year-old high school girl, and I knew I was not ready to be Miss America yet. So, I took a few years off from competing and concentrated on college. In 1994, as a graduating senior, it was the right time to return to the pageant competition.

When I was 23, I finally made it to Atlantic City to compete for the title of Miss America. You can only compete for the title once in your life, so I had to give it my all. What an incredible experience that was. The auditorium once served as an airplane hangar. It seats 25,000 people, and the stage is just enormous, a truly frightening prospect for most people. But during that time, I fully understood the Scripture that speaks of the peace that passes all understanding. It didn't make sense, but I was totally at peace—not nervous at all about standing on that stage and doing my best. When they placed the crown on my head, it was a dream come true.

The year of my reign was amazing. I traveled an average of 20,000 miles each month and was in a different state every 18-36 hours. I only had one day off per month. It sounds exhausting, but I was just so thankful for the opportunity to be Miss America that I think I lived on adrenaline for the whole year.

When I was crowned Miss America, I started to dream about where I might be on certain holidays. There would only be one Christmas, one birthday, and one Valentine's Day where I would get to be Miss America. On Valentine's Day, I wanted to be in an exciting place like Washington, DC or New York City. When I received my monthly schedule, I found out that instead of being in what I considered to be an exotic or romantic spot, I would be in Omaha, Nebraska. I was to find out later what an incredible sense of timing and direction God has.

At the airport, there was this guy who wanted to talk to me. He didn't know who I was, because I didn't wear my crown while I was traveling. He saw me go into the ladies' room, so he figured he would go into the men's room and emerge at the same time in order to meet me. But believe it or not, I was actually faster than he was! He checked all the gates in the area looking for me, and finally said to himself, *Well, Lord, I guess she wasn't the one.* He got on his plane and there I was—seated a few rows in front of him! When the plane was about to land, I needed to go to the rest room to freshen up as I was going to speak the moment I arrived in Omaha; and the only rest room was in the back of the plane (in this man's direction). When I came out to return to my seat, there was this man sitting in an aisle seat with his arm extended straight across the aisle blocking my way. A little forward, huh? Once we began to talk, I knew within 60 seconds that we shared a common faith and that we were on the same page in politics and religion. I just knew that we were cut from the same cloth. After about 15 minutes of talking he said, "It's Valentine's Day and it's a Friday night. If you're not doing anything, would you like to go out this evening?" That was our first date. I thought I wanted to be in some exciting big city on Valentine's Day. Who would have ever thought I would meet the man of my dreams on an airplane bound for Omaha, Nebraska?

By the time I gave up my crown as Miss America, Jon and I were dating seriously, and we knew that we were going to be married. In the same week my reign ended, Jon announced that he was running for governor of the state of Nebraska. So I went straight from one whirlwind to the next!

When I was in junior high school, I made a very important choice that affected my relationship with Jon and every other person I ever dated. At that time, I made a decision to abstain from drugs, alcohol, and premarital sex. Of course, this was not a very popular choice among my friends and classmates; many times I felt isolated and ridiculed by my peers. But God gave me the strength to resist those temptations. It was all worth it when I met Jon Christensen and walked down the aisle at our wedding as a 26-year-old virgin.

During the governor's race, Jon and I were interviewed by an Omaha newspaper reporter. He asked Jon what made me so special to him. Jon said, "It means a lot to me that she saved herself for marriage." A couple of days later, another writer for the same paper wrote a terribly scathing article about that statement, scolding us for being proud of my virginity. She even questioned whether purity was a smart choice or one that you would wish for in your future spouse. This launched a flurry of media activity, both positive and negative, regarding our stand for abstinence. When I was interviewed a month or two later by Dr. James Dobson from Focus on the Family, the abstinence speaking opportunities suddenly presented themselves. What was meant for evil, God turned into good for His Kingdom. Currently, I am a national spokesperson for purity and speak to young people all over the country about the importance of abstaining from premarital sex. I have seen thousands upon thousands of students pledge purity and give their lives to Christ because of one simple statement. God is definitely real.

There are so many other things that God has done in my life that show me He's real. After taking several years off from competing, I was interested in entering a local pageant in 1994—the Miss Florida State Fair Pageant. I put my application in early and made all the preparations to compete. A week before the pageant, I became sick and the doctors thought it might be mono. I was running a low-grade fever and was just exhausted. To top it all off, my voice wasn't sounding very good. The doctors put me on antibiotics, which didn't work at all. Three days before the competition, I was put on steroids to try and knock out the illness. Steroids, however, can have bad side effects, one of them being unusual weight gain. I gained 10 pounds in 24 hours. For the pageant, there was an opening production number and I had this cute little red dress to wear. The night before the pageant, I tried it on and couldn't even zip it! Obviously, that itself was a problem, but I also had to do a swimsuit competition and I was ten pounds heavier than normal! So, my mom and I knelt down in our hotel room and prayed, "Lord, I know that there are a lot bigger things to be concerned with around the world, but I know You called me to be here, and I know You have a plan for me. If you can find it in your schedule to help me lose ten pounds by morning, I would really appreciate that." The next morning I didn't wake up ten pounds lighter—I woke up twelve pounds lighter! Not only did I win that pageant, but I also won swimsuit competition!

Because I know He's real, my goal is not to be famous, make a lot of money, or be a household name. All I know is that I have to do what He has called me to do; however He wants to use me is my only desire. I don't know what God has planned for me, but I will continue to proclaim His truth wherever there is an opportunity. Jesus Christ is the only One who will never fail you or leave you. He loves you with an everlasting love. And most importantly, God promises eternal life to anyone who asks.

GOD'S ROAD MAP

The Holy Bible is a guide to help you live a happy and satisfying life. To learn more about the concepts presented in the chapter you've just read, take a look at these passages:

PURITY

God created us as sexual beings, and designed sex as a gift to be shared between a man and a woman after they are married. Within marriage, sex is designed to enhance intimacy, communication, and commitment, as well as to create life. In a world overrun with sexual images, maintaining purity is virtually impossible without the help of the Lord.

First Thessalonians 4:3-7

It is God's will that you should be sanctified: that you should avoid sexual immorality; that each of you should learn to control his own body in a way that is holy and honorable, not in passionate lust like the heathen, who do not know God; and that in this matter no one should wrong his brother or take advantage of him. The Lord will punish men for all such sins, as we have already told you and warned you. For God did not call us to be impure, but to live a holy life.

First Corinthians 6:13b,19-20

The body is not meant for sexual immorality, but for the Lord, and the Lord for the body....Do you not know that your body is a temple of the Holy Spirit, who is in you, whom you have received from God? You are not your own; you were bought at a price. Therefore honor God with your body.

HEALING

Healing can occur both physically and spiritually. The Bible is filled with examples of God's miraculous healings. He also heals us through the intervention of others, like the medical community or a trusted friend. But no matter in which way healing occurs, prayer is the key ingredient.

Mark 1:40-42

A man with leprosy came to Him and begged Him on his knees, "If You are willing, You can make me clean." Filled with compassion, Jesus reached out His hand and touched the man. "I am willing," he said. "Be clean!" Immediately the leprosy left him and he was cured.

James 5:13-16

Is any one of you in trouble? He should pray. Is anyone happy? Let him sing songs of praise. Is any one of you sick? He should call the elders of the church to pray over him and anoint him with oil in the name of the Lord. And the prayer offered in faith will make the sick person well; the Lord will raise him up. If he has sinned, he will be forgiven. Therefore confess your sins to each other and pray for each other so that you may be healed. The prayer of a righteous man is powerful and effective.

Clay Crosse

Dove Award-Winning Christian
Musician

A FTER over ten years of working the local music scene in Memphis, Tennessee, Clay Crosse had given up hope of a career in the national spotlight. But once the right ears in Nashville heard his soulful vocals, his career exploded. From 1994-2001 he had ten #1 singles, including megahits, "I Surrender All" and "I Will Follow Christ." Two of his albums had sales of more than 400,000 units.

Crosse has also participated in numerous high-profile special recording projects and compilations. He performed in the "Child of the Promise" and "The Young Messiah" tours among many others. He is the recipient of three Dove Awards, most notably, the 1995 award for "New Artist of the Year."

In addition to recording and performing, he has also spent the last three years leading worship at his home church, The Love of Christ Community Church. He has brought that love of worship music to his latest project, "Eternity With You: Live Worship." In 2005, Crosse and his wife, Renee, wrote the book, *I Surrender All: Rebuilding a Marriage Broken By Pornography*. For more information on his music and message, go to www.claycrosse.com.

I wish I had never seen porn. I know that I would be a better person if I had walked away from it and had never introduced it into my life. My wife and I had a tough couple of years as a direct result of porn, but what satan designed to destroy us is now glorifying the Lord.

Singing has always been a special joy for me. I remember walking home from school one day when I was in third or fourth grade just singing out. This guy heard me and said, "Man, that sounds just like on the radio!" Music was a big part of our family life, and I had a lot of cousins who would sing harmonies at family get-togethers. Those harmonies really caught my ear and eventually I began to sing with them. If nothing else, I knew I could carry a tune and my confidence grew.

When I was 15, I sang my first solo at church and the people responded really well. It became an addiction—I knew I had to do this! I could hardly think of anything other than seeing where my singing could go. Eventually God took me big places with my voice.

But it took longer than people think. I did quite a bit of local stuff, but my career wasn't like I wanted it to be. I wanted to make CDs and hear my songs on the radio. I wanted to be known outside of my hometown. I thought it could happen, but I was losing hope. In fact, I'd long since come to the conclusion that I was not going to make it full-time. I was going to be a guy working a normal job with musical talent on the side.

Nearly ten years after that first solo, some key people in Nashville finally heard me and began to show interest. A few years after that, I recorded my first CD. I got to leave my day job and go out on the road with some pretty major contemporary Christian artists. And before I knew it, I was a major contemporary Christian artist myself.

It was a whirlwind...I felt like an overnight success. But as I look back at all the years of singing in garage bands, in talent shows, and at every wedding and funeral that would have me, it had finally happened. After all those years of dreaming, God finally opened up a door and allowed me to pursue my music full-time. It was incredible.

I made several recordings and had some big number-one hits. My career was going great, but inside I was struggling. It's not such a nice thing to talk about, but for me, the struggle was mostly physical lust and sexual desire that got out of control. And pornography was the fuel that ignited that lust.

I'd first been exposed to pornographic magazines at a friend's house when I was in elementary school. Those images were burned into my mind forever. In junior high, high school, and college, I came into contact with those kinds of materials again; and the images began to affect the way I looked at women. As I grew older, pornography was something that only drew me further from Christ and drew me closer to myself. I became much more self-centered.

Truthfully, it wasn't like I got married in 1990 and started watching porn. When I got married, I *stopped* watching porn; I had been watching it up until then. My wife, Renee, and I didn't have premarital sex. So, I figured once we were married and I could have sex, I could put the porn away forever. I remained outwardly faithful to Renee, but my thought life was a real problem.

We slowly started taking on the attitude of a very casual Christian couple. We weren't careful about what we let into our home through television and movie choices. It started out very subtle—maybe just some normal network television shows that don't belong in a Christian's life. Then it regressed to the point where we were watching some pretty raunchy cable TV and movies—not pornography, but definitely movies that didn't glorify the Lord. We became very "open-minded" and were really pushing the limits. So, by the time 1996 rolled around, it was a very easy transition for me to see porn again.

But God loved me too much to allow me to go down that path. And He got my attention in a very real and powerful way through the one thing that mattered most to me—my voice.

I began having difficulty singing, and it really slowed me down musically. Some of the record labels stopped showing interest in me. I had always thought that if all else failed, at least I could sing. I used to find such strength in my voice, but even that was failing me. I was losing control of my singing; but I knew I had already lost control of my life.

I was weak, and I finally had nowhere else to reach, but for Jesus. I fell to my face sobbing and said the sinner's prayer. That day, I truly, completely, and wholeheartedly rededicated my life to Christ.

I came clean to my wife, Renee, in 1998. She was very upset, and it was tough for us as a couple to come out of that. But trust began to win out when she could see the changes taking place in my life and that my rededication was real. My priorities had changed. Things like reading God's Word and being the man God wanted me to be became much more important.

And other things changed as well—silly things like going to the movies. Renee and I used to see pretty much every major release available. On the weekend we'd go see a movie on Friday night, another on Saturday night, and often one on Sunday night. We didn't have much of a filter. After I rededicated my life, we didn't stop going to movies altogether, and we didn't throw our TV out the window, but we were more careful about what we allowed to come before us.

To this day, nobody knows what happened to my voice, physically. It's never been the same. But it doesn't take a medical doctor to tell me what happened—God was trying to get my attention. He loved me too much to allow me to go down that path of destruction. It really upset me, and I bet it upset Him to allow this gift that He had given me to be harmed. It had to hurt His feelings.

It makes me think of my eight year old. She is a really skilled athlete; she's good at basketball, soccer, and track. As her father, it would break my heart if I found it necessary to take that skill away to get her attention. That would take me to my knees. And I know that it was crushing to my Savior to have to do that to me. But He did it because He loves me. That's how I know He's real—He loved me enough to discipline me when I needed it.

My experience with pornography has taught me a lot. I would encourage everyone, particularly young men, to walk in wisdom. Pornography is not something you can participate in today and then it's over. It stays with you for a long time and shapes the way you view people and the way your character is built. I regret ever allowing porn into my life. And I can guarantee that many young men will feel the same way.

If you have already allowed pornography into your life, walk away from it now. And remember, that wherever we are on our walk, God is always there with loving arms. But there are consequences and repercussions to our bad choices. God will forgive you, but you will have baggage and will need healing to lead a healthy life.

Over a decade has gone by since I became a professional musician. I've been on countless stages and have recorded many CDs. I've had a life in the public eye. Those ten years have flown by. The life God gives us here on earth is brief, so take your decisions very seriously because we're not here that long. We're really just pointing to our true country...Heaven.

GOD'S ROAD MAP

The Holy Bible is a guide to help you live a happy and satisfying life. To learn more about the concepts presented in the chapter you've just read, take a look at these passages:

PORNOGRAPHY

According to a CBS news story in September 2004, Americans spend nearly $10 billion a year on adult entertainment. As a society, we have become increasingly tolerant and frighteningly desensitized to sexually explicit content. All in good fun? Hardly. Pornography destroys marriages and impacts our self-esteem...and it's a sin.

Proverbs 6:25-27

Do not lust in your heart after her beauty or let her captivate you with her eyes, for the prostitute reduces you to a loaf of bread, and the adulteress preys upon your very life. Can a man scoop fire into his lap without his clothes being burned?

Matthew 5:27 28

You have heard that it was said, "Do not commit adultery." But I tell you that anyone who looks at a woman lustfully has already committed adultery with her in his heart.

Titus 2:11-12

For the grace of God that brings salvation has appeared to all men. It teaches us to say "No" to ungodliness and worldly passions, and to live self-controlled, upright and godly lives in this present age, while we wait for the blessed hope—the glorious appearing of our great God and Savior, Jesus Christ.

DISCIPLINE

Just like an earthly father punishes his children when they do something wrong, God will discipline us for our own good. But God doesn't discipline us simply for punishment; it is to develop our character and help us learn to walk in His ways.

Hebrews 12:7-11

Endure hardship as discipline; God is treating you as sons. For what son is not disciplined by his father? If you are not disciplined (and everyone undergoes discipline), then you are illegitimate children and not true sons. Moreover, we have all had human fathers who disciplined us and we respected them for it. How much more should we submit to the Father of our spirits and live! Our fathers disciplined us for a little while as they thought best; but God disciplines us for our good, that we may share in His holiness. No discipline seems pleasant at the time, but painful. Later on, however, it produces a harvest of righteousness and peace for those who have been trained by it.

Billy Ray Cyrus

Actor, Hit TV Series "Doc" and Multi-Platinum Selling Musician

(Photo, courtesy of Billy Ray Cyrus Spirit Fan Club)

IN the early '90s, masses of fun-loving fans around the world lined up at dancehalls, parties, and concerts to participate in a wildly popular line dance called the "Achy Breaky." Billy Ray Cyrus' song, "Achy Breaky Heart," was a smash hit,

Topping both the U.S. Pop and Country charts and was the most successful country single released worldwide in 1992. The album it appeared on, *Some Gave All* sold over 14 million copies worldwide and held the #1 position on both Billboard charts for 17 weeks. His work has earned multi-platinum, platinum, and gold certifications all around the globe.

Cyrus' success in music eventually led him to acting, on the big and small screens and on the stage. He is probably best known for his role as Dr. Clint Cassidy on PaxTV's (now Independent Television) long-running hit series "Doc."

While he has received dozens of entertainment awards, he is most proud of the recognition he has received as a humanitarian, including the first ever Bob Hope Congressional Medal of Honor Society Entertainer's Award.

His most recent recording, "The Other Side" is an incredible testament to his love for God. Check it out at www.billyraycyrus.com.

＊＊＊＊

Ever since I was a little boy I could feel and hear this voice inside saying, "Someday God is going to use your life to do something for Him."

I grew up in Flatwoods, Kentucky. My Pap-Paw (grandfather) Cyrus was a preacher. My Pap-Paw Casto rode the caboose for the railroad and played bluegrass and country music.

My earliest memories are Saturday nights at my Pap-Paw Casto's house. He'd play the fiddle; my mom would play the piano; and my uncle would play the guitar. We'd sing "Won't You Come Home Bill Bailey?" and maybe some old Hank Williams songs. And then we'd listen to the Grand Ole Opry.

On Sunday mornings I'd be inside my Pap-Paw Cyrus' Pentecostal church, and we'd be singing hymns like "Old Rugged Cross" and "I'll Fly Away" and "Swing Low Sweet Chariot." My dad had a gospel quartet, and they'd sing just about every Sunday. When I was four or five, I started getting up there and singing with them. My earliest memories of life are based around music.

But my childhood was far from perfect. My mom and dad got divorced when I was around five. We were pretty poor at my house; I remember one time my mom sold the piano that her mother had left her, just so we'd be able to pay our bills, keep our house, and have some food on the table.

I remember once when Neil Diamond came to Charleston, West Virginia. As fate would have it, I won the last set of concert tickets they were giving away. Something incredible happened to me at that concert—I'll never forget it. Neil Diamond was singing his song, "Holly Holy Love." At that moment I felt like I was being embraced by one big set of hands. It was like something was all around me saying, "There's your purpose; that's what you're supposed to be. That's what you've always heard and felt since you were a little boy. Buy a guitar and start a band."

Within a matter of months, I was making my living playing music, and I've never stopped. But I wanted something more than those small clubs. As soon as I finished a gig on Sunday night, I'd take off and head to Nashville and knock on doors for a couple of days. I'd be so excited when I'd see Nashville in the windshield as I was coming into town. But then when I was leaving and looking at Nashville in the rearview mirror, I'd just feel like a kicked pup—like somebody had thrown scalding water on me and told me to get out of town. I took that as a sign to move to get a change of scenery.

I moved out to Los Angeles, but my luck out there wasn't any better. Instead of getting turned down in Nashville, I was getting turned down in Los Angeles. Between Nashville, Los Angeles, and my home base in Kentucky I had failed in just about every way you could possibly fail. I was miserable and headed for home with my tail between my legs.

Something told me that I should go back to that church where my grandfather was a preacher in Flatwoods. But it was strange being there without my grandfather. There was this other preacher just pounding the pulpit, just shouting that God loves a desperate man, and it was like he was talking right to me. I felt inside myself, I'm as desperate as I've ever been. *I'm as desperate as any man that's ever walked this earth.* I got up out of that same pew where I used to sit as a little boy, and I knelt down and said a desperate prayer. "God, help me. I can't do this anymore. I need help. I'm breaking."

I left that church and I went to play my gig that night in Huntington, West Virginia. Trust me, the devil sent every messenger he had to distract me from thoughts that were good or pure. He sent them all after me that night. But I made it out of there. Later, on my way to Nashville, I called the president of Mercury Records, and I told his secretary, "I'm desperate. I want to play Harold Shedd my very best song, and if this ain't good enough, then maybe I need to do something else."

And she set it up for me. I played him a song that I had written called, "Some Gave All" about a Vietnam veteran. At the end he stood up and said, "I'm going to structure you a little deal." And he got up and left the room. I figured he was going to come back and tell me I could sweep the halls or at best, maybe work with some writers. But when he came back into the room, he was with the vice president of the label. Imagine my surprise when that man shook my hand and said, "Congratulations, this must be a big day for you."

After ten years of being told "no" by everybody up and down the lonely streets of Nashville, somebody finally said, "yes." Look what God did for me once I asked for help!

My world went from its darkest point, to having the number-one album in the world for 17 weeks in a row just like that. I was even nominated for five Grammy awards. I knew I wasn't going to win a Grammy though. I told everybody in my interviews, "I'm not going to win a Grammy; I just thank God that I'm here."

For my performance on the award show, I wore a white t-shirt with the sleeves cut off that said John 3:16 in huge letters across the chest. I wanted to wear that shirt because I knew I wasn't going to get a chance to step up to the microphone and thank God, and I wanted everybody to know that I gave Him the credit.

As I'd expected, I didn't win. When I got into the limo after the Grammys were over, nobody was saying anything—not my manager, not the president of my record company, and not the owner. Finally I said, "At least I got to wear my John 3:16 shirt." And the president said, "Didn't you have something else you could have worn?" And there was just a hush in the car, obviously they were mad at me for wearing the shirt.

The next day I got up to catch an early flight. Everybody in the music business who was getting out of Los Angeles was on this airplane. Sitting in my seat I opened up the *LA Times* and got a look at the headline, "Cyrus Big Loser—Not Even God Could Help Billy Ray Cyrus Win a Grammy." And I just sat there. I thought I was going to cry. I was breathless and embarrassed in front of all those people on that plane. Everybody knew—they were all looking at the same newspaper. Suddenly, I felt a hand on my shoulder, and there stood Bob Seger. I'd been playing Bob Seger's music for ten years in the clubs, but I'd never met him. I turned and looked up, and he said, "Put that newspaper underneath your feet where it belongs." I'll never forget that.

One thing led to another, and I started doing a little bit of acting. And then, the next thing I knew, I was living up in Toronto starring in a television series. When I first did the pilot for "Doc," I certainly didn't think there would end up being 88 episodes. It has been a great experience.

The only thing I really regret from that rocket ride is that I didn't ever take the time to stop and smell the roses. I didn't ever take the time to just, you know, enjoy it. I was so busy making the next record, writing the next song, or doing the next show.

Right before Christmas 2002, I was up in Canada filming and something happened. I'm not sure what triggered it, but my inner voice said to me, "You need to make the record that you've wanted to make your whole life—and that's a gospel record. It's what you're supposed to do." And I was thinking to myself, *Cyrus, man, you haven't heard that voice in years. What makes you think you're hearing it now?* Within minutes my phone rung, and it was Billy Joe Walker, Jr., the legendary record producer known for his work with country stars like Pam Tillis, Travis Tritt, Tammy Cochran, and Tracy Byrd. He'd cut a lot of number-one records, but he'd never done a gospel record. Out of the blue he'd gotten the idea to do an inspirational record...and out of the blue, he thought of me to do it with him.

I say "out of the blue," but there are no coincidences, no accidents in my life. Everything happens for a reason. I made this record for a reason; *The Other Side* opened my eyes to what life's all about. And it's a beautiful thing.

The people at the record company had asked me if I could write a song about where I'm from, about my grandfather being a Pentecostal preacher, about my life, and my relationship with God. But I can't write a song on purpose; my songs come in moments of inspiration...or desperation. I got on my knees and prayed and said, "God, if You want me to write a song for this album, You have to give it to me. Because...what can I write that's worthy?" This song just came flowing out of me.

91

THE OTHER SIDE
by Billy Ray Cyrus

Oh I've heard about the streets of gold
Since I was just a kid
Stories that my grandpa told
The truths that he unhid
Preacher man sang a song of love
Our Savior was his pride
And he told of the perfect place
Just beyond the other side

Well there won't be no more sickness
Sorrow, death or pain
The sun will shine forever
No more darkness, no more rain
Glory hallelujah
Will echo through the halls
The other side is waitin'
Should our Maker come to call

The other side is perfect
It was made just for a king
At the right hand of Almighty God
The angels start to sing
And the light surrounds your very soul
The truth you cannot hide
The pearly gates will open
If you reach the other side

The wait'l sure be worth it
When you reach the other side
Oh, the other side

My world had been spinning out of control so much in the last ten years that I hit a couple of spots where I didn't feel like God could hear me anymore. But it wasn't that God wasn't listening; it's that I wasn't taking the time to be still and make sure that prayer was getting through. With that realization, I shifted my priorities. My family became my foundation, and my spirituality became my foundation. I started reconnecting back to life instead of being up there in the twilight zone on some rocket spinning out of control.

You know, we're only on this earth for a little while—make the most of it. And don't go it alone. I wish I would have known Jesus better back then, but I know Him now. That's what life on the other side is all about.

GOD'S ROAD MAP

The Holy Bible is a guide to help you live a happy and satisfying life. To learn more about the concepts presented in the chapter you've just read, take a look at these passages:

DISCOURAGEMENT

Do you ever feel like you just can't go on? Life can be absolutely debilitating sometimes, with disappointment around every turn. But God is right there alongside us to prop us up and help us go on. Lean on Him.

First Peter 5:8-9

Be self-controlled and alert. Your enemy the devil prowls around like a roaring lion looking for someone to devour. Resist him, standing firm in the faith, because you know that your brothers throughout the world are undergoing the same kind of sufferings.

Psalm 73:2-3

But as for me, my feet had almost slipped; I had nearly lost my foothold. For I envied the arrogant when I saw the prosperity of the wicked.

Second Chronicles 20:15b

Do not be afraid or discouraged because of this vast army. For the battle is not yours, but God's.

PERSEVERANCE

Persevering means to be courageous and faithful in the midst of trials. The outcome of your obedience may be a while off, but hang tough, God will see you through.

Second Peter 1:5-8

For this very reason, make every effort to add to your faith goodness; and to goodness, knowledge; and to knowledge, self-control; and to self-control, perseverance; and to perseverance, godliness; and to godliness, brotherly kindness; and to brotherly kindness, love. For if you possess these qualities in increasing measure, they will keep you from being ineffective and unproductive in your knowledge of our Lord Jesus Christ.

James 1:2-4

Consider it pure joy, my brothers, whenever you face trials of many kinds, because you know that the testing of your faith develops perseverance. Perseverance must finish its work so that you may be mature and complete, not lacking anything.

Philippians 1:6

Being confident of this, that He who began a good work in you will carry it on to completion until the day of Christ Jesus.

Charlie Daniels

Legendary Country Musician

CHARLIE Daniels is an American icon. His music—a combination of rock, country, bluegrass, blues, and Gospel—is as unique as he is. He's been making music for over 40 years now and has achieved far more in his career than he ever dreamed possible. His rebel anthems "Long Haired Country Boy" and "The South's Gonna Do It (Again)" propelled his 1975 album *Fire on the Mountain* to double platinum status. In the summer of 1979, Daniels recorded, "The Devil Went Down to Georgia," which became a platinum single, topped both country and pop charts, won a Grammy Award, earned three Country Music Association trophies, and pushed the album *Million Mile Reflections* to triple platinum. He has numerous other triple platinum, platinum, and gold albums. Daniels also earned a coveted Dove Award from the Gospel Music Association in 1994 for his gospel recording, "The Door." All told, he represents more than 18 million in record sales. Nearly 70 years old, Daniels still does over 100 shows every year.

Daniels is a true pioneer who has impacted the lives of everyday people everywhere. He is known as a man of strong convictions who loves his fans, his country, and his God. He just tries to be himself—the man God created him to be.

✦✦✦✦✦✦✦

I was born in 1936 in Wilmington, North Carolina, and I've lived in the South most of my life. I was raised at a time in the South when I didn't even know anybody who didn't believe in God. Things have certainly changed since then, but then everybody was a believer. Not everybody was a real hardcore Christian, living the life and all, but at least they were believers.

My family had a love for music, everything from pentecostal gospel, bluegrass, and rhythm & blues, and it's been a part of my life, all of my life. I started singing in church when I was just about four years old. I had to stand up on something so people could see me. I was probably off-key and out of whack, but I had the guts to do it. I kept at it—I learned to play the guitar, the mandolin, and the fiddle, and wrote my first song when I was 16. It's probably not something that the world would remember, but it was my very first one.

Of course, you do what you love, so once I started playing, that's all I wanted to do. I just kept heading in that direction, and I played whenever I could with whomever I could until it finally started moving into where I could get paid for it every once in a while. I moved to Nashville in 1967 and signed my first record deal in 1971.

My career has been an incredible blessing. But as I became more and more successful, I got away from my faith. I got so far off the path that you wouldn't have thought I was a believer. You know, it's just kind of a gradual thing. I never quit believing, but I really kind of got away from the Lord. I had my experiences—I did some drugs in times past, but it just didn't go together with a career. Finally, I understood that I had to get my priorities together. I was in the business to be a serious musician, not a partier.

I know God is real. I remember my wife was real sick one time. She was in the hospital; and we didn't know exactly what was wrong with her, but we knew it was something terrible. It turned out that she had some extremely bad infections inside that had to be taken care of pretty fast. I was at the hospital constantly, but I took a break and went home to get cleaned up. When I was in the shower, I said a prayer asking the Lord to heal her and give us the peace of knowing He had control of the situation. When I left the house to go back to the hospital, I knew she was going to be okay—I just felt it in my soul. It's one of those things God does for us when we're under stress sometimes. I was absolutely confident that she was going to recover—and she did.

I've traveled millions of miles, and I've been in some dangerous situations. But I've always known His protection. One of my favorite Bible verses comes from the 91st Psalm, "He who dwells in the shadow of the Most High will rest in the shadow of the Almighty." I committed it to memory years ago, and it's one of those things...I say it pretty often. God's protection has always been with me. It's just a matter of understanding that He loves us and He wants us to be safe. He will keep us safe if we just put our trust in Him. That's the thing...that's all there is to it. Prayer is a powerful thing.

I write a lot of story songs. I'd been wanting to do a Christian album for years because I had some things I wanted to say. I just thought a lot of people were falling through the cracks and didn't understand what faith was all about. So we recorded "Steel Witness" and "The Door" to talk to those folks. You see, one of the hardest things for people to understand about the Gospel message is that it is so simple; it's not the very complicated thing that we tend to try and make it. There's nothing you can do to make yourself a Christian; you just have to trust God that He is who He says He is, and He will do what He says He will do. There's no human act that you can do that can bring you to the Lord; you just have to say "yes" to Him. You just have to accept Him, and He will become a part of you. People think they have to be "good enough" to be a Christian. But we can never be "good enough"; there was only one person in the whole world who was, and that was Jesus Christ Himself. You're a sinner and I am too. When we accept the Savior, the sin is gone. That's what the Bible teaches. The Bible is not just pretty words that someone sat down and wrote one day. The Bible is God-inspired. It is real. And so is God.

HEART OF MY HEART
by Charlie Daniels

I was blinded by bright lights, lost in the darkness
And sin kept my life in a whirl
Lust, greed and money and sensual pleasures
Mark the boundaries of my narrow world
I was headed for hell but as far as I fell
Your Spirit still followed me down
Then when I hit the bottom and cried out for mercy
You picked me up off the ground

(chorus)
Heart of my heart, rock of my soul
You changed my life when You took control
Thy will be done, God's only Son
Faithful and true
Lord of all lords, King of all kings
The sweet sacrifice of praises we bring
Worthy's the Lamb, all that I am
I give to you
Satan kept telling me that it was too late
I'd committed the unpardonable sin
But I knew he was lyin' when I felt conviction
Tug on my heart strings again
I'm not proud of the past but I can't do a thing
To make up for the time that I've lost
Now my heart and my soul
And what life I have left
I lay at the foot of the cross

(chorus)
I give to You
Heart of my heart

GOD'S ROAD MAP

The Holy Bible is a guide to help you live a happy and satisfying life. To learn more about the concepts presented in the chapter you've just read, take a look at these passages:

PRIORITIES

What's really important in your life? If we're not careful, work can become our number-one priority, with our family in second place, and our faith a very distant third. By doing that, we're really missing the boat. However, if we put God first in our lives, everything else makes a lot more sense.

Joshua 24:15

But if serving the Lord seems undesirable to you, then choose for yourselves this day whom you will serve, whether the gods your forefathers served beyond the River, or the gods of the Amorites, in whose land you are living. But as for me and my household, we will serve the Lord.

Second Chronicles 1:11-12

God said to Solomon, "Since this is your heart's desire and you have not asked for wealth, riches or honor, nor for the death of your enemies, and since you have not asked for a long life but for wisdom and knowledge to govern My people over whom I have made you king, therefore wisdom and knowledge will be given you. And I will also give you wealth, riches and honor, such as no king who was before you ever had and none after you will have."

TRUSTING GOD

"Trust me." It's so easy to say, but so difficult to do because people let us down every day. How, then, can we trust in a force that we can neither see nor hear? The Bible teaches us that we can trust in God because His

Word is true. And His Word says that if we trust in Him, we will have eternal life. God is totally trustworthy.

Isaiah 26:3

You will keep in perfect peace him whose mind is steadfast, because he trusts in You.

First Peter 1:8-9

Though you have not seen Him, you love Him; and even though you do not see Him now, you believe in Him and are filled with an inexpressible and glorious joy, for you are receiving the goal of your faith, the salvation of your souls.

Andrew DeClercq

Former NBA Player, Orlando Magic

(Photo credit: Gary Bassing)

AT 6' 10" tall and weighing in at 255 pounds, NBA player Andrew DeClercq is a force to be reckoned with on the basketball court. Born in 1973 in East Detroit, Michigan, his family moved to Florida when he was 10.

DeClercq graduated from the University of Florida in Gainesville with a degree in history. As a Gator he scored more than 1,300 points, had 950 rebounds, and 175 blocked shots. In 1994 he was a member of the USA basketball team which competed at the Goodwill Games in St. Petersburg, Russia. DeClercq was chosen in the beginning of the 2nd round (34th overall) of the 1995 NBA draft by the Golden State Warriors.

After playing two years for Golden State, he was signed by the Boston Celtics as a free agent. Two years later, it was one more stint with the Cleveland Cavaliers before he found his home with the Orlando Magic where he played for five seasons. In 2000, DeClercq was named one of the "Good Guys in Sports" by *The Sporting News* for his outstanding character and civic responsibility.

About five years ago, I looked at myself in the mirror and didn't recognize who I saw. I wasn't living a lifestyle that I'd been taught to live while growing up. I called myself a Christian, but I definitely was not acting like one.

I guess you could say I grew up in the church. My dad was Catholic and didn't really go to church at all, but my mom grew up Baptist. And my sisters and I went to Sunday school every week and church every Sunday afternoon. I even sang in the children's choir...at least until they asked me to quit—seems I'm not a very good singer! I was saved and baptized when I was eight years old. Up through high school, I attended just about every church function there was.

Sports were also a huge part of my life—especially soccer. I started playing soccer when I was around six. I loved it so much, in fact, that I never even gave basketball a thought. But then I started to grow. In my 8th-grade year, I skipped a shoe size; I went straight from an 11 to a 13. By the end of the year, I was six feet tall.

I started the soccer season playing forward, and I just kept moving back in position as the season went by. I was so clumsy I couldn't handle the ball anymore. I kept pulling muscles because I was reacting to kids who were still 4'10", and I couldn't move as quickly as they could. I ended up going all the way back to goalie and realized it was probably the last year I was going to be able to play.

I also played basketball in my 8th-grade year but wasn't that good. I started my freshman year in high school at 6' 1-1/2", and by the end of basketball season, I was over 6' 5". So needless to say, with rapid growth like that, I couldn't really chew gum and walk over a line on the court at the same time! I was very clumsy.

By the time I was a sophomore, I was nearly 6' 7" and started practicing with the junior varsity team. Then fate stepped in. The power forward, center, and another player on the varsity team got injured and were sidelined. The coach had some of the JV guys come up and practice with varsity. They decided to keep me on there until Christmas; they really just needed another body. I wasn't a starter, but I did get a lot of playing time and gained a ton of experience playing against the older kids. I was supposed to go back down to the JV team after Christmas, but during my last game before the holiday break I ended up getting a breakaway dunk. After that, the coaches said there was no way I was ever going back to JV.

After my junior year, some colleges started noticing me. I got letters from over 200 schools. Just about every major Division 1 school sent a letter asking if I was interested in playing for them. I ended up choosing the University of Florida. It was close to home, but that's not why I decided to sign there. I really liked the head coach; I thought he could really teach me the game of basketball and help me get to the next level.

I started out majoring in civil engineering, but I just couldn't pass physics and play basketball at the same time. After the spring semester of my sophomore year, my coach told me I had a choice to make. He said if I kept going with engineering I would probably spend more time studying than playing basketball. He'd seen me too often falling asleep on the plane with my head in my hands halfway through a math problem. I would never survive doing both; I was burning the candle at both ends. He said if I really focused on basketball, I had a chance to play in the NBA. I have to tell you, I liked that idea—I liked it a lot!

So I changed my major to history—it was either that or geography. Since I figured I couldn't do much with either one, I chose history because I thought it was more interesting. It ended up being a good decision. I focused on basketball for the next two years and wound up getting picked up in the second round of the NBA draft by the Golden State Warriors.

I packed four suitcases of clothes, got on a plane, and flew out to California a week before training camp was scheduled to begin. I didn't have a place to live; I didn't have a car...I didn't have anything but my clothes. I managed to find an apartment, but since I didn't have a bed or any other furniture, I slept on the floor in a sleeping bag. All I had was a credit card with a $500 limit and it was maxed out...I was broke. I was out of funds until my first paycheck came on November 15. I remember that date—yes, I do.

Unfortunately, I started out the season on the injured list. I'd had mononucleosis at the end of my senior year and had been really sick over the summer. It was taking me a long time to recover so I concentrated on getting my strength back. I didn't play a whole lot that first year, but in my second year I had some really good basketball games. After that, I became a free agent and signed with the Boston Celtics. I was there for one full season, and then there was a lockout the following year. I played half of that lockout year in Boston and then was traded to Cleveland where I finished out the year. I played one more season for the Cavaliers until they traded me to the Orlando Magic. I've been on the Magic's roster for six seasons and in the NBA now for a grand total of 11 years.

Many people think being in the NBA sounds awfully glamorous. You do have a certain level of fame once people find out you play basketball. But I didn't like being in the limelight, so I stayed within a circle of friends. The problem was that this group could get pretty crazy. We'd stay up all night hanging out in bars. And when I started drinking, things really started going downhill.

In college I'd been a pretty good boy, not much of a partier at all. I didn't want anything to distract me from my goals in basketball, so it was easy to so "no" to temptation. It wasn't so much that I didn't want to get into trouble; I just didn't want to miss any games.

But when I got to the NBA, it was much harder to resist those temptations. I had the opportunity, and I definitely had the funds to explore and try new things. I did just about whatever I wanted and went places I never should have been.

There was a lockout in 1998/1999 and play was suspended. Normally, I would have stopped partying in the summer before the season started, knowing that I had to work out to get back in shape again. But this time the season was delayed, and I was free until the beginning of January. That meant that the party didn't have to stop. So, I kept looking for the next thrill, getting wilder and taking bigger risks. My friends and I sank to new levels of depravity.

One day I looked at myself in the mirror and didn't recognize the guy looking back. I knew I needed to turn myself around; I just didn't like who I'd become. I remember lying on the couch in silence that whole day not knowing what to do next. I compared who I was now to who I was when I came out of high school. Everything was out of whack; I wasn't the person I used to be. Even my thought patterns were different. It certainly wasn't how God wanted me to be living and I knew it.

Lying on that couch I prayed that God would straighten me out and bring me back to a place where my life was reordered properly. I started reading my Bible every day and taking nuggets from it to relearn some of those attributes and qualities—those boundaries that God sets for us. Matthew 7:13-14 told me what I needed to do to enter God's Kingdom: "Enter through the narrow gate. For wide is the gate and broad is the road that leads to destruction, and many enter through it. But small is the gate and narrow the road that leads to life, and only a few find it." I needed to get back on that narrow road.

I got away from that group of friends...for a while. During the off season, I went back to the beach where I was living. The problem was that on the beach there were so many little bars that I found myself getting back into the party scene. It was so easy to slip right back into the old routine. I had to walk away again.

It's been an ongoing process of slowly trying to fix the flaws in my character that would make me fall prey to that lifestyle. Now I've learned other ways to hang out with friends and have fun. I've grown so much in the last five or six years. My wife and I were married at the end of 2000 and we have a beautiful little girl. The whole process of my wife getting pregnant and watching her carry the baby was just so amazing. It has really helped me mature in my faith. Getting to know my daughter has definitely expanded my knowledge of what a father's love is.

Since I rededicated my life to Christ I have seen His presence in my life so many times—I know He's real. Looking back, I can definitely see many nights that He must have had some guardian angel draped over the top of me protecting me, keeping me alive, keeping me from making too many stupid mistakes or getting too far gone.

Partying can be fun for a little while, but there are repercussions to that sort of a lifestyle and those repercussions can be serious. I was very lucky; I had a couple of incidents where I could have been in the newspapers for DUI and just got lucky that a cop didn't pull me over that night. There were even times when I actually got into a car accident, but for some reason the police didn't test my blood alcohol level.

You see, everything's fun and happy when you're at the bar. But even though you might be the least drunk of every single one of your friends, you still shouldn't be getting behind the wheel of a car. When you're drunk, you don't make good decisions. Alcohol blocks those neural passageways that help you in the decision-making process. You have no boundaries. I count myself extremely lucky that I didn't get caught or have something terrible happen that would have changed my life or the lives of others.

Since I've been in the NBA, I've been asked to help out at many basketball camps and youth clinics. Typically, I'll teach them how to do a jump shot or a free throw or to dunk the basketball. After the clinic the kids get an opportunity to ask me some questions. I've become increasingly disturbed over the content of those questions: "What kind of car do you drive? How much jewelry do you have? What's the size of your house? How much money do you make?" I was telling the kids all about basketball, but I could see that I should have been telling them things they *really* needed to know. I needed to find a way to share my testimony with them.

The Fellowship of Christian Athletes (FCA) is my vehicle to reach out to schools and talk to kids. It's funny—I put my name on a list of potential speakers, and my phone's been ringing off the hook ever since. I'm not speaking because I want to; in fact, I hate speaking in front of groups. But I feel God has called me to do it. The kids need to hear that the lifestyle of the rich and famous isn't all it's cracked up to be.

Even though I changed my life and made the decision to follow Christ, I still struggle with the old temptations and the old sins. There is a consequence to sin—we have to face that. God will forgive you if you ask Him to and you will be washed clean. But you will also have to face memories for the rest of your life. The devil uses those feelings of shame and doubt to make you feel inadequate before God.

One of my favorite verses in the Bible is Second Corinthians 5:17, "Therefore, if anyone is in Christ, he is a new creation; the old has gone, the new has come!" Because I know I'm saved, that means I'm a new creation—the old stuff is gone and no longer part of me. That verse helps me remember where I was and how I was feeling when I was ashamed and guilty of sin. And at the same time, that promise is also encouraging, because I know I'm not that person anymore. I am a new creation in Christ. You can be too.

GOD'S ROAD MAP

The Holy Bible provides a road map to help you live a happy and satisfying life. To learn more about the concepts presented in the chapter you've just read, take a look at these passages:

BEHAVIOR

You've probably heard the saying, "Actions speak louder than words." What we do and how we behave tells the world who we are and what our values look like. The Bible is a manual that defines what's right and wrong—in other words, holy living. When we give our lives to Christ, we become a new creation.

First Peter 4:3-5

For you have spent enough time in the past doing what pagans choose to do—living in debauchery, lust, drunkenness, orgies, carousing and detestable idolatry. They think it strange that you do not plunge with them into the same flood of dissipation, and they heap abuse on you. But they will have to give account to Him who is ready to judge the living and the dead.

Proverbs 23:29-30

Who has woe? Who has sorrow? Who has strife? Who has complaints? Who has needless bruises? Who has bloodshot eyes? Those who linger over wine, who go to sample bowls of mixed wine.

REPENTANCE

When we repent, we admit that we have taken a wrong turn in life and have been living against biblical teachings. When you admit your sin and are willing to change, God can do wondrous things.

Second Corinthians 5:17

Therefore, if anyone is in Christ, he is a new creation; the old has gone, the new has come!

First John 1:8-9

If we claim to be without sin, we deceive ourselves and the truth is not in us. If we confess our sins, He is faithful and just and will forgive us our sins and purify us from all unrighteousness.

Acts 2:38

Peter replied, "Repent and be baptized, every one of you, in the name of Jesus Christ for the forgiveness of your sins. And you will receive the gift of the Holy Spirit."

Luther Elliss

Former NFL Defensive Tackle,
Denver Broncos
(Photo credit: Ryan McKee/Rich Clarkson
and Associates)

L UTHER Elliss has long been recognized as one of the fiercest interior defenders in professional football. A standout at Mancos High School in Colorado, the 6' 5", 318-pound Elliss earned All-League, All-Region and All-State honors in football. He was also a three-time All-League choice in basketball.

Elliss was recruited by the University of Utah and earned the Ute's Newcomer of the Year Award following his freshman season. He was selected All-WAC (Western Athletic Conference) after his sophomore, junior, and senior seasons. He was also a consensus All-American after his senior year.

The Detroit Lions selected Elliss in the first round (20th overall) of the 1995 NFL Draft. He was on the roster nine seasons with the Lions, earning the privilege of going to the Pro Bowl twice. While in Detroit, he was also awarded the Mike Utley Spirit Award three times by his teammates and was a member of the All-Madden Team. In 2004 he was released and picked up by the Denver Broncos.

A dedicated father of nine—five of whom are adopted—this gentle giant is a tireless advocate for kids and can often be found volunteering for various child-related charities.

✦❖❖❖✦

There have been so many times in my life where God has saved me. For some reason it just wasn't my time—God had other plans for me. It's been amazing to watch it all unfold.

I came from a big family filled with love. Our three-bedroom trailer was usually bursting with kids. There were six in my family, and we often had cousins adding to the mix. My hometown is Mancos, Colorado, a small town of just 800 people. Growing up in a small town was great; I had a lot more freedom than my kids do today. My parents didn't have to worry when I was gone all day with my friends. I was an adventurous kid—sometimes maybe a little too adventurous.

I've had some close encounters. I remember one day when my friend and I were down by the river smashing snakes. He was up on the hillside, and I was down low on the bank by the snakes. He picked up a pretty good size rock—he was struggling just to hold it up. When he threw it over the hillside toward the water, it hit me directly in the head—so hard it knocked me into the water. It was a miracle that I didn't have any serious injuries.

As a boy I spent a lot of time down by that river, sometimes when I probably shouldn't have. I remember one time in particular—one of those times when officials warned you to stay away because the currents were too strong. So, of course, my friends and I decided it would be fun to go swimming in that raging water. We made a makeshift raft and were going to navigate it down the river. But once the raft was built, everyone was too afraid to try it. To prove how brave (or foolish) I was, I said I'd do it. As soon as I got on the raft and got out in the current a little bit, the raft flipped over and threw me off. I went under the murky water. I couldn't see anything and I couldn't breathe. I was swept downriver by the current, and I didn't know how to swim. As I reached out my hand, screaming, "Oh God, please help me!" I caught a tree branch on the side of the embankment and was able to pull myself safely out of the river. I'd been carried over half a mile through the violent water and was bruised and battered and had cuts all over my body...but I'd survived.

The close encounters continued into my adulthood as well. I fell asleep at the wheel while driving late at night once and woke up as my car was careening across the median into oncoming traffic on the other side of the road. I was scared to death. When I was able to stop the car, I paused to thank the Lord for saving me. Shortly after I turned around and headed back down the road, I noticed that I needed gas. I pulled off at the next exit, and as soon as I stopped, all four of my tires blew out. When I looked at them, each tire had a stick gouged in it from my trip over the median. If they had blown while I was out of control on the highway, I would have had a very serious accident. Once again, it must not have been my time.

I've always loved water, particularly the ocean. In the summer of 1999, my wife and I were visiting some friends in California, and we spent the day at the beach. I'd been bodysurfing all afternoon at a legendary surfing spot on Newport Beach called "The Wedge." When it was time to head in, I thought I'd catch one last wave, and it turned out to be the biggest one of the day. I was riding solid on the wave, but then something went terribly wrong. I was positioned incorrectly, and the next thing I knew the wave slammed me into hard-packed sand on the ocean floor—headfirst. It stunned me for a minute; I was kind of floating. When I came to, I couldn't feel my extremities—I thought I was paralyzed. But then the pain came and while it wasn't overwhelming, I thought there was a possibility I had broken my neck or had some other serious injury. When I came out of the water, a little boy saw me and said, "Mister, are you okay?" "Yeah, why?" I answered. "Because you don't look okay." There was blood streaming down my face.

Later at the hospital they looked me over and didn't see anything terribly wrong. When they were ready to release me, I didn't feel right about it. There was something wrong with my vision, I could tell. They took x-rays and found out that I'd fractured my orbital bone. That's the lower bone that holds your eyeball up. It's an injury that boxers often get, from taking jabs in the face.

The surgeon later told me what incredible force it would have taken for me to break that particular bone in my face. It could have easily crushed my skull or broken my neck.

Looking back, I realize that God was shielding and guiding me even before I dedicated my life to Him. I grew up in a traditional Christian home. Mom and Dad encouraged us to go to church every Sunday, and I was a regular attendee. Even when my parents stopped going, I'd still go with my grandmother. It was just kind of what you did on Sundays. I wanted to do the right thing. To me it was just a religion; I didn't have a relationship with Jesus Christ at all. I didn't understand that; I don't think they explained it that well in my church. I went to church because it felt good to go. I thought that if I simply knew *of* Jesus Christ, I was good to go. But there is so much more to Christianity than that.

There was a lot of drinking and drugs going on in our small town, but that never appealed to me. I didn't party, mostly because I didn't want to disappoint God. I was trying to keep on His good side. I wanted to keep all the good marks and none of the bad marks. I was trying to work my way into Heaven.

Sports have always been a big part of my life. Because I lived in such a small town, we had only three sports in high school—football, basketball, and track. I played all three. The coaches liked me because I was one of the biggest guys in town. I started playing football in junior high school, and then in the summer before my 9th-grade year, I grew about seven inches. I was like a totally different person. I couldn't play my freshman year because I had Osgood-Schlatter, a disorder where the tendons stretch out too far. It was from growing too fast, kind of like growing pains, but much worse. My knees and elbows ached; there was no way I could play football that year.

It's funny, because football was never my sport of choice. I played just to have something to do and stay involved. Frankly, I played football and ran track just to help me with my basketball game. In the end I was offered a scholarship to play both football and basketball at the University of Utah.

In college I continued to read my Bible and was considered by many to be very "religious." It was a time in my life when I was seeking God and wanted to have a closer relationship with Him, but I still didn't know what that was supposed to look like. I got married in college, and my wife, Rebecca, and I bounced around between traditional churches, but never found what we were looking for. Now I understand why that church was so elusive. Once again, God had plans brewing that I knew nothing about.

I ended up being a pretty good college player and was blessed to be drafted by the Detroit Lions. I was blown away—only one percent of all college athletes make it to the professional ranks. I thought I'd go to college, hopefully play a few downs and get my degree. I never thought I'd make it to the pros. Even when they were starting to predict I'd get drafted, I still didn't believe it—not until my senior year when I was in the running for the Outland Trophy, which is awarded to the best offensive or defensive lineman in the nation.

Right after I started with the Lions, the team chaplain, Dave Wilson, introduced himself and invited Rebecca and me to the weekly Bible study he held at his home. At this point, Rebecca and I were continuing our search for a church in Michigan. My first year I went to those meetings consistently—after all, I wanted God on our side. God was my lucky rabbit's foot—I needed Him on Sundays! But I would purposely go to the meetings late and leave early. I would make sure I sat way in the very back so I could sneak out while they were praying.

But I was listening, and slowly the Word started feeding that desire I had deep inside of me. Dave was talking about everyday things that we all struggled with. Whatever we studied seemed to totally relate to where I was on my walk with God. I'd never experienced that before. I started going more and more, and eventually I was getting there early and staying to the end.

Dave and his wife, Ann, invited Rebecca and me to the church where he was a pastor, Kensington Community Church in Troy, Michigan. Now, we were used to very traditional churches, and this is a very contemporary, nondenominational church. During the services they do drama and play the Beatles—it's very modern. But to me, it seemed like blasphemy; I thought I would go to hell if I went there.

But Dave was persistent, so we gave it a try. Easter Sunday was the first time we went to Kensington, and it just blew us away. This was what

I'd been looking for! I leaned over to Rebecca and said, "Salt Lake City needs a church like this." That statement was a hint of things to come.

As we became regulars at church, I also emerged as a leader on the football team. It got to a point when Dave came up to me one day after practice and said, "Hey Luther, I need to talk to you." As he pulled me aside, he said, "I need to challenge you a little bit. You're a leader on the team and you go to chapel regularly. Everybody knows you're religious. But that's all it is—you're religious. You have to decide what you're going to do; you're straddling the fence right now. Until you give your life to Jesus Christ and have a personal relationship with Him, you're going to hell. You are satan's child, not God's child." I knew exactly what Dave was saying, and it scared me. I knew he was right.

I was a "Chreaster"—the kind of Christian who went to church on Sundays, Christmas, and Easter and thought I was doing all the right things. When I was in trouble, struggling with something, or afraid, I would call upon God. When things were going well, I didn't need Him.

I'd never given my life to Jesus Christ and accepted Him as my Savior. So that's exactly what I did, right then and there I asked the Lord into my life. I had the most incredible, peaceful feeling when I finished saying that prayer. I felt energized, like a veil was lifted and I could finally see clearly. That moment changed my whole entire life.

About a year later, Rebecca gave her life to the Lord as well. Our life as a couple changed dramatically once we started walking with Christ. Dave Wilson and his wife, Ann, challenged us to pray together as a couple. It was really hard at first—I had to be honest in front of my wife? But praying together changed our whole relationship; it became more real and more intimate.

I have always been told that my attitude and work ethic are my strengths. In fact, a lot of guys told me that my example on the field, even when I got a cheap shot, was one of the reasons they came to Bible studies and chapel. There were so many times on the field when I'd be frustrated or angry, but I kept control. I'd never been able to do that before. Instead of just getting mad, I tried to see people in God's eyes and not the way I would see them. That has changed my whole outlook on life.

There are so many reasons why I know He is real. My wife and I have a large family—four biological children and five adopted. When we first decided to adopt, God opened the door wide to confirm we had made the right decision. We heard a baby was available on a Tuesday. For the next two days we prayed about it and felt God say, "Yes, this is your guy." It takes most couples three or four months to complete the adoption process, but in a little over a week we had our precious little baby in our arms. It was just amazing.

I've been blessed with a lot of gifts in my life that have illustrated God's reality to me. But one of the greatest gifts came from a vision that started a series of events that could only have been orchestrated by God Himself.

As I mentioned earlier, in 1996, Rebecca and I visited Kensington Community Church for the first time. The service touched me in a profound way, and during that service God gave me a vision of what an impact a church like that would have in my home of Salt Lake City. But I didn't think anymore about it, until 2002 when God started laying it on my heart again.

The idea kind of gnawed at me, until finally I prayed, "Lord, do You want me to keep playing football, or do You want me to fulfill this vision You gave me a long time ago and start a church in Salt Lake City?" If He wanted me to plant a church, I knew I needed help...and lots of it. I had no background in that kind of thing. I started asking Dave Wilson a lot of questions, because he had been instrumental in the creation of Kensington. When I asked him if he wanted to go to Salt Lake City and start a church, I was surprised at his answer, "No, I just feel like God is calling me here in Detroit. But don't lose that vision. God is going to bring somebody to you."

One Sunday, Dave Nelson, another teaching pastor at Kensington, was preaching about his family's recent trip to California and how much his wife loved the mountains. As I was sitting there listening, I felt God clearly tell me, "This is him—call Dave and ask him to start a church with you in Salt Lake City."

Now, I knew *of* Dave Nelson and we'd played ball together and did some other church things together, but we were just acquaintances. I liked Dave. He was a good guy and a good athlete, and we had fun hanging out and talking; but I didn't really know him. But the prompting was so strong that on the way home from church I called him and left this message on his voicemail: "Dave, this is Luther Elliss. I want to know if you want to start a church in Salt Lake City. Give me a call. Thanks." That's it—that's about what I told him.

Amazingly, God was also speaking to Dave Nelson at the same time. Dave was feeling like it was time for a change. He felt like God was calling him to do something else then, but he didn't know what it was. He'd even been talking to the other pastors about starting another church in Michigan. But somehow he didn't feel like that was it.

Imagine his surprise, then, when he got to his office one morning and heard my message. He was blown away. He listened to it over and over again; he couldn't believe it. He called his wife, Susie, and said, "I just got this weird call from Luther Elliss, and he is asking if I want to start a church in Salt Lake City!" After praying about it for three or four months, we decided to go for it. And God has done some amazing things!

Thirty-five people came forward and said they would go with us to Salt Lake City. They gave up everything and trusted God. Most of them didn't even have jobs yet; they trusted God to provide for them when they got to Utah. And God has done that so far for every single family.

We talked with several church-planting organizations on what to expect of our new venture. Most of them said we could expect perhaps 200 attendees our first year. But I always felt, from the very beginning, that if we did this the right way, the church would be more like 700-1000 people in the first year. The church is called K2, and it's all about an adventure with God. The first service was held in September 2004, and by October 2005 we were averaging close to 1000 people. No church plant has had these kind of numbers.

God has blessed me immensely. It's a miracle that I have played professional football. After all, my dad is only 5' 8", 165 pounds soaking wet, a small man by most standards. I'm 6' 5", 318 pounds. If you see my family photo, everybody stands to my shoulders or shorter.

I look at my life and I just say, "God, thank You so much." What He's given us and allowed us to manage is truly amazing. I view the NFL as a platform to share my faith—I'm known as the preacher of the locker room! And that doesn't mean that my team is always going to win; God doesn't orchestrate everything. But I glorify Him even when we lose, even when we get blown out. I still say, "Thank You."

I'm in awe every day; every morning when I wake up I'm grateful that I 'm alive again and have a chance to serve another day. God hasn't blessed me for me; He blesses me to bless others. It's like that song, "Thank You," by Ray Boltz—when you get to Heaven, you'll meet this long line of people who want to say thank you for introducing them to Jesus Christ. That's one of the many great things we have to look forward to.

GOD'S ROAD MAP

The Holy Bible provides a road map to help you live a happy and satisfying life. To learn more about the concepts presented in the chapter you've just read, take a look at these passages:

PROTECTION

Do you know what? God can do anything because He created the world and everything in it—including you and me. When we put our trust in Him, He wraps His loving arms around us and sends legions of angels to protect us. Why? Just like a daddy who loves and guides us, the good Shepherd guards His flock.

First Samuel 2:9a

He will guard the feet of His saints, but the wicked will be silenced in darkness.

Psalm 121:8

The Lord will watch over your coming and going both now and forevermore.

Psalm 91:11

For He will command His angels concerning you to guard you in all your ways.

BLESSINGS

When somebody sneezes, we casually use the phrase, "Bless you." But what does it really mean to bless someone or be blessed yourself? Originally the phrase was used to wish health and abundant life for someone who was coming down with an illness. A blessing from God is so much more. It can be something tangible like work, food, family, but we can also be blessed by a personal relationship with the God of the universe.

Deuteronomy 28:1-4

If you fully obey the Lord your God and carefully follow all His commands I give you today, the Lord your God will set you high above all the nations on earth. All these blessings will come upon you and accompany you if you obey the Lord your God: you will be blessed in the city and blessed in the country. The fruit of your womb will be blessed, and the crops of your land and the young of your livestock—the calves of your herds and the lambs of your flocks.

Jeremiah 17:7

But blessed is the man who trusts in the Lord, whose confidence is in Him.

Psalm 84:11

For the Lord God is a sun and shield; the Lord bestows favor and honor; no good thing does He withhold from those whose walk is blameless.

Gloria Gaynor

Musician, Disco Hit "I Will Survive"

THE name Gloria Gaynor is recognized around the world. Her Grammy award-winning signature song, "I Will Survive" has been inspiring people for decades. In 1973 Gloria made history when Billboard created the Disco Action Charts. Her song, "Never Can Say Good-Bye" hit #1 on this chart and became the first dance song to reach #1 status in dance music. And this disco queen is still at it. In March 2001, nearly 30 years later, her single, "Just Keep Thinkin' About You," topped out at #1 on the charts. Her international hit "Last Night" with Giorgio Moroder debuted at #1 in Europe. She was the first artist to record an album especially for clubs, and the first to do a mega-extended, dance-medley party mix, releasing 12 dance singles that are collectors' items.

Ms. Gaynor has won numerous awards. In 2004 she was honored at the World Music Awards in Monte Carlo with the highly coveted LEGEND award, which was presented by longtime fan Price Albert. She has starred on Broadway in the longest running musical revue *Smokey Joe's Cafe*, on television in "That '70s Show" and "Ally McBeal." "I Will Survive" has been featured on the soundtracks of more than half a dozen major film releases.

After all this fame and notoriety, Gloria still says, "I can now sing 'I Will Survive' with true conviction because my strength to live and assurance that I will, comes from submission to the only One who can create life...Jesus Christ." Her complete story can be found in her autobiography, *I Will Survive*. For more information on Gloria's recordings and upcoming appearances, check out her website: www.gloriagaynor.com.

✦━❖┃❖┃❖━✦

When I was growing up, we were "poor but happy," as the saying goes. Children never mind or even know that they are poor, as long as they are loved, which we certainly were. My fondest memory of my childhood has always been of my relationship with my mother. We were always very, very close. She was really my best friend. I looked up to her—I almost idolized her. She was the one who loved me—unconditionally—no matter what I did. I saw her as being physically and morally strong, and I loved that about her.

From the time I was a little girl, I have never bowed to peer pressure to do things that my mother taught me were wrong. But of course, the other children didn't like me for that, and I really didn't have many friends. We always maintained this very strong, intimate relationship; but as I grew older, my mother's love was not quite enough. I wanted a boyfriend. Eventually I did try to keep male friends by becoming sexually active, and it still didn't work. I wanted to find a relationship that would carry me throughout my life, because I saw how lonely my mother was, and I never wanted to be that lonely.

I had two abortions by the time I was 21. During neither time was I having a happy, caring relationship with the father. Once, I broke up with my boyfriend after being intimate, and then I fell for the "let me help get you through it" line. I didn't really know whom the baby belonged to. I didn't want to marry either one of the guys, and neither one of them wanted to marry me. Abortion was illegal—a dreadful and awful experience in the 1960s. You'd go to some nurse's place and be given an injection, and then you'd go home. And soon the pain would start, and you were virtually alone. It was horribly painful, but I wasn't really aware of what was happening. I honestly thought it was just blood I was passing, because that's what they said.

For years I carried the guilt of these abortions around with me. I felt that God was punishing me for them. Even after I became a Christian, I still thought that that was why I didn't have any children. A pastor finally helped me to understand that when I accepted Christ as my Savior, I was forgiven for all my sins, even the ones for which I couldn't forgive myself. Christ died to pay for all my sins. I was free from all the guilt. I still wish that I had understood what an abortion really is, and not done it.

In terms of worldly success, the '70s was my decade. New York City became the center of the musical universe, the capital of nightlife, with a host of new stars, and I was right up there, shining among them. I had worked hard for many years trying to build a career, and it finally paid off; I had fame and fortune. But I also had troubles. I discovered too late that my manager had squandered all my money. He had guided me success-fully through my early years as a recording artist. I still pray for him, because once upon a time he was my friend, and I admired and loved him like a brother.

I seem to always have had a very strong belief in God...God, not Jesus. For some reason I never got hold of the idea of Jesus or thought anything about Him. But even as a very small child, I used to talk to God; and every night I would say my prayers, and felt He was looking out for me. Until the day my mother died, these nightly prayers were about the extent of my relationship with God. I would give Him my nightly grocery list, and in exchange I tried to be a good and moral person. That was the deal. But after she passed away in 1970, I became more and more aware of a great emptiness at the center of my life. I knew I was looking for something...missing something, but I didn't know what it was.

I had a growing desire to learn more about religion; I wanted to find somewhere I could belong, some kind of church community, although not necessarily a Christian church. I embarked on my search for a deep-er, more real faith. I started reading the Bible and attending church occa-sionally. At the same time I was looking into different religions: secular humanism, Buddhism, Islam, and transcendental meditation. I even tried

Hare Krishna and scientology, but none of it seemed to go along with what the Bible said. And even though I had never been a regular church-goer, I had somehow always believed that the Bible was real.

I continued my search for God in different faiths all through the '70s, until early in 1978 when things went *crash! bang! wallop!* I took a bad fall at a concert and ended up in the hospital for two weeks. Two weeks later I was released from the hospital the pain came back, and I was once again in screaming agony. I went back into the hospital and stayed for over three months. While I was in the hospital, I began to read the Bible far more carefully. And I left with a renewed faith in God. I was so grateful for my recovery. I felt perhaps I had been allowed to survive for some pur-pose. I still didn't know anything about Christ, but I felt much stronger in my faith in God.

In 1979, my husband, Linwood, and I became seriously rich. In addi-tion to "I Will Survive" being so big, Linwood was having success with songs by other artists in his publishing company. Linwood loved the fast cars, crazy lifestyle, night-and-day parties that sometimes went on for weeks. And he loved all the attention he was getting.

I've got to admit it—I loved it too...some of it...at first. I very much enjoyed my increased celebrity as an artist and the love of the fans. As my popularity increased, I was working less and enjoying it more. We were having great fun with the "in crowd." We were meeting people who were bigger stars than we were. We traveled in stretch limousines with iced bottles of champagne in the back. We were invited to wild parties, and we gave wild parties. We got into marijuana...well, we'd been into marijuana for a long time, but we got more free with it. And then we got into cocaine.

I hated cocaine. But using it was the only way I could keep up and be accepted by the others. And do you know what the terrible thing about cocaine is? Cocaine doesn't care if you hate it. You must have more. It made me feel as if someone were pushing me faster than I wanted to go. But then, to come down from it is even worse. So you have to have more, so you can stay up—until you've been high for so long you are exhausted and have got to get some rest. For me that was usually after two or three days, and then I'd have to sleep all night and all day. Then I'd wake up and start all over again.

We suddenly had all this money, and we were not experienced enough to handle it. I began to feel myself sinking into the depths of degradation. When you have a lot of money, there are always going to be people around flattering you so they can help you spend it, people whose only idea in life is to get high and stay high. I was allowing things to happen that should never have happened.

I'll say no more than this: Linwood and I gave a lot of parties; we took drugs; we spent a lot of money; and we drifted apart. People became far too deeply involved in our life, and I began to feel like "one of the girls" instead of Linwood's wife. The marriage wasn't doing at all well, and I felt scared and humiliated. Professionally things were going wonderfully, but back at home I felt split in two, almost like when I was a little girl.

It was really the money and high-rolling lifestyle that came with it that brought me to the major crossroads of my life. I could either take the attitude that life was a nonstop party, with champagne and cocaine flowing from the taps, or I could start really doing something about the aching void that had been growing inside me since I could remember.

Between 1979 and 1982, I was on a seesaw. I would start going to church for a few months, then I couldn't stand being left out of all the good times Linwood and our friends were having. I was an outsider even at church, because I didn't know any other Christians. So I was always on my own. I couldn't stand that, so I'd be back smoking and drinking and going to the parties and getting upset with myself and feeling guilty. So then, after a while I would start going to church again. You see, it wasn't about drugs, alcohol, or good times; it was about feeling left out, abandoned. In 1982, one of Linwood's girlfriends became pregnant, and had a baby daughter. I knew this way of life had to come to an end.

In 1982 I got saved. I had gone to a little Baptist church one day, and at the end of the service, they asked if anyone wanted to join the church and accept Christ as their Savior. I did want to join the church, but I wasn't interested in accepting Christ as my Savior—I didn't even know what that meant. Other people did go forward and they said that they believed that Christ had died for their sins, and risen again, and was forever interceding at the right hand of the Father. And I was thinking, *What are they talking about? I don't know about any of that stuff. What is all that?*

So I didn't join that day. I went home, but it bothered me. When I got home, I opened up my Bible and said, "God, I want to understand about this Jesus. I'm here. I'm listening. I want to hear from *You* about Jesus, because people make mistakes, people lie, people get confused; and I don't want to hear from the lady upstairs or the man down the hall. I want to hear it from You."

So the Lord began to show me. When I sat down at my dining room table that morning, the Lord used the Scripture to draw me to salvation. I began to sit down at my dining room table every time I had the chance, to spend an hour or two studying the Bible...and that's where I got saved. For two years the Holy Spirit led me through the foundations of the faith in Scripture. I feel very blessed, and unshakable in my faith. I didn't get it from my aunt, my mother, my grandmother, or the lady upstairs. Instead, the Lord Himself, the Holy Spirit, began to teach me.

I had met the Lord, and I was getting strength from the Lord; and there was no way I was going to turn back. Every now and then I'd hang out with the crowd, but I was with them, not of them anymore, and they felt the difference. I was still drinking a little wine, still smoking marijuana and cigarettes. I told myself that when I drank and smoked, I could get on a higher plane and be closer to God.

That all came to a halt one day after I remembered a conversation I'd had with a young woman at a dinner party the night before. The next morning, when I woke up, I thought, *There you sat, speaking about the Lord with such fervor and conviction—the only girl, the only person sitting at the table—with a whole bottle of liquor in front of you—and the only Christian. What a representation of Christ that must have been to that girl!?*

I fell on my knees and said, "Lord, forgive me. I am so sorry. And if You would take away from me the taste for alcohol—for champagne, I will never have another drink as long as I live." And that was the last time I took a drink. But that's not all.

I know He's real. I'd been smoking a pack of cigarettes a day. Anyone with a cigarette habit can tell you that even if you have the willpower to quit, for months afterward you still have a desire to smoke. When someone smokes around you, you want to just get a whiff of the tobacco. I had experienced that two or three times. I asked the Lord to take from me the taste for champagne. He knew that if I smoked, I'd drink. He, therefore, took from me the taste and desire for both, as well as marijuana.

The next evening, I stood in a backstage area cloudy with cigarette smoke and two bottles of Dom Perignon, and had no desire for either. As soon as I took it to Him, as soon as I said—and meant—that I was ready to be free from the desire for those things, Christ set me free. It was just as simple as that, and immediately the urge was gone. "Whom the Son sets free is free indeed." I call that a miracle, and I praise and thank Him for it. Hallelujah!

When I first sang "I Will Survive" in 1978, I sang it from the heart. I wanted to encourage everybody, including myself, to believe that we could survive. I'd had a lot of heartache and suffering, and I thought that I had made it through. What I didn't know then was how to survive, how to get better self-esteem. It has taken me a very long time since I first sang that song, to learn its lesson for myself. In the end, I have survived, but not through any power of my own. I have survived because after long years of loneliness, and insecurity, and lack of self-esteem, I learned to hand all of my burdens over to the Lord, and now I survive in His strength.

GOD'S ROAD MAP

The Holy Bible is a guide to help you live a happy and satisfying life. To learn more about the concepts presented in the chapter you've just read, take a look at these passages:

ABORTION

God's Word clearly states that all life is sacred, particularly that of the unborn child; therefore, abortion is a sin. Yet God also extends forgiveness...even for those who have had an abortion. He alone can heal the wounds left long after the procedure is over.

Psalm 139:13-16

For You created my inmost being; You knit me together in my mother's womb. I praise You because I am fearfully and wonderfully made; Your works are wonderful, I know that full well. My frame was not hidden from You when I was made in the secret place. When I was woven together in the depths of the earth, Your eyes saw my unformed body. All the days ordained for me were written in Your book before one of them came to be.

Jeremiah 1:5

Before I formed you in the womb I knew you, before you were born I set you apart....

Isaiah 1:18

"Come now, let us reason together," says the Lord. "Though your sins are like scarlet, they shall be as white as snow; though they are red as crimson, they shall be like wool."

GRACE

Grace is unmerited favor—or mercy we don't deserve. We don't have to do anything to earn God's love; by His grace He offers forgiveness and eternal life. To accept this gift, we need to simply believe that His Son,

Jesus Christ died on the cross to redeem of us our sins. And then we need to accept Him as our Lord and Savior.

Ephesians 2:8-9

For it is by grace you have been saved, through faith—and this not from yourselves, it is the gift of God—not by works, so that no one can boast.

Hebrews 4:16

Let us then approach the throne of grace with confidence, so that we may receive mercy and find grace to help us in our time of need.

Second Corinthians 8:9

For you know the grace of our Lord Jesus Christ, that though He was rich, yet for your sakes He became poor, so that you through His poverty might become rich.

Kabeer Gbaja-Biamila

NFL Defensive End, Green Bay Packers
(Photo, courtesy of the Green Bay Packers)

A FFECTIONATELY known as KGB, #94 Muhammed-Kabeer Olarewaju Gbaja-Biamila is an explosive, pass-rushing defensive end for the Green Bay Packers. In his parent's native Nigerian tongue, his name means "Big man come and save me," an irony for a guy whose main job is to take out the quarterback.

In 2004, KGB became the first Packers player to post double-digit sacks in three consecutive seasons. Only three other NFL players have done the same during that period. He made his first Pro Bowl appearance following the 2003 season, making him the first Green Bay defensive lineman to make it there since Reggie White did in 1998. Entering his sixth season in the NFL, he already stands third on the Packer's all-time sacks list at 50-1/2.

KGB grew up on the tough streets of South Central Los Angeles. At Crenshaw High School, he lettered three times each in football and track and was chosen as a National Football Foundation Hall of Fame scholar athlete. He was also one of 40 student owners of the nation's first student-run natural food company, "Food From the Hood." He appeared on the cover of

Newsweek magazine in recognition of the group's achievements. KGB was also honored on the magazine's "American Achievement Awards" which was nationally televised on CBS.

His success in the sport of football is enviable, but to Kabeer, the role model for everything in his life, both on and off the field, is Jesus Christ.

Before I knew Christ, I was leading a double life. On the outside, I was this clean-cut, wholesome athlete who said all the right words and was respectful to his elders. But behind closed doors, I was stealing, cheating, lying...and even killing. I was doing it all.

I grew up in a family with seven kids. My parents were born in Lagos, Nigeria and immigrated to the United States long before I was born. My mom was a Christian, and my dad is a Muslim. My mom was more of the spiritual leader of the household, and because of her faith, we went to church.

But for me, going to church was just checking in and checking out. There was no choice—I had to go. I have ADHD, so I always went to the bathroom to kill time. It was a good way of getting out of the service and not listening to the Nigerian pastor. He had a thick accent, and I was so focused on how he sounded and his outer appearance that I was totally blinded to the message. In the Bible, Jesus says, "He who has ears to hear, let him hear." My heart wasn't yet softened to hear God's Word.

I wanted to be more like my dad. He seemed perfect in my eyes, so calm and disciplined. Dad always had it all together, while my mom seemed to be struggling. The Muslim religion appeared more structured and organized—there was one god and everybody prayed to the East...simple. I have always had and always will have great respect for my father. To this day we have a very loving and rewarding relationship.

Looking back now, I can see the importance of being equally yoked in marriage. It's important for both partners to love the Lord, because in my weakness, my wife is strong. In her weakness, I am strong. But my mom was basically by herself. My dad was a good father, and he was the best husband he could be, but he was a Muslim and couldn't be there for her spiritually. They just served different gods.

Part of the Nigerian culture is the belief in voodoo and witchcraft. These types of practices are very common, and to most native people, they are not considered to be necessarily bad. My mother used to tell me that there is good voodoo, like going to a babaloa who would say charms to bring about success in business or in love. The witch doctor would just tell you to wear something around your neck and you'd have good things happen to you. It's a scam when it's all said and done, but a lot of Nigerians, especially women, get caught up in it. After I became a Christian, I showed my mom a passage in Leviticus that clearly forbids going to spiritualists. She had no idea it was wrong.

Even though my parents had different religions, it didn't seem confusing to me. They respected each other's views and had many similar beliefs. From my understanding as a kid, the only difference was that Muslims see Jesus as just another prophet and Christians see Him as the Son of God, or God in the flesh.

Like my dad, I called myself a Muslim, but I wasn't a practicing one. And also like my dad, I learned how to question Christians. It's not that hard to find "supposed" contradictions in the Bible. My dad told me what they were, and I went to my Christian friends and said things like, "Hey guys, look at the contradictions in your Bible!" I played devil's advocate, but I really believed what I was saying to them because I looked up to my dad.

My views of Christians didn't improve much when I left high school and went to San Diego State on a football scholarship. Before every game there was a chapel service; I went to it just to listen. A lot of the Christian guys would say things like, "I'm going to sin tonight when I go clubbing, but then God will forgive me." I was thinking, *Why would I want to be like them?*

But at the same time, I was no different than those guys. As a Muslim, what mattered was how I looked in front of other men. So, I had a clean-cut, good-boy image, but behind closed doors I was somebody completely different. I looked like a man of integrity, to the point where people thought I was still a virgin. Yet, I was having sex before marriage; I was cheating, stealing, doing it all. But since nobody saw me, it was as if I never did it at all.

I'd been doing wrong ever since I was a kid. There was this great guy named Mr. Reed at Audubon Junior High School. We used to call him "Mr. Audubon" because he had keys to the whole school. I started hanging out with him and became his helper; if he ever needed anything I'd get it for him. Sometimes he would give me the keys and I'd do errands. But when he gave me those keys, I would go to the cafeteria and steal food—whatever they had out. One time, I went around the school parking lot, popping people's tires with a blade for absolutely no reason. I wasn't thinking about what I was doing to them; I just wanted to see what it felt like.

My dad was the cook at our house, and with seven kids, we had to ask permission for the good stuff and he would give it to us individually; otherwise, somebody would get left out. I used to do things like drink the apple juice, fill it back up with water, and then hammer on the top so it looked like it hadn't been opened yet. I've also shoplifted and stolen from liquor stores. I was good at not getting caught.

But I've done far worse than steal a few trading cards. I got one of my girlfriends pregnant and she had an abortion. In my mind, that makes me a murderer—even though I wasn't a part of the actual procedure. It was my sin of having sex before marriage that put her in that situation. She didn't want to have the baby, and at the time, I was glad she had the abortion. Since then, I've asked God for forgiveness.

Yeah, I was leading a double life, big time. I was so much worse than those guys who were going to the clubs and then begging for forgiveness the next day. At least you knew where they were. But me, I was a snake; you wouldn't see me coming. Right behind your back I'd be stealing from you. On the outside I was a boy scout; on the inside I was a filthy dog.

I had a friend in college, a girl named Eileen who was the strength and conditioning coach for the football team. She was often the one I went to for advice when I was having problems with my girlfriends.

Toward the end of my college career I was training for the NFL and asked Eileen out. We went out several times, but every time she brought along a third party. And because that chaperone was there, I had a hard time showing Eileen my devious side. But one time, I convinced her to drive me home by herself and I had my chance. I tried to spit my game at her and make my move, but she shut me down. But as time went on, she was more willing to spend time alone with me.

Our relationship became more and more physical. Eileen was the strength coach at San Diego State, and I was a senior on my way out. That didn't look good—a coach dating a player. She'd come to my house, but nobody knew. I made sure she parked her car at a park and then I would pick her up there. Then we would sneak into my apartment. I did a really good job of keeping the whole relationship on the down low.

One such night, one thing led to another and we ended up in bed. As I was making my big move, she started to cry. I knew that Eileen was a strong Christian and that her faith was very important to her. I felt bad that I had caused her to stray away from her God.

Eileen knew what we were doing wasn't right. Even in Eileen's sin, God was real to her. And that inspired me. I wanted to have what she had. Eileen liked everything about me—I was a great guy in her eyes. But I wasn't a Christian, and she had people in her Bible study praying that I might find Christ. We still saw each other, but we were careful about not putting ourselves in compromising situations.

During my senior year, I met a man who would turn out to be very influential in my life. Gill Byrd was a two-time Pro-Bowler from the San Diego Chargers, and he led a chapel service before a game one day. He talked about how he had converted from Islam to Christianity. I didn't have much time to talk with him afterward, but he gave me his number. When I tried to call him later, the number was disconnected and I found out that he had moved to Green Bay. I didn't think anything more about it.

Then what do you know...two years later I got drafted by the Green Bay Packers and Gill was working there as the director of player development. Green Bay was the team I didn't want to go to; this California boy wasn't interested in a Wisconsin winter.

But it ended up being a blessing in disguise, because in Gill, I got to see a true Christian, living it and walking it, and he was cool. He was a strong believer in Christ, and you could see it in how he lived his life and how he treated his wife and kids. He took me in like I was one of his own sons.

I was confused—was the Bible right or was the Koran? I determined that I was going to prove that the Bible was a fake. Yet at the same time, I was searching for the truth. I got down on my knees, and although I didn't know exactly who I was praying to, I said, "God, whoever created Kabeer Gbaja-Biamila, please talk to me. I want to know who this Jesus is. Is He a prophet, or is He more than a prophet? I don't know and I want to know."

I didn't like to read back then, because my ADHD made it really hard to concentrate. The only book I'd ever read from front to back was Dennis Rodman's *Bad As I Wanna Be*. Then I picked up the Bible. In the Word it says, "Seek and you shall find." For five years, I'd been trying to seek, but I was really just looking. Most people who try to read the Bible get sleepy or distracted, especially during the first books of the Old Testament. But I was so focused on what I was reading, and I devoured Genesis, Exodus, Leviticus, and Numbers.

I became a Christian before I even got to the New Testament, because I was able to see God's mercy—and I was able to see Jesus there. I was able to see how events were actually connected; the Bible wasn't just a bunch of stories. And the most amazing thing was that everything prepared for the arrival of Jesus Christ. I saw Jesus in the Book of Isaiah—in the prophecy about a man who would come to die for the sins of the world. I was blown away.

As I was reading the Bible, God was literally talking to me. I realized that it wasn't contradicting itself at all, that it was legit. There's no way man could have written this Book, because all power of attorney was given to God. And that's not our nature; our nature is to be in control. But in the Bible it says God is in control of everything.

I already knew I fell short, because I knew my dirt. Little by little, God showed me that I was in no position to be judging other people—that I was the big hypocrite. I was truly humbled, and in spite of all of the wickedness I'd done, God loved me enough to go on that cross and die for my sins. As I was reading the Bible, He revealed Himself to me. "Kabeer—here I am."

After I read the Bible, Gill and I had some profound discussions. One ended in an argument when he offended me by saying that Allah is not the same God he served. How could he say that—when they're the same person? I was so angry, that I left his office for a while, and when I came back he had a friend with him. Dave Bratton was the first Christian I couldn't make stumble. He blew me away with his answers to my questions about the contradictions in the Bible. I was expecting him to say, "I'll get back to you with an answer," like everyone else did. Instead he opened up his Bible and showed me the answer.

And do you know what I realized? I realized that it didn't matter what the answer was; I was either going to accept Jesus Christ for who He is, or I was going to reject Him. I'd been doing things my own way for 22 years; I figured I should at least try God's way. That night I accepted Jesus Christ into my life.

A few days later, I had a chance to see God in action. I got cut from the Green Bay Packers; they put me on the practice squad. In college, I'd always had this attitude—it's not how you start; it's how you finish. So, I wasn't defeated...not yet. The team ended up drafting somebody in the first round for the only position that I could play—elephant end. As a matter of fact, there were four defensive ends all competing for just one spot, including this hotshot first-round draft pick.

But I couldn't worry about that. All I could do was be the best I could be and leave it in God's hands. And I did that. I kept my head focused on God. In Genesis, there is a story about Joseph. Despite the fact that his brothers mistreated him, he still had faith in God. And when he was brought to Egypt as a slave, Joseph prayed that he would find favor in the eyes of Potiphar, one of the Pharaoh's officials. And God did that. Eventually Joseph was in charge of everything in Potiphar's household. Then Joseph got thrown in jail and God allowed the warden to see favor in him. He was put in charge of all the prisoners. Eventually, Joseph was the second most powerful man in all of Egypt.

I remember saying that same prayer, "God, let coach Sherman see favor in me." The backup defensive end was traded to Miami, so that left the starter, John Thierry, Jamal Reynolds, and me in competition. I was doing really well in mini-camps and getting a bunch of sacks. I'd go in and get a sack on nearly every play. I got in a fight because the other players were mad at me; they thought I was jumping the count. But I just instinctively knew when the ball was going to snap—it was incredible!

The coaches were trying to groom the first rounder; they really needed to get him on the field so it didn't look bad if their big pick wasn't starting. So I wasn't getting very many reps. But when I was out there, I capitalized on it. Eventually, my reps increased and I got better. In my first game of the second season, I was the backup DE—only coming in on third-down situations. I probably only got 12 snaps in the whole game. I ended up getting three sacks against Detroit. In the next game, I got two sacks; in the next game another one; and then we played Tampa Bay and I got another three sacks.

In the course of the first four games of the season, I got nine sacks. Only two other people in NFL history have done that—Mark Gastineau and Kevin Greene. The only difference between me and them is that they were starters and I was the backup. I was a no-namer, so when I started getting these sacks, the announcers had to learn how to pronounce my name.

When I accepted Christ, one of the first people I told was Eileen. She cried again, only this time it was tears of joy. We'd been "seeing" each other for about a year, but neither of us had ever seen our relationship having a future. But slowly, God helped me realize that He'd put her in my life for a reason, and I wanted to marry her before I went back to Green Bay for my second season. I knew it was going to be hard living out there being single. When I arrived, I was so lonely. I tried to get her to come out and visit, but she wanted to wait a while.

After I knew I was on the team, I asked someone to send my dog, Nala, out to be with me. Unfortunately, the day that she was supposed to come was Tuesday, September 11, 2001. Obviously, she never made it.

You know the saying, "Idle hands are the devil's workshop"? Well, that Tuesday I had nothing to do; the tragedy of 9/11 was wearing on me, and it was our day off. In the past, I'd been sexually involved with a young woman in Green Bay. But when I became a Christian, I made a vow before God to stay away from her, and I hadn't seen her for more than six months. I even told myself that I wouldn't go to the bars anymore. But there was so much temptation! Yet I knew if I just kept my nose clean and went home right after work each night that I'd be okay.

I was frustrated and lonely because my dog wasn't there, and I was upset because I couldn't see Eileen. My loneliness got the best of me, and I picked up the phone and called that girl's number. "Oh God, I can't do this!" I said as I was dialing the phone. But luckily, the number was disconnected. I had to stay busy. I figured if I just went out, got something to eat, and did some errands, by the time I got home I'd be tired enough to go to bed.

But when I got home and pulled my car into the garage, that girl came up right behind my car! I didn't go to the party; satan brought the party to me. She hugged me, and I started telling her about Eileen, that I really wanted to marry her. But she said, "If she really cared about you, she'd be here right now." That's how I felt too. We went inside, and before you knew it we were in the bedroom and I'd turned off the ringer on the phone.

She was pursuing me and I was trying to hold back. But I wasn't very successful and right when I was about to make a big mistake, God put something in my brain—I was thinking that either she has a disease or she was trying to pin a baby on me. I told her to get out of the house.

When I checked the answering machine, I discovered that Eileen had been trying to call the whole time I was with that other girl. I felt so bad. I'd really messed up this time. I felt like there was no way I could serve God now. I couldn't be an ambassador for Christ, and I couldn't be with Eileen either. She deserved a better man than me.

I called Eileen and told her what happened. Of course, she wasn't happy, but God made her strong that day. The words that came out of her mouth were so powerful—I still can't believe it. I'd never experienced human forgiveness like that before. She said, "Kabeer, it's not about you; it's about Christ!" She still wanted to be with me, despite the fact that I had cheated on her.

I'd always thought that I was better than Eileen. I knew about her past; before she was a Christian, she'd been much more promiscuous than I'd been. She'd even cheated on some of her former boyfriends. I'd never cheated on anybody. So because of my pride, I thought I was better than her. But it's crazy how God will humble you. In this situation, Eileen could have easily judged me, but she forgave me, and I suddenly saw her in a different light. I felt like I was lucky to have her. Before, I thought she was lucky to be with me. God used that situation to humble me.

Eileen and I got married a month later. I really believe that if you are burning with passion, it's better to be married. That's why I was trying to marry her before the season. I knew I loved her; I knew I was burning with passion, and I didn't want to be in the situation where if I saw her, I couldn't touch her. Because touching her would lead to having sex.

I lost my virginity in college, and now I understand why God doesn't want us to have premarital sex. Because, I tell you, when you do get married, you bring all previous relationships to your marriage bed. On the day I married Eileen, October 12, I suddenly stopped desiring her sexually. We were now legally married, and I was no longer interested in her. When God says you can't have something, you want it. When God says you can have it, you don't want it. I thought there was something wrong with me.

And there was something wrong—I was afraid I needed Viagra. The only way I could respond to her physically was if I thought about other girls from my past, through pornography or things I'd seen on TV. I was thinking about other women while I was making love to my wife. I knew it was wrong, because the Bible says if you lust after a woman in your heart, you have actually committed adultery.

I told Eileen everything and together we prayed, "God, let it be my wife that I find refuge in and that I find pleasing. Let my wife, Eileen, be the one that I sexually have desire for and no other. God, forgive me of my past sins and all the junk that I put in my life." And in His awesome power, God restored our marriage. It's an awesome feeling when it's your wife alone who pleases you. If I had to do it all over again, I would abstain from sex until after we were married—just like God intended.

Through all of my experiences, I can see God's hand on everything—even during the tough times.

On December 1, 2002, our first son was born. That afternoon, we played Chicago, and after the game I received a call that my mom had been killed in a horrible car accident. She had received a phone call from a friend who needed her assistance. She was tired, and my dad told her that she needed to stay home and rest; but my mom insisted on going to help. On her way home, her car went out of control, struck a palm tree and blew up. The authorities think she may have fallen asleep at the wheel.

It was a very traumatic day. After that, I thought I just had to win the Super Bowl, that somehow that would bring meaning to her death. But the Packers were knocked out in the first game of the playoffs. I didn't handle it very well, and all the pain I'd been feeling came crashing down on me. Football had kept me busy, and now that it was over, I had to deal with the grief.

Eileen and I got into an argument. She kept saying, "Just trust in God." She said all the right things, but I just wasn't feeling it. I tried to get her to panic by leaving the house abruptly. She called and called, but I wouldn't pick up the phone. Instead, I was driving around town trying to get into trouble. I ran red lights and drove recklessly just begging the police to pull me over. I even tried to go to that girl's house, the one I had cheated on Eileen with, but she'd moved away.

Fortunately, God kept anything bad from happening to me that day. When I got home, I was able to pull into the garage without Eileen knowing I was there. I sat and listened to a song called, "My Life is in Your Hands," by Kirk Franklin about lifting up your hands to God and letting Him take your troubles away. It was all about trusting Him. And I started crying, bawling in that garage all by myself. That day, I felt God wrap His arms around me and tell me it would be okay.

Little by little, I'm changing and being molded into the man God wants me to be. Right now God is teaching me not to worry. Worry stems from my desire for control. I don't trust God enough to handle the situation. We put the burden on ourselves, when Jesus clearly tells us to hand our burdens over to Him.

God has shown me how to live my faith through my son Rashid. When he was younger, he would cry every time I would leave him. I'd have to sneak out of the house so he wouldn't cry all day. But now, I can tell him that I'm going to work and I'll be home later and he's okay. He has faith that I'll come back. It's the same thing with my faith—I can't see God and I don't always feel Him, but I know He's there.

As much as I enjoy football and my success, I know that those things won't last forever. There is one thing that will, however; and that's my relationship with my Lord and Savior Jesus Christ. That is my greatest victory.

GOD'S ROAD MAP

The Holy Bible is a guide to help you live a happy and satisfying life. To learn more about the concepts presented in the chapter you've just read, take a look at these passages:

SELF-CONTROL

Why is it so hard to practice self-control? Our sinful nature often gets the best of us, whether it has to do with sex, food, or alcohol. Self-control first requires that we understand how God wants us to live, by studying the Bible. We can then ask Him to lead the charge and give us the willpower we need.

Galatians 5:24-25 (NKJV)

And those who are Christ's have crucified the flesh with its passions and desires. If we live in the Spirit, let us also walk in the Spirit.

Romans 13:14

Rather, clothe yourselves with the Lord Jesus Christ, and do not think about how to gratify the desires of the sinful nature.

Second Peter 1:6 (NLT)

Knowing God leads to self-control. Self-control leads to patient endurance, and patient endurance leads to godliness.

MARRIAGE

In a culture where more than 50 percent of all marriages end in divorce, staying happily married can be a real challenge. Sexual sin is one reason for these dismal statistics, but so is a lack of commitment and selfishness. With God at the center of your marriage, you will be able to withstand any storm.

First Corinthians 7:2-5

But since there is so much immorality, each man should have his own wife, and each woman her own husband. The husband should fulfill his marital duty to his wife, and likewise the wife to her husband. The wife's body does not belong to her alone but also to her husband. In the same way, the husband's body does not belong to him alone but also to his wife. Do not deprive each other except by mutual consent and for a time, so that you may devote yourselves to prayer. Then come together again so that Satan will not tempt you because of your lack of self-control.

Matthew 5:27-28

You have heard that it was said, "Do not commit adultery." But I tell you that anyone who looks at a woman lustfully has already committed adultery with her in his heart.

Jason Hanson

NFL Kicker, Detroit Lions
(Photo, courtesy of Steve Kovich/Detroit Lions)

When it comes to putting the pigskin between the goalposts, they don't come much better than Jason Hanson. Considered one of the finest kicking specialists in the history of college football, this consensus All-American was chosen in the second round (56th overall) of the NFL draft by the Detroit Lions.

Going into the 2005 season, the 14-year veteran of the Lions is the team's all-time scoring leader with 1,336 points, the all-time leader in field goals (308) and extra points (412). In 2004 he became the 20th player in NFL history to reach the 1,300-point mark. Amazingly, Hanson has never missed a game in his 14-year run—that's 208 consecutive games! He has appeared at the Pro Bowl twice, and is a four-time winner of the Lions' Yale Lary Special Teams Player of the Year award. Hanson's field goal percentage is remarkable: inside the 50-yard line—.865; and .958 from inside the 40-yard line.

To Hanson, playing professional football is a privilege that holds a special responsibility. He helped establish Providence Youth Outreach in Pontiac, Michigan, an organization which helps at-risk youth, ages 12-22. He donates $200 for every field goal he kicks to the "Points for Providence" program. Hanson is also a popular speaker before youth and Christian groups in both Michigan and his home state of Washington.

One single kick can determine the fate of a whole game or even a whole season. As a kicker you can have weeks of glory; but if you miss the kick, you are the reason for the loss. Walking out on the football field at crunch time could be a completely nerve-racking experience. But I have learned over the years, that even if I lead the NFL in humiliation, my hope is not tied up in what happens on the field. My hope is tied up in Christ.

I was fortunate to have been raised in a Christian home with a brother, and a mom and dad who weren't divorced. I loved sports. My main sport was soccer, but I also played a bit of basketball. In high school, all my friends played football and eventually they coaxed me into giving it a try, "Why don't you come and play a man's sport?" Because soccer was in the spring and football was in the fall, I could play both.

I kicked right away. I tried some other positions, but my teammates had been playing for years so I was too far behind. Instead, I just concentrated on kicking the football. My junior year was great, and I had a lot of interest from colleges. It looked like I might have a future in the sport. But then I played really badly in my senior year, and most of the interest dropped. I was accepted at Stanford University, and the team said they were going to sign me. But I never heard from them again. As it turned out, one of my few remaining college options was in my home state of Washington at Washington State University. It was only 1 1/2 hours away and wasn't even on my radar screen. But by the end of the process, it just so happened that I had lots of academic scholarships there. And they were fairly interested in me playing football for them. So I decided to stay in-state.

College is one of the biggest reasons that I know God is real. I originally had no plans of going to Washington State, and in the end that's the door that was open for me. Now in retrospect, it seems like so much of it was God's planning. I was very successful in football there, and I met some very influential people in Washington, including my wife. *My choice would have been somewhere else, but God led me there.*

I walked on and made the Washington State football team right away and got a scholarship as soon as the season was over. And then the following year I did well. I was a consensus All-American, I was on the Bob Hope Show, and I was receiving all kinds of press, awards, tickets, and recognition. I was famous, young, and popular...and yet something wasn't clicking. My homework was still due, relationships were often a struggle, and the things inside my heart didn't change. I was getting the best that the world had to offer, but somehow it still wasn't enough.

On NFL draft day in 1992, I knew there were some teams interested in me, but I didn't know who would take me or when. There were definitely two or three teams that I thought were in the running. I thought one of those teams was going to draft me and out of nowhere came Detroit. I didn't know it at the time, but the Lions' special teams' coach was convinced that I was the guy they wanted and needed.

In the end, I was drafted by the Detroit Lions in the second round. My wife and I were sitting there looking at each other like, "Holy cow, where are we going?" We didn't know anything about the city so it was a big adventure. I have no doubt that God put us in Detroit. If I'd have picked, it would have been Miami or the Super Bowl champion or to stay home in Seattle. But we ended up in Detroit, and that's exactly where God wanted us.

When I was a kid, we went to church regularly. I suppose I was like most kids who thought Sunday school was fun, but the sermon was boring. There was a time around junior high when I began to realize that I wasn't saved or going to Heaven just because I went to church or because my parents were Christians. One summer I went to a Bible camp, and it was at that camp that I finally understood that it was *my* heart and *my* decision that mattered. I needed to decide if I believed that Jesus is who He said He is and that God is real, or if it was just going to be religion. It was clear to me that I needed to have a relationship with Jesus myself, not just practice a family tradition.

I did my biggest growing in college. I would never describe myself as being on the wrong side of the line of right and wrong, or going off the deep end. But you get to a point in college where suddenly you are making decisions on your own for what may be the very first time in your life. Suddenly, you are in total control over what you do, what you say, what you see, and what you think. In college, you are exposed to so many different things—ideas and philosophies and lifestyles—that you quickly come to a point of determining what you believe. And I came to really believe that what the Bible says is true and that my faith was real...that God is real. There was never a neon sign, lightning and thunder, or a dramatic conversion moment. It was more like a slow process of growth. I became convinced that it's not just a belief. I was sure.

For the last 14 years I've played professional football. And I've found that there's no peace in performance. And there's no peace in material things, because they're all so temporary. The fame, popularity, and possessions we get from the pro experience just don't last. And there's no peace in my field goal percentage. But I do have peace knowing that I have a relationship with God through Jesus Christ. In Philippians 4:7, the Bible talks about the peace that passes all understanding. There's no other place I've found that peace. I guess that's ultimately what has convinced me—knowing that who I am doesn't depend on my performance on the football field. It's not what the world says, but it is what the Bible says. And that's more important to me.

That peace carries onto the field. But it doesn't take away the adrenaline or the anxiety of that huge moment when I'm kicking the football. One single kick can decide the outcome of a game or even an entire season. It's tempting to use God as my rabbit's foot—you know, if I pray really hard, I will be successful. Maybe God does impact my games, but I know it's deeper than that—simply knowing that if I try my hardest and give my absolute best, that I can leave the results up to God. Who I am doesn't rest solely on my sports performance. Don't get me wrong—when I miss a field goal, I'm more upset than anybody. I take pride in doing my job the best that I can, but at the same time, I never despair. I know that being a successful football player doesn't answer the inner question of what happens when I die, how to have peace in my life, or who is going to forgive me. Fame and fortune are the wrong places to look for answers to those questions. I know that God has a plan and a purpose for my life, whether I'm a Pro Bowler or bow out on the football field.

I see God working in my life all the time. In the huge things like when there's an illness, we all go to God because it's so out of our control. But He's also interested in the smaller challenges in daily life. I know that when we have trusted God with every little part of our family's life, we've always had an answer. Like purchasing a home—what does God care about that? Yet when we were looking for a home in Detroit, we could see the doors open and close and found the perfect place where God wanted us to be. My family has experienced times where we could have just decided things on our own—we're intelligent enough to figure it out. But we stepped out and let God be in control, because we knew that the God we serve is real and that He would have a better plan for us than we could ever even imagine. That's something that has convinced me even more— the way He has taken care of the little things.

I don't know why I'm so extremely blessed. Sometimes it's overwhelming to think that God cares about me individually. Many think that Jesus is a myth or just another story, until they actually meet Him. I'm not going to claim that I understand everything, but to me it's not just a nice belief system or some kind of philosophy; it's really true. And I can claim that reality, because my relationship with Christ is true. God worked through my success to draw me closer to Him. And I'm never leaving His side.

GOD'S ROAD MAP

The Holy Bible is a guide to help you live a happy and satisfying life. To learn more about the concepts presented in the chapter you've just read, take a look at these passages:

SUCCESS

God doesn't measure success by the world's standards of fame and fortune. What truly matters is our godly success, not the size of our bank account or the number of trophies on our mantle.

Proverbs 16:3

Commit to the Lord whatever you do, and your plans will succeed.

Luke 12:15

Watch out! Be on your guard against all kinds of greed; a man's life does not consist in the abundance of his possessions.

Deuteronomy 6:10-12

When the Lord your God brings you into the land He swore to your fathers, to Abraham, Isaac and Jacob, to give you—a land with large, flourishing cities you did not build, houses filled with all kinds of good things you did not provide, wells you did not dig, and vineyards and olive groves you did not plant—then when you eat and are satisfied, be careful that you do not forget the Lord, who brought you out of Egypt, out of the land of slavery.

DECISIONS

Every day we make decisions—both big and small. It might be something as simple as what class to attend or something as important as whether or not you should get married. God wants us to consult Him on all decisions, not just the life-changing ones. And the biggest decision of all, is to accept Christ as your Lord and Savior.

Joshua 24:15

But if serving the Lord seems undesirable to you, then choose for yourselves this day whom you will serve, whether the gods your forefathers served beyond the River, or the gods of the Amorites, in whose land you are living. But as for me and my household, we will serve the Lord.

Psalm 25:4

Show me Your ways, O Lord, teach me Your paths.

Proverbs 3:6

In all your ways acknowledge Him, and He will make your paths straight.

Ken Hensley

Musician, Formerly with Uriah Heep
(Photo credit: Jørgen Angel)

Ken Hensley has been making music since his first real gig in 1960 as a 15 year old in England. After turning down an offer to become a professional soccer player, he devoted his entire attention to music. For the next few years he played with bands like The Gods, Toe Fat and Spice, and with rock greats who would later play with groups like Emerson, Lake & Palmer, Uriah Heep, and Jethro Tull. But Hensley is best known for his contribution to Uriah Heep, universally known as one of UK's most legendary rock bands. Uriah Heep was a highly original and innovative rock band. Their rise to the top was astounding, and they had many worldwide hits. Over the ten-year period he was with Heep (1970-1980), they recorded 13 studio albums and one of the greatest live albums of all time, *Uriah Heep Live—January 1973*. Hits like "Lady in Black," and "Easy Livin'," established Uriah Heep as one of the world's top bands and Ken Hensley as a highly respected songwriter. But after a time of this meteoric success, Heep began to self-destruct. Two band members were lost to drugs and alcohol, and Hensley left the band in 1980 needing to deal with his own personal issues. After moving to the United States to get a fresh start, he eventually joined Blackfoot, another hard rock band. After two successful albums with them, he left the band in 1985.

Hensley recorded more than 43 albums, with sales of over 40 million, had unimaginable fame and fortune, and lived life in the fast lane. He has also had four divorces and a cocaine habit. He kicked the drugs, remarried and found what was missing in his life. After many years of semi-retirement, Ken formed a new group called Visible Faith and recorded his first Christian album in 1999 aptly titled, *Glimpse of Glory*. In the end, Ken found his center in God and is the happiest he has ever been.

✦✛✛✛✛✛✦

I was saved in April 1993, at a very dark time in my life. After attending church in the hope of rescuing my marriage, I took some counseling from one of the associate pastors in which, among other things, he said to me, "I think what you need is a personal relationship with God." Of course, I was at a place where I couldn't imagine God wanting to have anything to do with me, but I honestly said to myself, "Well, Ken, you've tried everything else," and I prayed with him there and then. From that moment, my life changed and continues to change to this day, as through prayer and daily Bible study I learn more and more about my Savior as well as what He wants from me.

Before I was a Christian, I would often say in interviews that I believed that God was the source of inspiration for writing music and lyrics. I am now certain of it! I believe that my ability to write, record, and perform is a gift from God and that this gift is to be used to honor Him. In fact, I believe He is the source of all good things! But I am not the Bible-thumping type. I can only say that choosing to give my life to Christ was the most important and the most exciting thing I have ever done. I highly recommend it! I did the stardom thing, and I am thankful to God that I survived it! I would never want to go back to that way of life.

How do I know He's real? I can only tell you what has happened in my life, how many prayers have been answered, how many blessings I have received, how He ministers to my needs, and how He lovingly corrects me at all times—how He has changed my heart and my behavior and how He has helped me to know Him better over the years. He has gone from being all I had to all I need; and though I am a long way from where I need to be, I know I am on the right path, and I know He is in control!

How can you know He's real? If you don't (or won't) believe the testimony of witnesses, then you'll have to try it for yourself. If there is something (or anything) missing from your life, then what is there to lose? I had to come practically to the end of myself before I turned to God through Jesus, and it is ironic that we often turn to Him as a last resort when He should be first.

If everything is fine in your life, then ask yourself what's going to happen when you die...and believe me you have NO idea when that will be! There are few guarantees in life, but what is sure is that "every knee will bow" and we will all be held accountable for what we have done with and in our lives. I am a sinner, saved by grace through the blood shed by Jesus as He suffered and died on the cross. He died for your sins too, and you can be free of them by receiving Him as your personal Lord and Savior. If you don't believe me, give it a try. It is one thing you can do now and be certain you won't regret.

BELIEVE IN ME
by Ken Hensley

I opened up my heart today and Jesus was inside
I thanked Him for His presence there
And this was His reply

I am here, each and every day
As you sleep and as you pray
I'll protect you and I'll love you
Just believe in Me

I opened up my life today
And saw the highs and lows
And I prayed, my God
Forgive me for the wrong roads that I chose

He said that's all behind you now
Through your faith in My own Son
So believe in all that you will do
Don't repeat what you have done

For I'm with you each and every day
As you work and as you play
I'll protect you and I'll love you
Just believe in Me

I opened up my eyes today
And Christ was all around
And I prayed, oh Lord, give me Your song
And His voice came in a sound

I will give you words and melody
If you will give your life to Me
And I heard this sweet reminder
Of His promise to me...I am here...

GOD'S ROAD MAP

The Holy Bible is a guide to help you live a happy and satisfying life. To learn more about the concepts presented in the chapter you've just read, take a look at these passages:

CHANGE

Most of us resist change because it often causes stress. But it is one of the constants of life. Not all change is negative. When we become a Christian, God changes our hearts to be more in line with His will. For many, the change is extraordinary.

Second Corinthians 5:17

Therefore, if anyone is in Christ, he is a new creation; the old has gone, the new has come!

Hebrews 13:8

Jesus Christ is the same yesterday and today and forever.

ETERNAL LIFE

Is there life after death? There can be only two answers—yes or no. Some scientists say that near-death experiences are merely hallucinations caused by a lack of oxygen to the brain. The Bible talks about hell as eternal separation from God, and eternal punishment where there will be "weeping and gnashing of teeth." I don't know about you, but it's a place I'm not interested in visiting.

Matthew 16:24-27

If anyone would come after Me, he must deny himself and take up his cross and follow Me. For whoever wants to save his life will lose it, but whoever loses his life for Me will find it. What good will it be for a man if he gains the whole world, yet forfeits his soul? Or what can a man give in exchange for his soul? For the Son of Man is going to come in His Father's glory with His angels, and then He will reward each person according to what He has done.

Romans 6:23

For the wages of sin is death, but the gift of God is eternal life in Christ Jesus our Lord.

First John 2:17

The world and its desires pass away, but the man who does the will of God lives forever.

Bethel Johnson

NFL Wide Receiver,
New England Patriots

Bethel Johnson's is a true rags–to-riches story. He was raised in the crime-infested inner cities of Fort Worth and later, Corsicana, Texas, by a devoted single mother.

A true standout and local hero at Corsicana High School, Johnson led his football team to the Class 4A state title game. He is the all-time leading receiver in the history of the school.

Johnson was recruited by Texas A&M to play football. He connected on 117 passes for 1,740 yards and 11 touchdowns, setting a school record. Because he'd been plagued by several serious injuries, his draft prospects were uncertain. But he knew God had a plan for him to play professional football, and he wasn't disappointed.

The New England Patriots selected Johnson in the second round (45th overall) of the 2003 NFL draft. As a rookie, the wide receiver led his AFC peers with a 28.2-yard average kickoff return. That same year Johnson played in his first Super Bowl game in Houston, only a few hours away from home. He entered 2005 as the NFL's top active kickoff returner. Johnson has his own website, www.catch81.com.

The devil has been trying to take me out for a long time. He knows God has a purpose for me, a purpose that is going to affect him in a major way. It started from day one. When I was a couple of months old, my mom was driving while holding me over her shoulder. The car stalled and she got stuck on the railroad tracks. Finally, after frantic attempts to get the car started, she managed to pull off the tracks, just as a train came barreling toward us. The train hit the back of the car and spun it around. Then the car flipped over. But mom held onto me and I was fine. We both were. That was just God...He has had my whole family covered since the very beginning.

Looking back, I can really see how God was protecting my family and me while we were living in one of the most dangerous neighborhoods in Texas. I grew up in a real bad area of Fort Worth. My sisters and I would have to fight somebody every single day. The neighborhood was filled with drugs and violence; people were getting shot and killed all the time. To me, it wasn't anything out of the norm for us to witness things like that. As a child, growing up in the inner city, that was part of daily life.

As a single parent, my mom raised five kids—four girls and one boy. I admit it was tough though, but more so for my mother. But I learned a lot from my mother by growing up in our situation because she displayed unbelievable strength through the hard times. When faced with adversity, she never showed any signs of weakness, only the will to survive. We didn't have any money, and she constantly had to make sacrifices for her children. My mom was young; she had all five of us by the time she was 28. So she was a younger mother trying to work, raise kids, and still be young all at the same time. I learned what unselfishness is by watching her.

I grew tired of fighting with other kids every day. When I was eight, I asked my mom if we could move to Corsicana, Texas so we could be with some of our family. My grandmother, aunts, uncles, and cousins all lived there. A week later, Mama packed us up and we left.

Being in Corsicana was great; we didn't feel like we were all alone in this world. But we still lived in a rough part of town. My teen years were my wildest ones. During those years, a lot of things happened to me. My most vivid memory is the day I got shot.

I was breaking up a fight between one of my "supposed" friends and my cousin. My cousin went home, and the other guy did too. But the other guy came back with a group of guys...and a gun. He and I were friends, so I tried to talk him into putting the gun away. At one point in the conversation I turned my back on him, and when I turned back around, he shot me twice. One bullet hit me in the neck, the other in my side.

I didn't know I'd been shot; I couldn't feel it at the time. But as I headed back to the basketball court where I'd been hanging out, I felt blood pouring out my side and knew something was wrong. Instinctively, I headed toward home to tell my mom. I thought I could make it down the street, not realizing how bad it was. But someone I knew grabbed me, put me in their car, and drove me to the hospital. I am grateful that they did because I don't think I would have made it home.

After I was shot, I had a hard time trusting people. I was a bad guy, real bad. Someone could say to me, "Man, I'll kill you," and it usually led to a fight. If I felt my life was being threatened, I'd take the initiative and defend myself by any means necessary. If they were going to do something to me, it wasn't going to be easy because I stayed on guard. I had a reputation to protect.

During my freshman year in high school, my mom and sisters moved back to Fort Worth. I stayed in Corsicana because I didn't want to leave; but eventually the complications with my living situation forced me to join them. And once I got back to the city, I got involved in some gang stuff. Fortunately, the other guys in the gang didn't allow me to get too involved with some of the activities. I played basketball, and back then I was real good at it. A few members of the gang recognized my potential as an athlete and not a gang member. They kind of steered me in the direction of a sports future, basically looking out for me. I wanted to do all the things they were doing, but they wouldn't let me. I thank God for allowing them to be my eyes when I couldn't see my future. My future could have turned out totally different.

By my sophomore year I moved back to Corsicana. I tried basketball once again, but when I didn't make varsity, my future in basketball ended...but it didn't end my future in sports. I'd been playing baseball and football since I was 10 years old and running track since I was 13, so I had options. Baseball was my favorite. I played centerfield. But they play too many games in baseball and ran too much in track, so football seemed more attractive.

I knew from the first time I put on pads at 10 years old I was destined for the NFL. Since the age of 5, I always knew that I was going to be the one to make a difference for my mom and my family. My goal has always been to find a way to help my mom get out of her situation. And I was focused. I knew we didn't have to accept living in the projects; we didn't have to accept what society handed us. I could make a difference and change our situation. It took me the next 19 years to get there, but it got done.

To other people, though, I seemed very much *out* of focus. In their opinion, I'd be lucky if I lived to see 18. I was a child who just didn't care and had absolutely no respect for authority. It all stemmed from the trust issues I developed growing up. I think I was just basically misunderstood as a child. A lot of people couldn't handle me; and when they handled me wrong, there was a big problem between me and that person.

I was blessed to have somebody step into my father's place, the father I never knew. And he helped lead me in the right direction. He had been my baseball coach since I was around 11. He saw something in me that my mom didn't even see. And he wouldn't let me give up on myself, no matter what happened. He made sure I was going to reach my full potential in life. He and my mother were the only two people I never wanted to disappoint in life. That's why I never got into selling drugs, killing, stealing, or robbing because I didn't want my mama or my coach visiting me in jail. My life would have turned out a little different if it weren't for them.

Football really kept me off the streets. I'd played running back since I was 10. Then midway through my junior year, they moved me to wide receiver, which I hated because we were not known for passing the ball. But that quickly changed. During my senior campaign, as a receiver, every team in the country was recruiting me; I was one of the top prospects coming out that year.

I chose Texas A&M because of their loyalty to me. Texas A&M began recruiting me when I was a running back, although I wasn't that good. When I moved to wide receiver, all the other schools jumped on the bandwagon. But A&M had been there from the very start. After I met the coaches on my recruiting trip, I knew it was the place for me.

As a freshman I was a top recruit, which meant I had status on campus and the opportunity to get the girls. Frankly, I played my role perfectly. I was so prideful and arrogant, to the point where I just became too difficult to deal with. At this point in my life, God and church were the furthest from my mind.

There were a couple of teammates who used to come over and hang out with us, but then there was a sudden change in both of them. They were no longer into the things that we had going on at our house. Later that year, they started inviting me to church. But I was having too much fun; there was no way that was going to happen.

I didn't grow up in a Christian household—not by any means. I honestly didn't know about church until I was 8 years old when we moved to Corsicana. That's when my aunt started making us go to church. It seems like we were there every other day. We'd be outside playing, having a great time and Mom would call us into the house to change clothes and go to church. I used to hate it so bad. It seemed to me that church never ended; we'd get there early for Sunday school and by the time we got out of regular service it was time for the evening service. It never ended. We just had to sit there all day and it was so *boring*, especially for an active child like myself. So I vowed that I'd never go to church when I was older and could make my own choice.

So when my teammates kept asking me to go to church, I wasn't overly enthusiastic. There would be times when they'd see me on their way to church, and I'd just be getting in from the party I was at on Saturday night.

Eventually, I gave in and went to a few services. Strangely enough, every time I was there, it seemed like the preacher had been out on the town with me the night before—He was talking about everything I'd been doing. I always felt convicted when I went to church, and when they did the altar call to give your life to God, I felt Him tug at my heart. But I pushed that prompting away. I was worried how my girlfriend and friends would react if I became a Christian.

Eventually, the tug on my heart was too strong to resist, and the opinions of my girlfriend and friends no longer mattered to me, so I answered the call and took the necessary steps toward salvation. That was December 12, 1999, two months before my 21st birthday. I had been so excited about being able to buy alcohol with my own ID, but suddenly, turning 21 didn't have the same meaning.

When you first receive God, you're on fire and you want everybody to be saved. But I never had the knowledge to take on all of God, and I never knew how to study the Bible. The Bible says God's people perish from lack of knowledge. I was one of those people. After I got saved, I didn't know what I was supposed to do next. I took the steps necessary to give my life to God, but I never took the steps necessary to keep going.

This was my biggest problem.

When I was a kid, I went to church sporadically. And even when I did go, I didn't pay any attention. So I don't remember any of the instructions on living a Christian life. But I do remember this: Somebody once told me that all you have to do is give your life to God, and then you can do whatever you want. And when you die, you're guaranteed to go to Heaven. So of all the things I could have learned about God, I picked up on the wrong thing! Salvation should be more than an insurance policy.

I was on fire for a good six to seven months, but when there was a bump in the road, I fell off. I wouldn't tell people the things I was struggling with. The devil wants you to feel ashamed of what you've done, so you won't ever go to your brothers and ask them to pray for you. The enemy doesn't want you to confess your faults one to another like the Bible says. In James 5:16 it says, "The effectual fervent prayers of the righteous availeth much" (KJV). In other words, the prayers of a believer are powerful and effective. Satan knows that, so he doesn't want it to happen. He brings up the past to keep you from going forward with God. You don't speak as boldly about God when you've got something hanging over your head. You think, *Man, I can't say nothin'; I'm just as bad.* That's what I struggled with—being ashamed of myself. I felt unworthy to serve God and I totally backslid.

The thing is, once you take that power away from satan—the power of him holding something over your head—he really doesn't have anything left. Once I took that power away and said, "You will not make me feel ashamed of what I have done; you will not make me feel ashamed to serve God; and you will not make me feel unworthy," things changed. If I struggle with anything, I can go to my brothers in Christ. I can call my mom or the pastor of my church and ask them to pray for me. When that happens, satan's power is gone.

Well, God dealt with me and I got back on track. Then things started happening. I had multiple injuries in college. There were two that really turned people away about my future in the NFL. First, I had my spleen removed after it ruptured, and I ended up red-shirting that year. When I came back, I had a bowel obstruction, so I had to have surgery again. These operations were only nine months apart. Now, there were a lot of skeptics out there that year, but I ended up having a great senior campaign, even breaking school records.

One Sunday, I was at church with one my friends, and right in the middle of worship, the preacher stopped the service and called me to the front. He asked me if I fast and pray. "Yes," I replied, and then he said, "God told me you'll be drafted in the late first or early second round." Right there in front of the congregation he prophesied over me, so I knew that's exactly what God was going to do, and I stood on that.

It was nothing but God that got me into the NFL, because a lot of teams were skeptical due to my injuries. But I didn't listen to the media. I remember them talking so bad about me, but they had no idea who I served. Instead, I listened to what God said, and God said I was going to be drafted late first, early second round.

The day of the NFL draft came. On pick #43 or #44, I went to the restroom and saw one of my friends get drafted to Washington. As I was walking out, I got a call on my cell phone welcoming me to the New England Patriots. I was surprised it was New England because they had pick #56 or something like that, and I knew we weren't that late in the second round. But they had traded up to draft me at #45. I was chosen in the first part of the second round just like God said.

Once I got my signing bonus, I took care of my mama long before I took care of myself. She had been driving a car that she'd gotten from the members of the church. That's why I love my church, because they didn't have much to give her, but they took care of my mother. They made sure she had transportation. I told her to pick out any car she wanted. And I bought her a new house. My mom's happy now; she finally has a sense of security. Nobody can take those things away from her ever again.

You see, my mother has always been the leading lady in my life. I love my mama. She's told me that she's proud of me, but I wouldn't expect her to give me all kinds of praise. She knows everything comes from God. God blessed her with me, and through me, God made a way for her.

My rookie year was a tough one for me spiritually. I was so far away from home that I couldn't just drive home anytime I wanted to, like when I was in college. When I got to New England, I started hanging around with the wrong type of people. And like the Bible says, bad company corrupts good character. I had a good character and I had good intentions, but I was hanging around with the wrong crowd. I was either going to affect them, or they were going to affect me.

When I finally joined my mother's church in Texas, things turned around. They don't care who I am; they tell me when I'm doing wrong and what the consequences are. That's what I need. I don't need someone to sugarcoat the truth.

And the truth is that life is hard. I've seen more, and been through more than people over twice my age. But all along, God was there. He didn't let anything happen to me because my job wasn't finished. I just had to find my way to Him. He waited patiently, because God knows everything. He knew exactly when I was going to come around; He knew when I was going to backslide; and He knew what it would take to bring me back to Him. God has used my life to show the world what type of God He is. My career...no...my life is a blessing from God and it's a dream come true.

Yeah, the devil wanted to get rid of me, but God had other things in mind. And my story's not over yet.

GOD'S ROAD MAP

The Holy Bible is a guide to help you live a happy and satisfying life. To learn more about the concepts presented in the chapter you've just read, take a look at these passages:

SATAN

Just as God is real, so is His enemy satan. The evil one's goal is to trip us up and separate us from his archenemy, God. Watch for him and arm yourself with God's truth and protection.

John 8:44

...He was a murderer from the beginning, not holding to the truth, for there is no truth in him. When he lies, he speaks his native language, for he is a liar and the father of lies.

First Peter 5:8-9

Be self-controlled and alert. Your enemy the devil prowls around like a roaring lion looking for someone to devour. Resist him, standing firm in the faith, because you know that your brothers throughout the world are undergoing the same kind of sufferings.

Second Thessalonians 3:3

But the Lord is faithful, and He will strengthen and protect you from the evil one.

TRUTH

The Bible says that the reality of Jesus is absolute truth. Through study of His Word and our own personal relationship with Him, we are free to discover that truth.

Second Timothy 3:16-17

All Scripture is God-breathed and is useful for teaching, rebuking, correcting and training in righteousness, so that the man of God may be thoroughly equipped for every good work.

First John 1:1

That which was from the beginning, which we have heard, which we have seen with our eyes, which we have looked at and our hands have touched—this we proclaim concerning the Word of life.

John 18:37

...Jesus answered, "You are right in saying I am a king. In fact, for this reason I was born, and for this I came into the world, to testify to the truth. Everyone on the side of truth listens to Me."

Al Kasha

Academy Award-Winning Songwriter

A l Kasha has achieved phenomenal success as a writer in film, television, and theater. An award-winning songwriter, he has had hits for the last five decades—a very rare achievement. Kasha has won two Academy Awards—the first in 1970 for the theme song, "The Morning After" from the movie *The Poseidon Adventure*, and in 1974 for the song "We May Never Love Like This Again" from the hit movie *The Towering Inferno*.

With over 30 motion pictures to his credit, Kasha has lent his considerable talents to films such as *All Dogs Go to Heaven*, *Giant of Thunder Mountain*, and *Rudolph, the Red-Nosed Reindeer*, an animated movie musical starring John Goodman and Whoopi Goldberg. Dozens of stars have recorded his songs, including Elvis Presley, Frank Sinatra, Johnny Cash, James Ingram, Melissa Manchester, Marilyn McCoo, Sammy Davis, Jr., Aretha Franklin, Sheena Easton, Julian Lennon, and Donna Summer. Kasha is also the author of four best-selling books.

In November 2004, Kasha won an ASCAP Country Award for "Streets of Heaven," sung by country singer Sherrie Austin. The song, which he cowrote with Austin and Paul Duncan, was voted the Number One Christian Country Song for the year 2004 in *Power Source Magazine*. And to top it all off, his Tony award-winning musical production, *Seven Brides for Seven Brothers* embarked on a new national tour in 2005. When he is not busy writing hit songs, Kasha can be found speaking to churches, universities, and executive ministries around the world on being a Christian living in Hollywood and overcoming agoraphobia. For more on his fascinating life and healing, take a look at his website: www.alkasha.com.

✦·⊹·┼·⟩⟨·┼·⟩⟨·┼·⊹·✦

One out of every 18 people in America has a phobia of some kind. I am one of them. My bout with agoraphobia, an abnormal fear of open or public places, was particularly debilitating because I was a public figure. But the day I met Jesus, that all changed.

I was born in Brooklyn, New York. My father was a violent alcoholic who beat up my mother, my brother, and me nearly every day. The police were at our home often, but it made little difference. I come from a strict Jewish background; my grandfather was an Orthodox rabbi, and he was heavily into God's law.

We were lucky to live across the street from a movie studio. When we were children, my brother and I often played extras in various movie trailers. One day, a man at the studio heard me sing, and my show biz career began. At 16 I started writing songs; before long, my songs were being recorded by some of the top names in the music business. By the time I was 22, I was a record producer and enjoyed a very rewarding career in New York during the musical heyday of the 1960s. In 1968 I moved to Hollywood to pursue a career in the motion picture business.

I am fortunate to have achieved a great deal of success in the industry, including two Academy Awards. But even though I've had a great deal of recognition for my body of work, my whole life was based on the bondage of achievement. I never truly felt the peace that I had once assumed would accompany that kind of acclaim. Always striving for the next level of achievement only produced more emptiness inside. During the time I was busy winning Oscars, my father was dying of cancer. I was completely overwhelmed by the burden of balancing work and my personal life which resulted in serious depression and illness. I was afflicted with a disease called agoraphobia, a paralyzing fear of being in public places. People with agoraphobia have severe anxiety-ridden panic attacks when out in public so they tend to stay home where they are more comfortable. I reached a point where I could barely leave my house. Even my previously happy marriage was falling apart. It was total emotional paralysis.

My wife and I separated for a month. While I was on my own, I spent a great deal of time reevaluating my life. One sleepless night, when I was feeling particularly lost and alone, I started flipping through the channels. I ended up watching Rev. Robert Schuller share a Scripture from First John 4:18-19 that turned my life around: "God's perfect love casts out fear." It struck me since I certainly knew what it meant to be paralyzed by fear. After listening to him, I understood that the opposite is also true; fear casts out love. I got down on my knees, placed my hand on the television, and began to pray. "If there is a Jesus, please reveal Yourself." All of a sudden, a tremendous, all-enveloping warmth overtook me. I was in an air-conditioned apartment with the windows glued shut, and suddenly they began to shake and open. A blinding light poured in, and I felt a powerful pressure in my chest. I couldn't breathe! I knew something beyond my comprehension had just taken place.

The next morning I gave my life to Jesus. Afterward I felt peace while driving for the first time in a year. (Driving had long given me terrible anxiety attacks.) But not everybody was thrilled with my conversion. I'm a Jew who came to Christ working in a predominantly Jewish industry. Many of my colleagues thought I was just going through a phase and would come back to my senses. The first few years after I became a Christian, a lot of people wouldn't hire me even though I'd already won two Academy Awards. But I prayed to the Lord to make my work better than ever, and I kept having hits year after year.

Since I met Christ, my life has changed greatly, to the point where I can now comfortably travel around the world speaking about agoraphobia and the deliverance of fears. I am also an ordained minister and speak about being a Christian in Hollywood. There are so many Christians who come to Hollywood to try and make it in show biz—not an easy thing to do for anyone. But for a Christian, it is especially difficult. Ceil and I even started a Hollywood Bible study to help minister to and encourage other believers in LA. The meetings are still going to this day. Christians belong in Hollywood, as long as there's not too much Hollywood in the Christian. Christians not only belong in Hollywood, they are *needed* in Hollywood.

While I am still a successful songwriter, my real passion is sharing my story and my faith. My ministry, Faith Over Fear is a healing ministry. One of the things I most love about the Lord is that He talks to the unapproachable. Jesus would talk to all kinds of people—rich, poor, lepers, prostitutes, and even tax collectors. He loved everybody. We are all children of God...and it doesn't matter what denomination you are. I believe in Christ, not in Christianity.

My transformation has been nothing short of extraordinary. Jesus Christ healed me of the most profound fear—a fear that completely gripped me and nearly destroyed my life. He has given me a talent and a career that continues to be highly rewarding. But most importantly, He has given me a platform to share His love and power with a hungry world. If He would do all this for me, imagine what He could do for you. Remember, fear casts out love; but love, His perfect love, casts out fear. Don't be afraid to accept Him.

GOD'S ROAD MAP

The Holy Bible is a guide to help you live a happy and satisfying life. To learn more about the concepts presented in the chapter you've just read, take a look at these passages:

FEAR

Al Kasha shares his victory over agoraphobia, a debilitating phobia that caused him to fear being in public places. He was able to conquer that fear only through the saving grace of Jesus Christ. We all have fears— fear of failure, fear of being alone, and fear of the future. But there is one thing we need not fear—our destination for eternity, if we only trust in Christ for our salvation.

Psalm 46:1-3

God is our refuge and strength, an ever-present help in trouble. Therefore we will not fear, though the earth give way and the mountains fall into the heart of the sea, though its waters roar and foam and the mountains quake with their surging.

John 14:27

Peace I leave with you; My peace I give you. I do not give to you as the world gives. Do not let your hearts be troubled and do not be afraid.

DELIVERANCE

Christ can be victorious over any foe, whether it is an illness or satan himself. The Bible promises victory over the greatest battle of all—death, that through Christ, we can spend eternity in paradise with Him.

Psalm 103:2-4

Praise the Lord, O my soul, and forget not all His benefits— who forgives all your sins and heals all your diseases, who redeems your life from the pit and crowns you with love and compassion.

Psalm 40:1-3

I waited patiently for the Lord; He turned to me and heard my cry. He lifted me out of the slimy pit, out of the mud and mire; He set my feet on a rock and gave me a firm place to stand. He put a new song in my mouth, a hymn of praise to our God. Many will see and fear and put their trust in the Lord.

Jeremiah 30:12-13,17

This is what the Lord says: "Your wound is incurable, your injury beyond healing. There is no one to plead your cause, no remedy for your sore, no healing for you....But I will restore you to health and heal your wounds," declares the Lord.

Corey Koskie

Major League Baseball Player,
Toronto Blue Jays

(Photo, courtesy of the Toronto Blue Jays)

Corey Koskie is a baseball anomaly. He didn't even play high school baseball. Shoot, they didn't even have high school baseball where he grew up! Longtime third baseman for the Minnesota Twins, Koskie was raised on a farm outside the small town of Anola, Manitoba, just 20 minutes east of Winnipeg. Like most Canadians, he was a huge hockey fan and was also a top-notch Junior A player. And when that season was over, he concentrated on competitive volleyball, eventually earning a scholarship in that sport to the University of Manitoba. The only baseball he played was in a summer club program.

Miraculously, Koskie was drafted by the Minnesota Twins in 1994, making his major league baseball debut in 1998. He was the first native Manitoban to hit the major leagues. In 2001, he was selected as the Manitoba Sportswriters and Sportscasters Association's Manitoba Male Athlete of the Year. Also in 2001, he became the first American League third baseman and second third baseman in Major League history with over 100 runs, over 25 homeruns, over 100 RBIs, and over 25 stolen bases. After seven highly successful seasons in Minnesota, Koskie was picked up in the fall of 2004 by the Toronto Blue Jays.

※※※※※※

Growing up I never thought I would play professional baseball...but God had a plan.

Like most Canadian boys, I was a huge hockey fan and idolized guys like Wayne Gretzky. I played Junior A hockey up through my freshman year in college, but I was also big into volleyball. I played competitively beginning in 9th grade; I played on a high school team, a provincial team, and a club team. I ended up getting a scholarship to the University of Manitoba, which had the #1 volleyball program in the country. I basically played at the highest level you can for that age group. We won many national championships and even played in international tournaments.

All this time I was just kind of messing around with baseball. I had fun playing it during the short Canadian summers. There was no organized high school team, so if you wanted to play baseball, you played town ball. We played a couple of games a week in June, July, and early August. We didn't even have any practices; we'd just show up 45 minutes before game time and warm up.

So imagine my surprise when I got a call from the baseball coach at a small junior college in Boone, Iowa. He'd heard about me and invited me to go down and try out for his team. He called every day, sometimes twice a day. "Are you coming down...are you coming down?" There I was with a full volleyball scholarship with the #1 team in the country being asked to move to some little town in Iowa to try out for a baseball team with no guarantees...and with no scholarship money in the offer. I'd even have to take out a student loan to play there.

And imagine my head volleyball coach's surprise when I walked into his office and told him I was quitting volleyball to go to Iowa. "What?" On the way home that day I couldn't believe what I'd just done. The coach called my parents and tried to get them to talk me out of this crazy idea. But for some reason, I wanted to do this. I remember praying about it, "God, what should I do here? What do I do?" I didn't have any idea if this was the right thing to do or not; I just did it! Knowing how things have turned out, I guess it was my destiny.

When I first went down to Iowa, there were like 75 or 100 guys trying out for this baseball team. I was like, "What am I doing here?" After the first day of training camp, I told my parents I thought I wanted to go home. But they convinced me to stay one more day, and things actually got better. I started having some fun.

I was down there for a year when the doctor found a tumor in my leg. It was benign, but in order to remove it, they had to take pretty much my whole bone. There was just a little bit of bone left on the back side of my shin. It was tough because I was supposed to play on the Manitoba baseball team in the Canada Games that summer. The Canada Games is like a mini–Olympics; teams compete from every province in the country. It is very much like an Olympic experience. There is even a village where only athletes are allowed. I really wanted to participate in the Games. I knew there would be a lot of pro scouts there since all the best baseball players in Canada under the age of 20 would be participating. The coach of the team had a decision to make. He either had to choose me for the team in the hopes that my leg would be good enough to play on or choose another guy—a pretty good player, in fact. For some reason, he took a chance and chose me.

That's one way I know God is real—His healing hand. On June 4, I had my surgery. The doctor told me I would be fully recovered by September (eight and one-half weeks). But the Canada Games were being held the second week of August. God managed to heal me early, and I was not only able to participate but did fairly well. Team Manitoba finished 4th. The head coach of the National Baseball Institute saw me play. NBI is a training facility where elite players in Canada go to hone their baseball skills. I'd always wanted to play at the NBI because many players get drafted by pro teams from there. When they called and offered me a spot at NBI, I was pretty much, "I'm coming!"

Because I had played only club ball growing up, I'd never really had any formal training. As a matter of fact, the coach of the NBI told me that I threw like a little girl! My throws were all over the place. Instead of stepping with my opposite foot, I stepped with the foot I threw with. No one had ever taught me the right way before. I was 20 years old, and after years of playing the game, I finally was taught the proper footwork. It was amazing. I could throw the ball across the diamond more consistently. I was amazed at how much I improved.

After a year at NBI, it was time for the professional draft. The papers had me slotted to go in the first couple of rounds which would mean a lot of money. I was all excited; I'd pretty much already spent the money. But when I didn't get any calls that first day, people were pretty surprised. On the second day, the Minnesota Twins drafted me in the 26th round. Looking back now, I realize it was all part of God's plan.

A few months later, I was off to Elizabethan, Tennessee to play professional baseball for the Twins low A farm team.

After five years in the minors, I was called up to the big leagues—the Minnesota Twins. It wasn't really what I expected. You expect so much, and ultimately it's still just baseball, you know. It's like AAA ball but nicer hotels and more people to watch you play. I started having a lot of anxiety about stuff; I couldn't eat and I couldn't sleep. I don't think it was about performance. In fact, when I got to the ballpark, I seemed to calm down. I knew this was no way to live. I'd been raised Catholic and we went to church every Sunday because my mom took us. It made me feel good to go to church. So I went to baseball chapel every Sunday through the minor leagues, but it didn't really have any affect on me. It just seemed like the right thing to do...I didn't get it. But I had a hitting coach named Bill Springman, and I could tell he had something I didn't have. I started to ask him questions about Jesus and that's when my faith really started to develop.

The first part of the season was real nerve-wracking. I was wondering what was going to happen. There's a lot of pressure and temptation at this level. I've seen a lot of guys who have done great in the minor leagues but have done nothing at the big league level. I didn't want to be one of those guys. I started to study the Bible, and my faith kept growing. I was also praying a lot with the team chaplain when I got to the big leagues. This time in prayer brought me such tremendous peace. Through prayer and petition, I had a peace that no matter what happened I would be alright. It was one of those things I had to give up to Christ because I knew I couldn't control the situation. I understand now as a Christian that I should pass everything before the throne. That's one very important lesson I've learned.

I still have trouble with anxiety; it's a constant battle for me. I worry most about my kids. Being a father is a big responsibility. I pray for protection over my family every single day. And I know satan's going to throw stuff out there to make me nervous. He really can get me when I'm tired and worn down. But we have to remember that 99.8 percent of our fears don't come true. The Bible talks about how we can find comfort knowing that there are people all over the world going through the exact same thing we're going through. When I think I am at my lowest point and that I'm going through this alone, I remember that brothers and sisters around the world feel the same way.

They call this the age of anxiety. First it was The Great Depression, then the Cold War. This is the age of anxiety because people just can't handle the pressures of this hectic American lifestyle. I can't imagine how people who don't have Christ in their life handle those pressures.

In 2004, I had a lot of injuries—a problem with my hamstring, a bruised sternum, and then finally a high ankle sprain when an opponent slid into me at third base. I missed three weeks just before the end of the season heading into playoffs. I focused a lot on prayer during those three weeks. I was praying, "Lord, I realize I'm not going to be able to do anything to finish out this year without Your hand on it. My timing's all messed up; I missed three weeks while other guys are at their best getting geared up for the playoffs. I'm not going to be able to do anything without Your blessing." When I came back after my ankle healed, I didn't miss a beat; I was right back in stride. He sure answered my prayers that time.

How do I know He's real? It's hard to explain to people who have no idea what a relationship with Christ really feels like. If I talk about how the peace of God came over me, some won't understand. It's almost that we fight with God until we get to the point where we have nowhere else to go and it's totally hopeless. Then we give Him a chance. That's the whole thing—our human nature fights it. We think we're independent creatures—we can do this, we can do that. And then we get to the point of our life where we throw up our hands to God and recognize that the only way to get through life is through Christ. It's too bad that it takes us so long to figure that out.

Life as a professional athlete can be stressful, especially when it comes to moving to a new team. Change can be hard and filled with anxious moments. But I know I can always lean on my faith. Worrying about something just shows a lack of trust in the Lord. God has been in my past; there's no reason He's not going to be there in my future—whatever that is. He's in control. After all, who'd have ever thought a kid from rural Canada who played pickup ball games in the summer and threw like a little girl would become a professional baseball player. He really knows what He's doing. I'll stick with Him.

GOD'S ROAD MAP

The Holy Bible is a guide to help you live a happy and satisfying life. To learn more about the concepts presented in the chapter you've just read, take a look at these passages:

WORRY

In this fast-paced world of ours, anxiety is epidemic. To treat it, we use a variety of therapies, including prescription drugs and alcohol. Left untreated, worry robs us of our joy. Is there a cure? All we really need is a relationship with the great physician, Jesus Christ.

Philippians 4:6

Do not be anxious about anything, but in everything, by prayer and petition, with thanksgiving, present your requests to God.

Matthew 6:25-34

Therefore I tell you, do not worry about your life, what you will eat or drink; or about your body, what you will wear. Is not life more important than food, and the body more important than clothes? Look at the birds of the air; they do not sow or reap or store away in barns, and yet your heavenly Father feeds them. Are you not much more valuable than they? Who of you by worrying can add a single hour to his life?

First Peter 5:7

Cast all your anxiety on Him because He cares for you.

STRESS

"Stressed-out" has become the catchphrase of the last decade. We all feel it—pressure from competing elements of our lives...work, family, even church. Americans are stretched beyond our capacity. It's time to do two things: Simplify and give it up to God.

Second Corinthians 4:8-9

We are hard pressed on every side, but not crushed; perplexed, but not in despair; persecuted, but not abandoned; struck down, but not destroyed.

John 14:1

Do not let your hearts be troubled. Trust in God; trust also in Me.

Psalm 62:2

He alone is my rock and my salvation; He is my fortress, I will never be shaken.

Jonny Lang

Blues Guitarist and Recording Artist

Jonny Lang has been called a prodigy, a virtuoso, and a once-in-a-generation blues artist. Whatever label you apply, his extraordinary talent is the real thing. Lang catapulted into the music spotlight when he was only 13. Critics and fans alike were astounded by his soulful playing and gravelly vocals. He sounded more like a 40-year blues veteran than a teenager from the plains of North Dakota.

His debut solo album, *Lie to Me*, was recorded when he was just 15 years old. It went platinum, as did the following year's release, *Wander this World*. Lang spent his teenage years with guitar legends like B.B. King and Buddy Guy and toured almost non-stop with the Rolling Stones, Aerosmith, and Sting. Altogether, he's recorded five albums and earned a Grammy nomination.

Lang's accolades are far-reaching. He was named the Best New Guitarist in *Guitar* magazine's reader's poll and was also named to *Newsweek's* Century Club of the 100 Americans expected to be influential in the next millennium. He was even profiled in *U.S News and World Report*.

His latest recording chronicles his incredible spiritual journey and is due out in early 2006.

Between the drinking, the drugs, and my fascination with magical religions like witchcraft, I was about as far away from God as I could possibly be. But my family kept praying for me, and I know God honored their prayers and snatched me up out of all that. I don't think I could have written a better storyline than what God has given me.

I spent my childhood on a farm outside the small town of Casselton, North Dakota, an agriculturally rich spot in the heart of the Red River Valley. My father was a farmer as was his father before him. I probably would have been a farmer too. But instead, I found music.

My parents had a huge pile of records. They listened to a lot of Motown, Steely Dan, Stevie Wonder, and Otis Redding. My mom is a great singer. She even went down to Nashville to cut a demo at one point and took a shot at a music career. But she chose to raise a family instead of pursuing music. So I've been around music my whole life.

When I was 12, my dad took me to see a band some of his friends were in called the Bad Medicine Blues Band. It was the first concert I'd ever been to and I was thrilled. The guitar player, Ted Larson, really inspired me; I wanted to be just like him. My dad gave me a guitar for my 13th birthday, and I was fortunate enough to take lessons from Ted.

It wasn't too long before they asked me to join the band and changed the name to Jonny Lang and the Big Bang. About a year later we made an album together called *Smokin'*.

I got involved in "adult" activities at a very young age. I started drinking and smoking cigarettes. But there was an unwritten rule in our band that there was no drinking the day of the show. So I managed to keep things in check…for a while.

After about two years of playing together, we went down to Minneapolis to take part in a showcase event. There were a bunch of record labels at the show looking for new acts to sign. I ended up getting signed as a solo artist by A&M Records.

What happened to me after that is almost a blur. The first album we did together, *Lie to Me*, debuted at #1 on Billboard's New Artist chart. My next album was just as successful. The excitement and pressure of being with a major label definitely changed things. I was on the road constantly, playing with musicians twice my age in places where they check your ID at the door. But it didn't matter how old I was because I was the headliner.

By the time I was 17, I was an alcoholic and smoking two packs a day. I also started doing drugs. It was mostly marijuana, but there were other drugs as well. In my position, anything I wanted was just handed to me. I used cocaine, ecstasy, and hallucinogens. I really loved to be high. It got to be such a problem, that if I wasn't high, I didn't feel normal.

Despite the fact that my parents divorced when I was young, they still tried to get me to go to church with them and have me attend Sunday school. But I never really had an interest in religion. I saw things that really burned me and turned me off to Christianity, especially hypocrisy. However, what turned me off the most about Christianity was that I'd never seen the power of God move. It was just a lot of going through the motions but not experiencing His power or His presence. I thought the miracles you saw on TV were just hoaxes. And I certainly wasn't interested in being held accountable for my actions, which is basically what it all boils down to.

If anybody tried to talk to me about God or Jesus I would say things like, "Okay, I've heard that one and I'm not interested." I got involved in a lot of less accepted forms of spiritual expression that I thought were the right path. I guess you could call it witchcraft, for lack of a better term. And through those rituals I had experiences and saw things that were so powerful. Now this was real! But I found out later where the real power is.

When I was 16, I met the most wonderful girl in Los Angeles while on tour and became great friends with her and her family. I fell in love with her right away, but she was scared of me. Who could blame her? Eventually we started dating. When I was in town, her family would try to get me to go to church with them. But I was thinking, *Don't even try.* I'm just so thankful that they loved me because I was such a mess. They loved me through all that and God gave them a heart to stick with me.

I'll fast forward a bit. Haylie and I had been broken up for a period of time, but I was still real tight with her family. In fact, her father, Cliff, was like a second dad to me. That sometimes made it kind of uncomfortable between me and Haylie.

Cliff had become very sick; he had Hepatitis C and cancer all over his body. It got so bad that He was being cared for by hospice nurses in their home. I had a break in my schedule and was able to go to California for a visit.

One night while I was there, I decided to go out with a friend of mine to get high. We went to his apartment, but before we had a chance to do anything, the phone rang. It was Haylie's mom...Cliff had just died. I remember feeling relieved, because he had been suffering so much, struggling for every breath. Honestly, I was more worried about interacting with Haylie and her family than I was about Cliff actually passing away. I didn't have very much backbone, and I wasn't prepared to deal with the whole situation.

But I had to go back to the house. While I was walking out in the hallway of my friend's apartment building, I was suddenly hit in the stomach by the most incredible force. It spread from there and filled my whole body. I had this soundness of mind and this extraordinary peace that I just couldn't explain. It was an incredible feeling.

After a few minutes, I started rationalizing—it was probably just some sort of primal instinct that comes out to help cope with the death of a loved one. In my mind, I tried to find a natural explanation for it. I certainly never thought it might have something to do with God.

When I got back to the house, everybody was just beside themselves. I was not the kind of person who could deal with those kinds of emotions. But whatever had happened to me in that apartment hallway gave me a special wisdom to handle it. Everything I said was the perfect counsel— wisdom that I just did not possess. For some reason I had the most remarkable heart to be the counselor. I was even using words I'd never used before! At one point I said out loud, "Who are you?" Thinking back on it now, I can almost hear God chuckling in the background.

After a little while, the pastor of their church came over. I was upset at his presence; I figured he would just fill them with false hope and say things like, "Cliff is in a better place now." A better place? I didn't believe that. Cliff was just dead—end of story.

We all went into Cliff's room and gathered around his body. The pastor started singing "Amazing Grace," and I started rolling my eyes. But it was their dad; who was I to make waves? So I mumbled the words too. When the song was over, that same peace hit me again—and this time it hit the whole room. Everybody went from being completely hysterical to poof...the grieving was done. Again, I figured it was just something therapeutic to help them manage.

When people from the morgue were coming to remove Cliff's body, I thought it would be best if Haylie didn't see that. So I took her to the backyard. We talked about what had been going on that night and our memories of her dad. All of a sudden, I got hit in the stomach again with that tremendous force. It was almost like I had to throw up; I couldn't keep it down any longer. Bursting out of my mouth came the word "Jesus!" right in the middle of our conversation. The power of God hit me so hard that I started shaking in my chair. It was like somebody grabbed my shoulders and shook me forcefully back and forth. It didn't hurt, but it was violent.

Yet at the same time I felt total peace. He didn't say, "Hey, this is Jesus" or anything, but I knew it was Him. I heard Him say to me, "You don't have to have this if you don't want it." I was completely and utterly amazed, and I definitely wanted it. I wanted it more than anything I'd ever wanted in my whole life. I kept shaking and shaking until I fell to the ground. I gave my life to Christ right there at that moment.

While I was lying on the grass, a filmstrip was playing in my mind. Memories of all the times I'd persecuted Christians came clearly into focus. I remembered how I'd told my dad he was crazy for what he believed. Later, I called my dad and told him I'd given my life to Jesus. Do you know what he said? "Yeah, I knew that would happen someday." You see, they'd been praying for that moment all along.

At Cliff's funeral a few days later, I confessed publicly that Jesus was my Lord and Savior. Haylie and her mom almost fell off their chairs. Even though Haylie had been sitting next to me when I had my encounter with the Lord, she doesn't remember anything about it. In a court of law, I'd probably be overruled—there's no proof of what happened. But I know it happened; it was a private, supernatural moment between me and almighty God.

What's so miraculous about this whole experience is that I had not been pursuing God. I despised Him. I was living with total hostility toward God, yet He still loved and delivered me. While I was shaking, I was actually being delivered of all the addictions and demons inside me. From then on, I had absolutely zero cravings for the drugs, the alcohol, or the tobacco. The best recovery program in the world can't claim that.

He also healed me of another thing that night—dyslexia. My whole life, this learning disability had prohibited me from sitting down and reading a book; it was just too frustrating. But when Jesus touched my life, He healed me of dyslexia and gave me a heart to read the Bible. More importantly, He gave me the ability to comprehend it. So what the enemy meant for evil, in the area of my reading comprehension, God meant for good. The first book I ever really read was the Bible—what a great place to start!

The most convincing reason that I know He's real is that I know the person I was before I met Him. I know the way I thought and the way I conducted my life. That old person was replaced with a brand-new one, a person who was willing to conform to the image of Christ. All the sermons in the world could not have convinced me of that. But He convinced me Himself and I know the truth. I've witnessed so many wonders and miracles and God just proves Himself to me constantly. There's nothing that could convince me otherwise. Jesus is the living God.

GOD'S ROAD MAP

The Holy Bible is a guide to help you live a happy and satisfying life. To learn more about the concepts presented in the chapter you've just read, take a look at these passages:

OCCULT

It all seems so innocent—palm reading, tarot cards, fortune-telling, psychics; but it can lead to so much more. Satan uses these tools to soften you, and to get you to open the door to your soul just a crack. Don't do it. Allow only the things of God through that door.

Leviticus 19:26b

Do not practice divination or sorcery.

Second Chronicles 33:6

[Manasseh] sacrificed his sons in the fire in the Valley of Ben Hinnom, practiced sorcery, divination and witchcraft, and consulted mediums and spiritists. He did much evil in the eyes of the Lord, provoking Him to anger.

First Chronicles 10:13-14

Saul died because he was unfaithful to the Lord; he did not keep the word of the Lord and even consulted a medium for guidance, and did not inquire of the Lord....

WORLDLINESS

Worldliness means to be devoted to the ways of the world and earthly pursuits rather than to the ways of God. As many celebrities will attest, the rewards of the world are far too fleeting, while the rewards of a relationship with God are priceless.

Job 21:11-15

They send forth their children as a flock; their little ones dance about. They sing to the music of tambourine and harp; they make merry to the sound of the flute. They spend their years in prosperity and go down to the grave in peace. Yet they say to God, "Leave us alone! We have no desire to know Your ways. Who is the Almighty, that we should serve Him? What would we gain by praying to Him?"

Psalm 49:16-20

Do not be overawed when a man grows rich, when the splendor of his house increases; for he will take nothing with him when he dies, his splendor will not descend with him. Though while he lived he counted himself blessed—and men praise you when you prosper—he will join the generation of his fathers, who will never see the light of life. A man who has riches without understanding is like the beasts that perish.

Kerry Livgren

Songwriter and Band Member of the
'70s Super Group, Kansas

Kansas was undeniably one of the most influential rock groups of the 1970s. Still a staple on classic rock radio stations, this progressive rock band is known for its breakthrough sound and sweeping lyrics. Founding member Kerry Livgren was the band's primary songwriter, lead guitarist, and keyboard player.

Their self-titled debut LP appeared in 1974, and by 1976 they were propelled to stardom with the release of *Leftoverture*, which reached #5 on the Billboard Pop Chart and has sold over three million copies. The smash hit from that album, "Carry On Wayward Son" topped off at #11 on the singles chart. The follow-up album in 1977, *Point of Know Return* was even more successful; it reached #4 on the charts with megahit single "Dust in The Wind" coming in at #6. Altogether, Kansas has eight gold albums, two triple platinum albums, one platinum live album, and one gold single.

Livgren has also produced numerous solo albums, receiving a Dove Award for Instrumental Album of the Year in 1989. Much of his time now is spent producing his own original work and that of several other talented artists through his record company, Numavox Records. Find out more at www.numavox.com.

I am amazed at the diversity of beliefs I have embraced and rejected. A relentless pursuit of meaning drove me down a variety of Western and Eastern paths, all coming to dead ends. But what I found in 1979 was not another end, but the beginning of a new life that gets richer with each passing month.

My first electric guitar was one I made myself. I taped a low quality microphone to the inside of a guitar, plugged it into an old Sears amplifier, and my guitar was complete. Popular English groups like the Yardbirds and The Kinks had a strong influence on my music, but the musical and philosophical romanticism of composers Wagner and Strauss and philosophers Nietzsche and Rand profoundly affected my music and my developing worldview.

Although I was a poor student in high school, I went to Washburn University, in part to quench my raging thirst for knowledge. But the more courses I took, the more confused I became. My college years turned out to be the bleakest time of my life. I felt a tremendous urge to justify my own existence. I wanted to know who I was as a person, why I was on this planet, and what I was going to do with my life.

Only one course came close to satisfying some of that urge. Not surprisingly, it was a course on world religions. It opened up new realms of thought for me, since each of these religions dealt with the basic questions I was beginning to struggle with. The last religion we examined was Christianity. Strangely, I found it to be the least compelling and interesting of all the world religions.

I was raised in the Lutheran church, but in the early '60s I drifted away from Christianity. It wasn't in vogue. Instead I dabbled in about every Eastern religion out there—Hinduism, Buddhism, Taoism, and Zen. My worldview was composed of various elements drawn from the East and the West. But I was never able to fit Jesus into the picture.

The first version of the band Kansas was formed in 1970 by combining the best members of two rival bands—my band called Saratoga and another band called White Clover. That first year was by far the most bizarre period in my life. We were surrounded by people who were heavily into drugs, and I was completely immersed in that culture. We lived in a very communal fashion with people continually coming and going. We had animals, frequent guests, stragglers, and hitchhikers. It became the scene of every form of hedonism and the center of the hippie culture in Topeka, Kansas.

Our band achieved a measure of popularity, but because our music was so unusual there were few places we could play. We had set out to become the most controversial group ever to hit the Midwest, and we achieved that goal. After some personnel changes, Kansas clicked. A demo tape of the band found its way into the hands of record publisher Don Kirshner, and he sent a representative out to see us perform.

When we heard that an agent from a major record company was coming, we took some steps to prepare; we publicized that there would be free beer at the concert! When Wally Gold arrived to check us out, he thought we were the most popular band in the five-state area. Not long afterward,we received a momentous phone call from Don Kirshner saying that he wanted to sign us to a recording contract. We were off to New York to record our first album.

Kansas gradually built up a kind of cult following and developed its own distinctive audience. As this was happening, we were all getting increasingly engulfed in the whole process of becoming a major rock band. It was a very exciting lifestyle. With the success of *Leftoverture*, and the release of our first big hit, "Carry On Wayward Son," we had a tremendous sense of accomplishment. We had gone from playing small clubs in rural Kansas, barely surviving on a diet of rice and beans, all the way to recording a gold album and joining the upper echelon of recording artists. We had overwhelming success on our next album, *Point of Know Return*, as well. The single "Dust in the Wind" went gold and the album reached triple-platinum status. Kansas was riding on the crest of the wave.

My desire to find religious truth during this period was actually heightened by our success. The only thing I could really cling to was the tremendous emotional experience that resulted from creating music. In a real sense, music became my god. And knowing that my lyrics were having a profound effect on the lives of many people, I felt compelled to accelerate my search to find the truth. Many of our fans thought I was some kind of a prophet. I felt like a sham and hungered more than ever to discover the true God.

I had already tried Christianity and found it wanting. As a result of the Jesus movement of the late '60s and early '70s, I had come to stereotype Christians as falling into one of two extremes. A Christian was either a hypocrite who went to church on Sundays as a social maneuver, or a wild-eyed Jesus freak who fanatically threw tracts at people on the street. I had not yet met anyone who could offer an intelligent defense of the Christian perspective.

In 1977, I discovered a book that convinced me I had reached the end of my quest. It was called the *Urantia Book*, a 2,097-page cultic volume that appeared to have all the answers I was looking for. *Urantia* is an ancient name for the planet Earth, and the *Urantia Book* believes that no one religion has all of the truth. The basic theme of this book is the proclamation that all men are indwelt by divinity and are involved in a very gradual process of achieving complete God-consciousness. I became convinced that the book could not have been written by men or human inspiration.

Two years later, Kansas had become one of the most successful and respected rock bands in the country. I enjoyed a real sense of artistic fulfillment; my marriage was going well; I had achieved financial prosperity; and I thought I had discovered the real meaning of life as an Urantian. The summer tour of 1979 changed all that.

We were touring with a band called Louisiana's Leroux. The lead singer, Jeff Pollard, and I struck up an instant friendship. Jeff was a Christian and we often debated the merits of Christianity and the *Urantia Book* for days at a time. Although I would try as hard as I could to swing him over to my side of the fence, I started noticing these feelings in me that actually wanted him to be right. I think I knew in my heart that he was right, that the Bible was the Word of God. Jeff was essentially telling me that I had been deceived by the *Urantia Book*.

No one wants to admit that he has been taken for a ride. The internal turmoil taking place inside me was bewildering, and as the days wore on, I grew more and more upset. Jeff gave me a very clear explanation of the Christian Gospel, and for the first time, I understood what it meant— what actually happened on the cross 2,000 years ago, who it was who died there, and why.

Now, while I was responding to all of this on one level, another part of me kept saying, "My God, you can't become a Christian! What would everybody think?" Because of my image of what Christianity meant, my concept of what Christians were like, and what it would mean socially, economically, and personally for me to become one, the thought absolutely terrified me. I began to get more agitated and emotionally upset. It was as though a thousand pounds was weighing down on my shoulders. I knew I was heading toward a significant conclusion, but I didn't know what it would be.

At the end of our time together, Jeff and I parted ways, and I continued our summer tour. I'll never forget what happened at my hotel in Indianapolis. It was about 3:00 in the morning on July 24, 1979. As I was sitting on my bed with open books laying all around me, I came to the conclusion that if it was really true, I would have to face up to it and become a Christian regardless of the consequences. It was time to quit fooling around. If this was the real God, then I wanted Him. I said, "Lord, if Jesus Christ is Your Son, then I want to know Him. If He really is the living God, my Redeemer and my Lord, then I want to serve Him with all my heart."

Words fall pitifully short when I try to describe what took place after that prayer. I was overwhelmed. Laughing and crying at once, I felt that that huge weight on my shoulders was suddenly taken away forever. This time I knew that my quest had reached an end; the years of searching were over.

I was so excited that I felt like running out into the hall and waking everybody up to tell them what I'd found. I couldn't contain myself, so I sat blubbering on the bed until I realized I'd better get some sleep to be ready for the concert the next day. So I lay in bed, turned out the light, and said a prayer of thanks to God for saving me after all those years of stumbling.

The moment I woke up I thought, *I'm a Christian. Where do I go from here?* The first thing I decided to do was to try to go and have some breakfast. So I stepped out of my room into the elevator and went down to the lobby. As the elevator doors opened downstairs, I saw Christmas decorations all over the hotel. Loudspeakers were blaring, "Joy to the world, the Lord is come, let Earth receive her King." It was the end of July—I honestly thought I had lost my mind!

As I walked off the elevator, my eyes began to fill with tears. For the first time in my life I understood what the words "Joy to the world" really meant. I asked the waitress what was going on with the decorations. She replied, "Well, it's an annual custom we have. It's called Christmas in July."

I don't know if the Lord worked out my conversion to happen on Christmas in July in Indianapolis, but the impact was profound. I had come to the end of a very long road, but this end was in fact the beginning of a much more exciting walk with God. I knew that He was going to change every aspect of my life—my music, my marriage, and my relationships with family and friends. Even if He wanted me to give up music, I was willing to do so, because it would be worth giving up anything for Him. I had never felt like that before; I had been a grabber, not a giver.

Years later I still feel like my life is a piece of music that has just reached one of the grand climaxes that I've always loved. When all is said and done and my life is over, all that will have truly mattered is that I made a choice in this life to believe in and serve the Lord Jesus Christ. And I know that this life is nothing compared to the life He is preparing for me in Heaven.

ENDNOTE

1. Chapter content was extracted from Kerry Livgren's autobiography. Kerry Livgren and Kenneth Boa, *Seeds of Change: The Spiritual Quest of Kerry Livgren*. Nashville, Tennessee: Sparrow Press, 1991.

GOD'S ROAD MAP

The Holy Bible is a guide to help you live a happy and satisfying life. To learn more about the concepts presented in the chapter you've just read, take a look at these passages:

WORLD RELIGIONS

In the material world of entertainment, nontraditional religions are all the rage—scientology, Kaballah, The Book of Urantia, Bhagavad Gita, and new age spirituality of all types. What most of these practices have in common is that they are centered on the empowerment of self. The Word of God is very clear—there is only one way to get to Heaven, and that is by acknowledging and receiving Christ.

Exodus 20:3-5

You shall have no other gods before Me. You shall not make for yourself an idol in the form of anything in heaven above or on the earth beneath or in the waters below. You shall not bow down to them or worship them; for I, the Lord your God, am a jealous God....

Zechariah 14:9

The Lord will be king over the whole earth. On that day there will be one Lord, and His name the only name.

John 14:6

Jesus answered, "I am the way and the truth and the life. No one comes to the Father except through Me."

SALVATION

Sin can cause broken relationships and struggles in our lives. More importantly, it separates us from God and eternal life. But through His death on the cross, Jesus Christ provided a way for us to be victorious over sin. He offers us salvation, that by accepting His gift we can be reborn into a new life and share eternity with Him.

John 3:16

For God so loved the world that He gave His one and only Son, that whoever believes in Him shall not perish but have eternal life.

Romans 10:9

That if you confess with your mouth, "Jesus is Lord," and believe in your heart that God raised Him from the dead, you will be saved.

Leon Patillo

Musician, Formerly with
Latin Rock Band, Santana

Leon Patillo was the lead vocalist for the prolific Latin rock band, Santana in the mid-1970s. He helped bring several albums to life including *Borboletta* (gold), *Festival* (gold), and *Moonflower* (platinum). In 1978 he left the band, partially because of his newfound Christian faith. He released his first solo album, *Dance Children Dance* through Word Records in 1979. He has since released seven more recordings including such hits as "J.E.S.U.S.," "Cornerstone," and the famous wedding song, "Flesh of My Flesh." Leon has performed at such venues as Radio City Music Hall, Madison Square Garden, the Hippodrome in England, and numerous halls and churches throughout the world. He was also invited to perform at the Pope's homecoming in Poland. Patillo hosted a weekly TV show, "Leon and Friends," which aired on TBN and JCTV.

Patillo works with Koinonia Foster Homes and has helped place over a thousand homeless kids in loving Christian homes. He also works with World Vision whose mission is to help the world's poor by meeting their immediate physical needs. To learn more about his ministry and his music, go to www.leonpatillo.org.

My musical career was inspired by a grammar school teacher named Miss Hughes. She believed that every kid had a special gift. One day she sat down at the piano and started playing. I was sitting beside her and my hands started doing what her hands did. I thought she was doing the coolest thing. I started taking classical piano lessons from a tough German teacher, and my parents really made me practice. I remember sitting at the piano in front of our big bay window hating it because all the other kids were outside playing football. But soon the other kids were coming inside to listen to me, telling me what a special gift I had.

My mother was a Baptist and my dad was a Methodist. So from Sunday to Sunday, I would go to either one church or the other. And then, if they both didn't feel like going to church, they would send me down the street to the local Catholic church. So I got a chance to have Methodist, Baptist, and Catholic in me all at once. We eventually settled in the Methodist church because we wanted the family to be together. By the time I was 14, I started a youth choir in the church. I learned a lot about harmonies and putting sounds together in that choir.

I formed a group called the VIPs and we performed at dances around the San Francisco area. Eventually I moved to L.A. and got hooked up with a producer named Richard Perry who produced a lot of groups and worked with the Pointer Sisters. He got me singing background and doing arrangements with Martha & the Vandellas and the Pointer Sisters. I also had my own group called Creation and we were down there working the circuit.

Then came my big break. A friend of mine who was part of the Santana Band ended up in jail right when the band had really started to take off. When he got out of jail, they wouldn't let him back in the group. He asked me to help him with his own record, so I helped arrange some of his songs, added a few of my own, and then sang them on his album. Well, I came to find out that he really wasn't producing the album for himself at all; instead he wanted to take these songs and sell them to Carlos Santana. He took the album up to Carlos' house, played it for him, and Carlos said, "The album's okay, but boy, I've got to get a hold of that guy singing!" So that's when he called me. Carlos Santana called me to see if I would come up to his home in northern California and talk about getting involved in his group!

I'll never forget going to his house. We went down to his private studio and he started playing this new song and telling me what the lyrics and melody went like and I started singing along. We were singing songs like "Black Magic Woman," "Oye Como Va," and "You Got to Change Your Evil Ways." And then I sat down and played a song I'd written, and he absolutely loved it. He didn't know I could play the organ too. And then those magical words, "This is cool, so you can play and sing with us." That was it—I was in. And that was the true beginning of my professional career. We toured all over the world together and did three albums, *Borboletta*, *Moonflower*, and *Festival*.

Shortly after I became involved with Santana, I started dating a girl in San Francisco. Her brother, Richard, was a Christian, and I really felt like he was a little too much on my case. I basically just tried to find a way to avoid him. It seemed like every time I came to the house he was at the front door. If I came to the side door, he was there. If I came up through the basement, he was there.

After he ministered to me for about an eight-month period, I decided I would go to a Bible study with him to get him off my back. The meeting was in a little coffee shop up in the Haight Asbury district of San Francisco. They spoke a great word about the difference between the flesh and the spirit. It was just right on the money. I thought maybe at that meeting they were going to try and convert me. But instead they just had a short prayer, and boom, we were out.

When we got back to his house, we sat in the car in his driveway and he asked me, "How did you like the meeting?" I had really been thinking about what they said about the rewards of the flesh and the rewards for being close to God. So when he posed that question in the driveway I said, "You know, I really, really enjoyed it, and I think I learned something about my life." Richard asked me if I wanted to make a commitment to the Lord right there and then. But I said, "Well, I don't know if that's going to work. I'm lead singer for Santana now and you know what that's going to bring about for me." Every lyric, every song, and every place we go and thing we do would cause some sort of chasm in my faith.

But there couldn't be any harm in saying a little prayer, could there? It sounded like a logical thing for me to do, so I said okay. Now I wasn't accustomed to holding a man's hand so I kind of shriveled away when he was trying to reach for me. But we started to pray and BAM! God just did it right there in the car! I had this tremendous physical feeling of a weight falling off me. It wasn't just words; I could feel it happening! It was just like I was free to go into a whole new side of life that I had never experienced before—this time, with God in it.

In his house there was a piano and something made me go to that piano and start playing a song just right out of my fingers and out of my mouth and out of my soul. The words were, "We must believe, we must believe in Him and praise His name." It just came right out as if it was a song that I had heard all my life. The next thing I knew there were three or four of his family members gathered around the piano utterly amazed. They had all seen me leave the house cussing and smoking, and now here I was singing praises to God!

That was when I knew that God was real. He had taken this gift of mine and had shown me why the gift was inside of me. He was able to take something that I thought was so individual and so personal and inject Himself inside of it and then express Himself through it. As the years have gone on, the songs have gotten better as well as my relationship with the Lord.

Now my conversion experience was very special to me, but it didn't go over that well with the rest of Santana. It was particularly tough because Carlos was a Buddhist, and it caused a little bit of a conflict whenever spiritual things came up. But for the most part, we found a way to make it work. We were writing songs together, and we'd have to try and find a medium ground when it came to certain songs. I had one song called, "You Are My River." It was saying that you are my river, keep on flowing through. To him it meant one thing and to me it meant something else. So that's how we wrote.

We took Earth, Wind and Fire on their first trip to Europe. I had just become a Christian and really felt like it was something that I wanted to start introducing to others. I kept hearing a voice inside of me saying that this was too good of a thing to just keep it to myself. I needed to pass it on to others. When I went over to say hi to Philip Bailey, Andrew Woolfolk, and Larry Dunn from EWF, I had my Bible under my arm, and they asked me about it. After a few minutes of talking, the suggestion came up to have a Bible study during the six weeks we were on tour. And we did just that. Nearly every night after the concert we would meet in one of our rooms and study the Book of John. Before the trip was up, those three guys received the Lord, and it was just a marvelous thing.

After we returned from Europe, Philip had the idea to hold a concert together on neutral ground so his friends would come. We decided to call it Jesus at the Roxie. The next thing we knew the word was out. There was going to be one 8:00 show on a Friday night, but because there was so much interest, we ended up doing a double show that night and two more shows on Saturday night. People stood out in the rain just because they wanted to come in. I'm talking about people like Jim Brown, Della Reese, Smokey Robinson, and Marilyn McCoo—the list goes on and on and on. I was absolutely blown away that He would use me in this kind of a setting.

I think this whole business of me witnessing to Philip and the other guys from Earth, Wind and Fire kind of disturbed Carlos Santana because I ended up getting fired from the group. But I think Carlos realized that there was something missing, and he called me back three or four months later. I came back and wrote about three fourths of the *Festival* album, the last album I did with them. But I was really onto a different mission by then, and I knew I couldn't go back to the group to be the vocalist.

Back in the early '90s I was approached by TBN about doing a show called "Leon and Friends." I went on a boat trip with several others to strategize about the show and how we could secure the involvement of the charity I was helping, Koinonia Foster Home. This trip was going to be taken by mostly couples with only a few singles like myself. I'd been through a divorce just a few years before this, and I didn't feel like I was ready to meet anybody new. But trying to keep an open mind, when I got to the boat I said a quick prayer, "Lord, surprise me."

The next morning, all the couples were hanging out together and I hunted around for a piano to kind of have some time alone. When I found one, I sat down and started writing a song, and this guy came up and sat down beside me and started singing along. The next thing I knew, this young lady started coming toward us. She had this beautiful smile and to me she was kind of like walking in slow motion right at me. But she cut away and sat down by this guy who was singing with me. I was disappointed; I figured he was her husband. But he introduced me to her as his sister! Remember when I said that prayer, "Surprise me"? Well, He certainly did. I am now happily married to my fabulous wife, Renee. She's another reason why I know that God is real. I'm so thankful to God for sending me Renee.

My life since Santana has been incredible. I continue recording and touring, but now all the glory goes to Christ. And because I am open to it, I continue to see the reality of Jesus nearly every day.

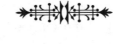

GOD'S ROAD MAP

The Holy Bible is a guide to help you live a happy and satisfying life. To learn more about the concepts presented in the chapter you've just read, take a look at these passages:

TALENTS

Most of us have a desire to excel at something—academics, sports, music, or our work. God has placed within His people special gifting. The key is to take that talent, whatever it is, and use it for His glory. Only then will we feel true fulfillment.

Matthew 25:29

For everyone who has will be given more, and he will have an abundance. Whoever does not have, even what he has will be taken from him.

Romans 12:6-8

We have different gifts, according to the grace given us. If a man's gift is prophesying, let him use it in proportion to his faith. If it is serving, let him serve; if it is teaching, let him teach; if it is encouraging, let him encourage; if it is contributing to the needs of others, let him give generously; if it is leadership, let him govern diligently; if it is showing mercy, let him do it cheerfully.

Ephesians 4:11-12

It was He who gave some to be apostles, some to be prophets, some to be evangelists, and some to be pastors and teachers, to prepare God's people for works of service, so that the body of Christ may be built up.

GOD'S PLAN

As children of God, we are part of His divine plan. Isn't that extraordinary? But in order to have the proper end result, we need to consult the building plans—the Bible, and speak daily with the Architect.

Jeremiah 29:11

"For I know the plans I have for you," declares the Lord, "plans to prosper you and not to harm you, plans to give you hope and a future."

James 1:5

If any of you lacks wisdom, he should ask God, who gives generously to all without finding fault, and it will be given to him.

Heather Powers

Christian Musician, Formerly with
Huey Lewis and The News
(Photo, courtesy of Erick Anderson)

Singer/songwriter Heather Powers draws inspiration from a troubled past. Her compelling life saga includes assault, rape, addiction, divorce, emotional breakdown, and utter brokenness. While her story is often incomprehensible, she focuses not on the trauma, but on the amazing restoration and redemption she has experienced.

Powers has shared the stage with the likes of Huey Lewis and The News, Roby Duke, and Dennis Agajanian. She has also led worship at many different churches and for events and conferences around the nation. She currently leads worship at her home church, aCROSS Marin Fellowship in Marin County, California.

In early 2004, Powers' song, "Little Bit of Heaven" became the first single off of her self-titled debut album. Her new recording, "Lay Them Down" was released in late 2005. Through this record, it is Powers' desire to be a blessing to those who are struggling and to encourage them to lay whatever they've been through at the foot of the cross. It worked for her, with miraculous results. For more details, go to www.powersongs.com.

Everyone has their own rock bottom. My descent was a long, slow, and anguishing one. When I hit the bottom, I hit it hard. But in the end, Jesus Christ lifted me up and rescued me. And He reminded me on that day, that He'd always been there waiting for me.

I have a very rich Christian heritage. My father is a pastor, as was my grandfather and my uncle. My dad actually started Insight for Living with Chuck Swindoll, and worked with him for many years. So, I probably had the ideal upbringing in terms of being in a Christian family and learning Christian values.

Being a pastor's kid, I was involved in music from my earliest memories. I began playing piano and guitar, and I knew from a very early age that music was my life's aim. I was even on a Christian television show for a while, called "Day of Discovery."

Growing up, I always felt like I was in a fishbowl being looked at from the outside. Because of my dad's role in the church, I felt an intense pressure to keep up appearances and play my part as a preacher's kid.

Two very significant things happened to me around the time I was going through puberty. When I was 13, I was home alone one evening with my brothers and sisters while my parents had gone out. There was a man who had been stalking me for a while, and that night he'd been eyeballing our house and was able to find a way in. He came into the house with his pants undone and tried to sexually assault me. Fortunately, my little sister woke up, and we created enough commotion that he finally fled. We found out later that he had raped the girl above us the week prior.

As a young woman entering adolescence, I was coming into so many new sensations and feelings that I'd never experienced before. I was becoming aware of my body and all the changes it was going through. When you are 13, you're awkward and unsure of yourself and terribly modest. I'd been so protected, so sheltered, and this experience traumatized me at a very impressionable age.

The man was never caught. My sister and I were so disturbed by what had happened that we both slept at the foot of our parent's bed for six months. They didn't know how to get me the help I needed. Instead, we all just kind of believed that the Lord would take care of it.

About a year and a half later, when I was 15, something else happened—something even worse. My parents had gone out of town, and I was staying with a friend of mine. I took advantage of the fact that my parents were gone and went out on a group date that I knew I shouldn't have been on. Six or seven of us went to Disneyland for the day, and in the evening went to a park to play "capture the flag." My date and I were "hiding" in the dark for the game, and we started kissing. He became very aggressive, and when I objected to his further advances, he ignored me and became increasingly more vicious. In the end, he raped me. I was battered, bruised, and horrified. Worse yet, I was ashamed that it could have even happened, especially by someone I liked and knew fairly well.

It took me six months to tell my parents what happened because of the guilt and shame that I felt. I'd been disobedient by going out on the date in the first place, so I felt like I got what I deserved. I didn't think they'd believe me anyway. As it turns out, that boy had been involved with similar situations before. However, I never pressed charges against him, because by the time I told my parents, I didn't want to go through any more heartache.

These two traumatic events, happening so closely together, caused me to suppress a lot of emotion. I didn't get any help from the church, because at that time, people just weren't open to discussing things like rape in the Body of Christ. As far as church goes, I think there's much more awareness and counseling available now. Honestly, nobody knew what to do with me. I learned that the Body of Christ can be very judgmental and tough on those who are struggling. So I never alluded to the fact that I was hurting.

Shortly after the rape, my dad took a senior pastor job at a church up in Grass Valley, California. It was a really tough move, because it uprooted me from everything I knew and all of my friends. It was like starting all over again.

When I was 16, I met a young man and we started dating. We became physically involved very quickly. After years of counseling, I now understand that when your innocence is taken away so violently, you have a warped sense of what sex is and you misuse it. I was never going to let anybody hurt me that way again, so I was proactive instead. I was in charge of my own sexuality—nobody else.

Michael and I got married two years later, and had both of our children by the time I was 23. My choice to get married came from me wanting to escape all the other stuff going on in my life. Looking back, I certainly wasn't ready for the responsibility of being a wife and mother.

Ever since I'd been a little girl, I'd had excruciating headaches. When I turned 13, and the two incidents of assault happened, my headaches increased in severity to the point where they became debilitating. By the time I was 19, I began to be hospitalized for migraines.

The headaches were so severe that they would knock me out for days at a time. I have a family history of migraine, so my doctors knew that was a component. But they couldn't figure out why they couldn't get them under control. The headaches got progressively worse resulting in hospital stays for weeks at a shot.

The pain was so agonizing that I threw up constantly. So they gave me anti-nausea drugs along with narcotics for the pain. It was kind of a balancing act. They tried many different medications, including Oxycontin, Vicodin, and Soma, but nothing was really working.

Oxycontin is a drug that has ruined countless lives. It is synthetic morphine, and people find it impossible to get off of it. It's a long-acting drug, so that you aren't constantly having highs and lows. So you're basically just high all the time and don't even know it. And you need more and more to make it work. I was in and out of the hospital from the time I was 19 until it all blew apart when I was 28. By then, I had a full-blown addiction to prescription medications.

I was a shell of a person for many years. I had two little ones at home, but I was so incapacitated that I couldn't care for them. Fortunately, I had a wonderful family that pulled together and stepped in when it was necessary. I was numb and drugged up most of the time. A lot of my life went by while I was lying on the couch. As you can imagine, my marriage wasn't doing too well by this point; neither was my job. My husband, Michael, and I led worship at our church.

Even though I was taking all these medications, my condition wasn't getting significantly better. We would find things to keep the pain at bay for a time, but it would get worse again. Then my doctor had an idea. She had a feeling that there were some other things going on that were making my headaches worse.

She put me on an antidepressant, and when my serotonin (a natural hormone that enhances our sense of well-being) levels finally came up, I had a vitality that I hadn't felt for a long time. I hadn't realized how numb I'd been. And I wanted to feel again! I didn't care if it was pain; I just wanted to feel something.

So, I weaned myself off the Oxycontin and all the other painkillers. I did it all by myself, and the fact that I was able to kick them was a miracle in and of itself. It was brutal; the withdrawals were very painful.

By the time all the narcotics were out of my body, my doctor had been steadily bumping up the antidepressant dose, until I was taking four times the amount I should have been. As a result, I literally went crazy. I started having frightening manic episodes and ended up in a psychiatric hospital. Part of being a patient there was participating in therapy. I found out that so much junk had long been buried inside of me, and I had been suppressing a great deal of guilt and shame. It all came out—raging. The more guilt and shame I felt, the further I ran, until I came to the point where I walked out of my life completely.

For a year and a half, I abandoned my life. I filed for divorce, left my kids with my husband, and quit my job. And I started to use illicit drugs and live a very promiscuous lifestyle. I basically reclaimed my adolescence and did all those things that teenagers often do. I pulled out all the stops.

I met a guy named Josh, and we partied together constantly. The life I was leading was in very dark territory, especially the abuse of methamphetamine. Like so many other women, I got sucked into using meth because I wanted to lose weight...and I did. I lost 40 pounds. But I lost so much more.

This preacher's kid was on a serious downward spiral. Despite the drugs, Josh and I were still able to function in society. Nobody would have ever guessed what we were doing. We were living two different lives.

One night I sat in a cold bathtub for hours and sobbed. My life was a complete disaster and I was miserable. I was absolutely, spiritually dry; there wasn't anything left to fake. I knew so profoundly at that moment though, that the Lord had never left me; it was I who had walked away from Him. I knew also that there wasn't anything I needed to do in order to clean myself up so He would come and rescue me. That was the beginning of a slow journey back to the Lord.

I told Josh I was done partying and I meant it. There were a few bumpy weeks where I had to literally pray my way through each and every day, but the Lord thoroughly delivered me from all of my addictions.

But He wasn't finished with me yet. I didn't do drugs anymore, but I did drink wine. I thought wine was okay, because it's culturally acceptable. I could get away with drinking it with dinner and with friends, and nobody would think twice about it.

But the Lord dealt with me on that too. He said, "If you are going to totally trust Me, you've got to give up all those things that you think are going to provide relief and let them go." That was such a tough thing to do. Wine was my last safety blanket, my comfort in a cup. I was afraid to give it up because I didn't know what life would be like without it.

But I did give it up, and officially declared my day of freedom. When I stepped out in faith, God met me in such a powerful way. He took away all the desires to live my old life and replaced them with Himself. And it was such a different relationship than I'd ever experienced with Christ before, because all of a sudden, it wasn't about anybody else, and it wasn't about Christian culture. It was just He and I. I had alienated myself so thoroughly from the rest of my family that He was really all I had left. He became more real to me than anything I could see.

Giving up wine was the absolute turning point in my walk with Christ. The day it happened, my prayer life was revolutionized. It caused me to see the Lord in ways that I never did before. That day—my freedom day—I realized that my life really wasn't mine. And that was okay. I felt like I was walking under God's mercy and I saw what He had saved me from. I knew that God would use those years when I had disobeyed, and had failed so miserably, as trophies of His grace and mercy.

I was still with Josh during this time. When I told him I was done partying with him, he thought it was great because it would help him slow down too. But it was just the opposite. Instead, he started using the amount that both of us had been using before, and he went deeper into the lifestyle. Only now, he had to hide it from me.

He was on methamphetamine and GHB and was drinking a case of beer a day just to try and get calories in him. He had withered away to just 140 pounds. The only people he could really party with were these weird, underworld types. His drug dealer even told him to quit and stopped selling to him. You know it's bad when you've gotten too extreme for your drug dealer.

Josh became very ill with a serious strep infection that wasn't healing. It was heartbreaking to watch him go down the tubes so quickly. I didn't know what to do. I finally told his parents what was going on, and we were able to get him into a rehab facility close by in West Marin.

God was so sovereign in this situation, because if we hadn't gotten him into treatment Josh wouldn't have lived much longer. He had such a severe infection going on and he still continued to abuse his body. I can remember sitting in the intake interview seeing that Josh was ready; he knew it was a life-or-death situation. He was in rehab for a month, and in September 2005 he celebrated five years of sobriety. We're now happily married.

During this whole ordeal, I'd still been pursuing my music. My band had a benefactor who heard the music I wrote and ended up paying for a record to be made. He happened to live next door to Huey Lewis and took our demo tape over to him for a listen. Huey loved it and got us in touch with one of the guys in his band, Johnny Colla, who is the sax player and cowrote many of their hits.

I started making a record with them and working at their studio, and eventually, they asked me to open for them in concert. I'd always had affirmation of my musical talent within the church, but this was the first time I'd felt validated in the mainstream world. It was a crucial time in developing my confidence.

But my music career never went anywhere, and I was terribly disappointed. For a couple of years I was silent. I gave up music entirely, because it just hurt too much. I had tried for so long and had some measured success, but I was embarrassed and humiliated that it wasn't progressing faster. For so long, my identity had been wrapped up in my music. Because I was a charismatic person and outwardly gifted, I was able to fool people into believing that everything was rosy. So music became a huge part of my persona. Throughout all of my trials, music has been the one safety net I've had. So when I gave up music, I mourned the death of it.

I understand now that the Lord was not going to let those doors open until He had all of me. He made that very clear. When I got to the point where I gave up my music and the control of my life to Him, He began opening the doors of opportunity once again.

My ex-husband, Michael, started calling me asking me why I wasn't doing any music. He wanted to know what was going on. "God has given you this gift and you need to do something with it." After several of those phone calls, we formed what is our band now. I know it's unusual that my ex and I are in a band together. But we're still very, very good friends. We're both remarried and we co-parent the kids. We are blessed to have a very close and healthy relationship.

Our friendship is miraculous on several levels. During the height of my addictions, I was on staff with him at our church. I left him and our kids, and walked out of our life completely. So when I fell, I did it very publicly. It was amazingly brutal at first, humiliating and horrible. Everyone knew about it and saw the journey unfold. Many of our old friends on staff, and in the congregation, walked through that journey with Michael on the other side of it, supporting him.

But God has really used this story to reach a lot of people and change a lot of hearts. It has caused people to realize that no matter who you are, if you open the door even just a crack to the enemy, he'll take you down in any way he can. None of us is immune to it.

Now the Lord has brought some incredible opportunities before our band. And the greatest part is that we can't take any of the credit. From the get-go, from the forming of this group, it has been surrounded in prayer. We knew that if God was going to do anything with it, it was going to have to be completely His and not about us. So from the very beginning we started praying that way. "Lord, use what You've given us and show us what we need to do." It is totally mind-blowing to see the doors that He's opened in such a short period of time.

Most importantly, it's remarkable that I'm even here to share this. He's taken a life that was a complete mess and is using it to glorify Himself and to minister to other people. He's real in so many ways, but mostly in the fact that I'm alive at all. And so is Josh; there's no reason he should be still alive either. The Lord has healed my body and my relationships and brought music back into my life. The whole thing is really a miracle.

There's nobody on this earth that God can't rescue. He's in the business of reaching in and resurrecting new things. If He did it for me, He can do it for you too.

GOD'S ROAD MAP

The Holy Bible is a guide to help you live a happy and satisfying life. To learn more about the concepts presented in the chapter you've just read, take a look at these passages:

REBELLION

Heather shares a heartbreaking story of sexual assault, addiction, and recovery. Even though she was raised in the church and believed in Christ from an early age, she turned her back on God. Ultimately she was saved when she chose to stop rebelling and gave up the control of her life to someone who could better manage it—Jesus Christ.

Isaiah 59:2

But your iniquities have separated you from your God; your sins have hidden His face from you, so that He will not hear.

Hebrews 3:12-14

See to it, brothers, that none of you has a sinful, unbelieving heart that turns away from the living God. But encourage one another daily, as long as it is called Today, so that none of you may be hardened by sin's deceitfulness. We have come to share in Christ if we hold firmly till the end the confidence we had at first.

Jeremiah 3:22a

Return, faithless people; I will cure you of backsliding.

ADDICTION

Addiction is on the rise—addiction to drugs, alcohol, sex, even work. On our own, we are often powerless to kick these compulsions. But nothing is too big for God to handle.

Romans 6:19-20

I put this in human terms because you are weak in your natural selves. Just as you used to offer the parts of your body in slavery to impurity and to ever-increasing wickedness, so now offer them in slavery to righteousness leading to holiness. When you were slaves to sin, you were free from the control of righteousness.

Romans 8:5-8

Those who live according to the sinful nature have their minds set on what that nature desires; but those who live in accordance with the Spirit have their minds set on what the Spirit desires. The mind of sinful man is death, but the mind controlled by the Spirit is life and peace; the sinful mind is hostile to God. It does not submit to God's law, nor can it do so. Those controlled by the sinful nature cannot please God.

Rudy Sarzo

Bass Player with DIO, Formerly with
Ozzy Osbourne, Quiet Riot, and
Whitesnake

Rudy Sarzo has been an internationally known professional musician for more than two decades. A sought-after bass player, Sarzo has rocked stages with many big-name bands. He made a name for himself with Ozzy Osbourne's band in the early '80s. Sarzo was also a member of Quiet Riot and recorded the smash album *Metal Health*—the first heavy metal debut recording to reach #1 on the Billboard charts. The band is probably best known for their megahit "Cum on Feel the Noize." From April 1987 to September 1994 he was a member of Whitesnake. Sarzo is currently a member of the multi-platinum heavy metal group DIO. His recordings with all of these artists combined have sold over 30 million copies.

Sarzo has been involved in numerous world tours and MTV music videos and was voted 1983's #1 Bassist in *Circus Magazine*. In addition to these musical accomplishments, Sarzo is a long-time bass instructor and Digital Media clinician/spokesperson for such products as Sony Pictures Media Software's Acid, Vegas, DVD Architect, Sound Forge, and Ulead's DVD Workshop2. Find out more at www.rudysarzo.com

God does unbelievable things for me...every single day. And I can't wait to see what the rest of my life will look like.

I was born in Cuba. As a child I went to catechism and had a typical Latin Catholic upbringing. In the Catholic religion there is a lot of icon worshipping. I remember walking into my grandmother's house and the first thing I'd see is a life-size image of Jesus on the cross suffering. That is a very powerful image for anyone to see, but especially a child. It was scary—very gothic. Catholic churches are filled with images like that, which as an adult I can better understand. I remember when I was nine years old getting ready for my first communion. But in order to have my first communion, I also had to have my first confession. The thought of the priest in the confessional booth was just a little scary and very intimidating. There he was asking me to tell him about my sins. As a kid I never thought I was doing anything wrong or the least bit sinful. So my first reaction was like "I have nothing to confess." But they made me feel guilty because they told me I was born a sinner. So there I was, just nine years old and already on the wrong path. I had a hard time understanding that concept. It made me feel more afraid of God than anything.

When I was ten, we left Castro's Cuba to get away from communism. At the time, the government was taking kids away from their families and sending them over to Russia and things like that. So in order to avoid that, my parents started the process of getting us out of the country. This was back in 1961, so it took a couple of years through the legal channels. Like many other Cubans we went to Miami. We loved America. This was the time of the Beatles playing on the "Ed Sullivan Show," so rock and roll was a big thing. Back then, kids could really communicate with each other through music. And like so many other kids, I wanted to be in a band. I started out playing the guitar, but since there were so many other guitar players, it was suggested I switch to the bass to get more gigs. My career was kind of like an evolution. I played in party bands, and then I started going to clubs and so on. After awhile, I left Miami to pursue my career in Los Angeles. In the '70s, that's where the music industry was at; it was where all the musicians were gathering; it was the thing to do.

Over the years I started discovering my own faith, different from what I learned as a child. I started reading the Bible and found out that my direct link to God was through Christ. I learned that I could have a relationship with the Savior. But still, things were kind of disappointing for me, and my career wasn't going where I wanted it to. I was 30 years old by then. (In Hollywood years, I was like 80!) Up to this point, I hadn't recorded an album or been on tour. Finally, I made my peace with God. If I was going to make it, that was fine and I'd be eternally grateful. But if I didn't make it, that was fine too. My relationship with God was the most important thing in my life. I basically turned it all over to Him. I had a whole new attitude; this was a defining moment.

Less than a week later I got a phone call that changed my life. My friend, Randy Rhoads, was in Ozzy Osbourne's band, and they needed a bass player. He recommended me, and after an audition, I became the newest member of Ozzy's band. If it wasn't for Randy, I wouldn't have made it in this business. I'd have ended up playing conga drums in a salsa band in Miami. He was completely, 100-percent responsible for me meeting Ozzy Osbourne. And I got thrown into the most incredible, wacky world. It was like going on the biggest roller coaster ride of my life!

My professional career was launched. I think it is more than a little ironic that it was this particular band that started it all, a band known for being dark and full of occult symbolism. But because God put me there, I learned a lot about people, especially about perception—perception of the unknown. Somehow musicians are held up to a different standard than other performers. For example, an actor like Bella Lugosi can get away with playing some dark and evil characters and people don't assume he is evil as well. Or if you have someone on Broadway playing Dracula, most people in the audience don't think he is really a vampire. But if you are a musician and you play a character like that, you must be bad. A guy like Alice Cooper isn't the same as the character he played on stage. And neither was Ozzy. It's all just a show. Ozzy recorded a song called Mr. Crowley on the *Blizzard of Ozz* album. It was all about Aleister Crowley who was a famous English writer and occult figure. The lyrics to the song are actually anti-occult and critical of Crowley, but because Ozzy was singing it, people just assumed the opposite. The song is all about questioning the occult, not promoting it.

While on tour in 1982 with Ozzy's band, we experienced a tragic loss. The band was in Florida, and my longtime friend, Randy Rhoads, was killed in a plane crash. He was with two other people in the plane when it clipped the band's bus where Ozzy and several other band members were asleep and then crashed into a nearby home. The home was gutted by fire, but everyone managed to escape. All three on the plane were killed. Randy was only 25 years old. When something like that happens, you never forget, and you start looking at life anew. It's a gift—something you don't take for granted. After the crash, one of the first things I saw Ozzy do was go to church and pray. People don't know that; they don't see that side of him.

After the plane crash, I fulfilled my commitment and then left the band. It was just too hard to continue without Randy. Performing material that he wrote was a daily reminder of my lost friend. When you live through something like that, you never forget the smells or every little detail of that horrid day. It's with you forever; you just learn to live with it.

I rejoined Quiet Riot, with whom I'd played before I met Ozzy. We had a huge hit, "Cum on Feel the Noize." It was kind of like an anthem that a lot of people connected with. That album was the first heavy metal debut to reach #1 on Billboard. I felt very blessed to have that opportunity and success. Eventually I left the band and joined Whitesnake. We played together from 1987 to 1994. It was a great time.

I think God gave me a wonderful gift to be able to work as a musician; that's the only thing I've ever been successful at. As musicians, we're so blessed to do what we dreamed of doing when we were kids. Playing the same stages as my heroes—that was sacred ground to me. That's where the magic happens. Even though I go into different areas of the music industry, I'm always ready and willing and open to keep playing...as long as my fingers keep moving.

I don't consider myself to be of any particular religion—I'm a Christian. I read my Bible every day and just follow the Christian teachings. My faith has always been at the core. I've always known where I had to give credit for my success. It's been a gift—a true blessing. I've had a lot of ups and downs, but I've always had the same faith. And I truly believe

I would have kept the same faith whether I had "made it" or not. It was too strong—too clear.

Religion is a very personal experience. I don't think anybody can actually sit you down and tell you that you have to do this. I think as human beings we are always looking for direction and guidance. It is within us to realize that it doesn't stop here—that there is something bigger and more powerful than us. Sometimes when you go through life and no matter how hard you try, things don't happen the way they should or the way you want them to happen. I have worked harder at my failures. When it's the way it should be, when it's what God has planned for you, it's so easy! You just show up and do what you are supposed to do. And when it's not the way it should be, you are just beating your head up against the wall.

I know Jesus is real because I can feel Him, I can see Him. After Christ rose from the dead, He gathered His apostles together one last time. Thomas said that he wouldn't believe He was real unless he could put his finger in Jesus' wounds. He believed because he saw Jesus in the flesh. Well, at the risk of sounding a little wacky, I have visions and I know He is real because of them. They are unexplainable really. I've had some prophetic visions that I didn't understand when I originally saw them, but they have come true. These visions are a spiritual gift, and they are very comforting. Through them I can communicate directly with God. It happens all the time now. There is basically a presence that I'm aware of through meditation. There are things around us that we are not aware of; we are just too concerned with the here and now to see them. But there is this great presence all around us. Now I know how to look for it.

My life continues to be a spiritual journey—every day. It's very exciting and wonderful to see what He is doing in my life. I try to devote my day to God as much as possible. It's the least I can do for all the things God has given me.

GOD'S ROAD MAP

The Holy Bible is a guide to help you live a happy and satisfying life. To learn more about the concepts presented in the chapter you've just read, take a look at these passages:

LEGALISM VERSUS A PERSONAL RELATIONSHIP WITH CHRIST

Focusing too much on rules and rituals within a denomination makes it more about the religion itself than about the relationship. The whole point of Christianity is to develop a personal, one-on-one relationship with God through His Son, Jesus Christ.

Romans 5:10-11

For since we were restored to friendship with God by the death of his Son while we were still his enemies, we will certainly be delivered from eternal punishment by his life. So now we can rejoice in our wonderful new relationship with God—all because of what our Lord Jesus Christ has done for us in making us friends of God.

Mark 7:8

You have let go of the commands of God and are holding on to the traditions of men.

Romans 1:21-23

For although they knew God, they neither glorified Him as God nor gave thanks to Him, but their thinking became futile and their foolish hearts were darkened. Although they claimed to be wise, they became fools and exchanged the glory of the immortal God for images made to look like mortal man and birds and animals and reptiles.

Galatians 2:20

I have been crucified with Christ and I no longer live, but Christ lives in me. The life I live in the body, I live by faith in the Son of God, who loved me and gave Himself for me.

SPIRITUAL GIFTS

Spiritual gifts are special endowments that Christians receive from the Holy Spirit. Many of them are supernatural in scope, like Rudy Sarzo's ability to see visions.

First Corinthians 12:7-11

Now to each one the manifestation of the Spirit is given for the common good. To one there is given through the Spirit the message of wisdom, to another the message of knowledge by means of the same Spirit, to another faith by the same Spirit, to another gifts of healing by that one Spirit, to another miraculous powers, to another prophecy, to another distinguishing between spirits, to another speaking in different kinds of tongues, and to still another the interpretation of tongues. All these are the work of one and the same Spirit, and He gives them to each one, just as He determines.

John Schneider

Actor and Musician Best Known
for Roles on "The Dukes of Hazzard"
and "Smallville"
(Photo credit: Patrick Ecclesine)

John Schneider is best known for his role as Bo Duke, the fun-loving, fast-driving, country heartthrob on the wildly success-ful '80s TV series, "The Dukes of Hazzard." His boyish good looks graced the covers of everything from teen magazines to lunch-boxes, and had girls swooning from coast to coast.

In a career spanning more than three decades, Schneider has starred in six TV series, five miniseries, four feature films, one soap opera, 14 movies, and numerous Broadway musicals. He is now entering his fifth season playing Clark Kent's father, Jonathan, on the hit WB series, "Smallville."

A respected singer and songwriter, Schneider has also released 11 solo albums, including a number-one compilation and four #1 singles. He and his wife, Elly, have recently created Johnenelly Productions. Their mission is to develop programs that show and espouse valued families.

Schneider is also recognized for his noteworthy charity work. In 1982, he and Marie Osmond cofounded the Children's Miracle Network. Nearly 25 years later, the organization has provided more than two billion dollars to fund children's medical facilities across North America. For more information, go to www.john-schneider.tv.

❋❉⟨⟩❉❋

I'd heard they wanted to cast real southern people from the ages of 24-30. I was 18 and from New York—a perfect fit. I let my beard grow, grabbed a beer, and in my best southern accent, I told the directors I was a 24 year old from Snellville, Georgia. And it worked. For six seasons I played the part of Bo Duke on the hit series, "The Dukes of Hazzard."

While I was playing Bo, I was also working on my music career. So when "Dukes" ended, I decided to focus on music for a while. Within a month, my first single with MCA, "I've Been Around Enough To Know," went number one. I went out on the road and had a great time.

But I started to realize that in order to make a career out of being on the road, you had to get involved in things. I was never a drug culture person, but I could understand how people could get involved in that. It's not so much the singing on the road that's the cause of people's downfall; it's the spare time in the hotel and on the bus. You're really only busy for an hour or two a day. And I think that's when people often wind up saying, "I've got to figure out a way to show up for work and not have to really *be* there." Once you have that thought, it's the beginning of the end. I started having those thoughts and I knew that I needed to get off the road, or drugs would be the next logical step. If I would have stuck with it, I would have probably been tremendously successful *and* miserable. Instead, I met my lovely wife, Elly.

God was never a big part of my life until one day I saw a big musician help a little old man up off the floor. I saw that there was purpose and acceptance on a level that I'd never seen before. And then all of a sudden, everything made sense to me—you know, that "could have had a V8" sort of moment.

Johnny Cash was that man. I lived with him and his wife, June, for a while about 15 years ago. It was really delightful to see someone who was actively involved in his design from God. That doesn't mean that he didn't step out of that design occasionally, and it doesn't mean that he didn't blow it. But he knew where he was in the job—in the walk, or the jog, or the sprint that is a relationship with God. Johnny Cash had a big influence on me from the time we did Stagecoach together until the time I moved away from Nashville and away from his house.

Before I met Johnny, I thought to be a Christian you had to be smiley and happy and wear your sweater tied around your neck. And that wasn't going to happen for me. If that was the kind of army Jesus was trying to gather, then He'd have to go to another camp. But Johnny proved to me that you didn't have to check your masculinity at the door when you became a Christian—because Johnny was every bit a man.

When I got saved, I got on board in a big way because I've always been very purpose-driven. And what I've learned is that God is up to something, and we all are part of it. Now, on the surface that sounds really simple, but it's really not how people act. People act as if *they're* doing something, and *God* is part of it. They act that way in prayer; they act that way in church; and I hear that from the pulpit more times than not—that God is interested in your circumstances and wants to help you out. That's not it at all. God designed us for a purpose that *He* has, something that *He's* doing, not something that we're doing. So our job, then, is to discover the design God has for us because only then can we be effective people—not only for ourselves, but for His Kingdom.

Finding your purpose is really kind of simple. You have to look into yourself, into your history, and figure out what you were made to do. Look back in your childhood and think about what you wanted to be more than anything in the world. In the Bible it says, "God will give you the desires of your heart." That doesn't mean God will give you the stuff you want. It means that God will put into your heart what your desires, and therefore your purpose, will be.

That's what happened to me. I wanted to be an actor from the time I was eight years old. It wasn't because of anything; it was just there. And I never turned away from it. Most people turn away from those dreams because along the line somebody tells them they can't do it. As soon as you are in touch with those God-given desires of your heart, there is a legion of bad, satanic forces that will come and try to put out that fire.

Because I never got out of my design, it made me ready to meet Christ on the day that I did.

People want to know that they're part of something and yet I hear them fight it. "God, if You can just help me get this done, then I'll be free to do what You want." God is not going to help you cut your grass! He's going to help you cut His grass. He'll give you the lawn mower and the fertilizer and teach you to take care of His grass, not yours. We need to get it through our heads that it's not about us.

God used me for years and years before I knew Him. He didn't wait until I said, "Jesus Christ is real." He did not render me ineffective until that day. He used me the whole time. When I look back, I think, *My God, You're smart!* No wonder this happened and that happened. Like the biblical character Joseph, I look back on all the trials, tribulations, victories, and successes, and understand now what they were all about.

Being a Christian doesn't mean I smile all the time. I've got stuff going on and too many taxes to pay. But I'm fighting the fight, you know? And I know that if I keep fighting, one of these days I'm going to start to see the fruits of the battle.

Christians have bad days too. But let's track a couple of Jesus' bad days. All of our worst days put together couldn't equal one of His last couple days. What makes us think we should have it easier than Him? No matter what kind of day I'm having, I have the peace of knowing I have a personal relationship with Jesus Christ. And that makes all the difference.

My coming to faith has affected what I do for a living in a big way. I feel like I've gained a whole lot of wisdom from the ups and downs I faced in the Hollywood spotlight—wisdom that God is now using to help others. People know there's something different about me on the set. When you become a Christian, you are quite a bit more aware of other people's needs and their difficulties. Your job, no matter what it is, becomes your mission field. It becomes your pulpit. Wherever you are, you're a representative of Christ. And now I'm playing fathers all the time, which is really fantastic. I think that's largely because of the combination of respect, purpose, and discipline I get when I read the Bible. I try and use our heavenly Father's example when I play these characters.

You could say I've been transformed, but words are so tricky. It's not so much how He can transform you; it's why. Why bother? "For God so loved the world that He gave His only begotten Son (John 3:16)...okay...why? Is it because I'm really great? No, I don't think so. Is it because I'm really special? No, I don't think so. Is it because I'm really valuable to the Kingdom? Yeah, I think so! My transformation wasn't about me. It wasn't for me. It happened so that through me, God could impact His Kingdom.

God expects something out of you. In fact, God is like the dad out in the backyard doing chores. When the kids finally wake up on Saturday morning, the dad thinks, *I'm so glad you woke up because I've got all this stuff to do. Come on, let's go!* And the kids whine. That's what we do when God has work for us. But we all have a part to play. And it's time we learned our lines.

GOD'S ROAD MAP

The Holy Bible is a guide to help you live a happy and satisfying life. To learn more about the concepts presented in the chapter you've just read, take a look at these passages:

PURPOSE

We are all searching for our purpose in life. When we finally understand that our true purpose is to live for God and introduce others to Him, everything else becomes much simpler.

Romans 8:29 (NLT)

For God knew his people in advance, and he chose them to become like his Son, so that his Son would be the firstborn, with many brothers and sisters.

Second Thessalonians 1:11-12

With this in mind, we constantly pray for you, that our God may count you worthy of His calling, and that by His power He may fulfill every good purpose of yours and every act prompted by your faith. We pray this so that the name of our Lord Jesus may be glorified in you, and you in Him, according to the grace of our God and the Lord Jesus Christ

FRUSTRATION

Being a Christian doesn't mean we won't have bad days. Modern life can be very frustrating, from the taxes we pay to the traffic on the freeway. But remember, frustrations are temporary and can be overcome; we just need patience and perseverance. Jesus had one of the worst days in history, but He rose again to sit at the right hand of God.

James 4:1-3

What causes fights and quarrels among you? Don't they come from your desires that battle within you? You want something but don't get it. You kill and covet, but you cannot have what you want. You quarrel and fight. You do not have, because you do not ask God. When you ask, you do not receive, because you ask with wrong motives, that you may spend what you get on your pleasures.

Isaiah 53:7-9

He was oppressed and afflicted, yet He did not open His mouth; He was led like a lamb to the slaughter, and as a sheep before her shearers is silent, so He did not open His mouth. By oppression and judgment He was taken away. And who can speak of His descendants? For He was cut off from the land of the living; for the transgression of my people He was stricken. He was assigned a grave with the wicked, and with the rich in His death, though He had done no violence, nor was any deceit in His mouth.

Ricky Skaggs

Grammy Award-Winning Country
and Bluegrass Musician
(Photo credit: Erick Anderson/eafoto.com)

Ricky Skaggs has been called "the man who put bluegrass back on the map." This highly accomplished singer/instrumentalist first appeared onstage with the legendary Bill Monroe when he was only five years old. During the early years of his career, he worked with bluegrass pioneer Ralph Stanley and J.D. Crowe & The New South.

In the late 1970s, Skaggs turned his attention to more mainstream country music, first as a member of Emmylou Harris' Hot Band and later as a solo recording artist. As a country artist, he recorded 14 albums and had 12 #1 singles including five in a row: "Crying My Heart Out Over You," "I Don't Care," "Heartbroke," "I Wouldn't Change You If I Could," and "Highway 40 Blues."

Skaggs made a huge decision in 1997 to go back to his musical roots—bluegrass music, and established his own record label—Skaggs Family Records. Since then, he has recorded seven bluegrass albums of his own and nurtured the careers of numerous other artists, including the Del McCoury Band, Mountain Heart, Jerry and Tammy Sullivan, Melonie Cannon, Ryan Holladay, and family band Cherryholmes.

All told, Skaggs has ten Grammy Awards, a Dove Award, eight Country Music Association (CMA) Awards including Entertainer of the Year in 1985, eight Academy of Country Music (ACM) Awards, eight TNN Music City News Awards, and nine International Bluegrass Music Association (IBMA) awards. In 2003, he was included on CMT's list of the "40 Greatest Men of Country Music." That's a lot of trophies to put on your shelf. But Skaggs knows that his true treasures lie in Heaven. For more information, go to: www.skaggsfamilyrecords.com.

✦·⫶·┃⫶┃⫶┃·⫶·✦

I've been singing in church since I was three or four years old. My mom would hold me up in her arms in front of the congregation, and I would sing harmony with her and my dad. Harmony—it's amazing to think about it! But what's even more amazing, is that after the services, these old preachers would come and pray and speak the word of God over me. They'd say things like, "God is going to use you in your life. He's going to use your music. He's going to use your talent and your gift to bring people to the Kingdom." Being a little kid, my mind did not comprehend that. But my spirit was saying, "Yeah and amen" to every one of those words. It's a wonder to see how that prophecy has come true.

The Baptist church I grew up in was very charismatic. When the church service would start, everybody would get out of their pews and come up front to gather around the altar. They'd find a spot wherever they could and get down on their knees or prostrate on their faces to pray. It was real fire-and-brimstone, hell-and-damnation, wrath-of-God kind of preaching. You know, it scared me to death. Ours was a freewill Baptist church; we called it "foot-washing Baptist." It was so powerful to see old men wash the feet of young men or young men wash the feet of their fathers. It was humbling.

My mother was a real prayer warrior. I had an experience as a tiny boy that has impacted my Christian faith ever since. One day, I came inside from playing and was looking for my mom but couldn't find her. Finally, I went to my parents' bedroom. The door was open a crack, and I peeked in and saw my mother down on her knees, praying. She had this beautiful glory on her face; it was lit up with the most beautiful light…like a ray of sunshine from Heaven. And the tears were running down her cheeks, but they weren't ordinary tears. They were like gold—golden drops. The sight of her stunned me. I knew I was in the presence of God.

She was praying for my dad, and my brother, and my sister. And then I heard her call out my name in prayer. She was asking the Lord to keep His hand on my life and that some day, when I reached accountability, that I would know Him. It was a powerful thing. I knew Christ was real when I saw God on my mother's face.

My dad was a welder and worked away from home most of the time. He'd come home on Friday night and then spend Saturday at home with us. Then he'd have to get up at 3:00 or 4:00 on Sunday morning and start driving to his jobsite. He'd drive all the way from Kentucky to Detroit or Chicago on two-lane roads. That was long before we had interstates. It was an eight to ten-hour drive just to get back to wherever he was working—jobs were hard to find in those days.

I think he'd been saved as a young man, and I know that he and mom went to church when they first got married. But because of his work schedule, he didn't often have the opportunity to go to services. One night, when I was about 13 years old, I was at a revival with my family in this little town real close to where we lived. I saw my dad go forward and rededicate his life to the Lord.

Now, the Lord had been dealing with me already. I'd been "white knuckling" on the pews every night during the altar call. I knew that I needed to go and give my heart to the Lord too, and I really felt the Holy Spirit drawing me to make a decision. But being just 13, I thought, *What could I have done so bad that I really needed this?*

After I saw my dad go forward that night, I realized if it was that important for him to take that walk and make a commitment publicly to everyone in the community, then it was important enough to me.

The next night our family was singing at the service. Every time I sang those songs about the Lord, my heart would be warm and full. And my spirit would just burn inside—I was so under conviction. That night I went forward and gave my heart to the Lord and just cried at the altar like I'd murdered someone.

I came back home and a friend asked me, "How do you feel now?" It was all so new and different. I'd never really studied the Bible, so I didn't know how I was supposed to feel. Was I supposed to feel like a new person? Was I supposed to never think a bad thought again? "You must not have got saved then, if you don't know how you feel," he said. That statement sowed a little seed of doubt into my heart. And my heart was so tender at the time, so freshly plowed by the Lord. That seed came in, took root, and started to grow. I agreed that I probably hadn't been saved at all.

When I was 15, I started working for bluegrass pioneer, Ralph Stanley in his group, Ralph Stanley and the Clinch Mountain Boys. I was young to be traveling with a bunch of old men who were drinking. I'm amazed that my mother and dad even let me go with them. But they were good to me and watched over me.

I drank some, but realized that wasn't what I wanted to do—mostly because of my mother. It was like she would read my mail—not literally, but she could read my "spiritual mail." She would tell me that she saw me in a dream, and I was doing something I shouldn't have been doing. I knew that whatever I did the Lord was going to reveal to my mother. Oh man, did that keep me on the straight and narrow! My mother was a faithful prayer warrior for me, and in the end, the Lord made sure her prayers got answered.

For a good while, probably until I was 18 or 19 years old, I lived with a whole lot of doubt in my heart. I was a good kid; I just wasn't sure of my salvation. I felt like if I died I would be lost. Two of my close friends, Sharon and Cheryl White, started talking to me about the joy they had in the Lord. And I saw the joy they had. Cheryl bought me a new Bible, the NIV version. What it did for me was take the King's English, more like what Jesus spoke, and turn it in into a language that I could really understand. I started reading the Word and eating it up. Once I got the Word in me, I realized that the devil had been a liar all those years. I had made a commitment to Christ, and He had not forgotten that. I rededicated my life to the Lord and was baptized. After that, I started to fall in love with the Lord and had a romance with Him for the first time ever.

You see, I realized He wasn't mad at me. I thought He was, because I had made a commitment and turned my back on it somehow. I thought I did it wrong when He did everything right. Finally, I understood that it's not about what we do. It's about His grace and sacrifice. Jesus loved me.

In my mid-20s the Lord started opening doors for me in Nashville with country music, and it's been a whirlwind ever since. The life I live now, I live by the Son of God. Not one of us can live the Christian life without Christ in us. Christ in us is the hope of glory. Like Paul said, I was buried and raised to newness of life because of His resurrection. You can't kill a dead man; I'm already dead. So it's Christ who is living in me. None of us can live a perfect, sin-free life. But when you become a Christian, you are just not a slave to sin anymore. As long as the devil rules the darkness of this world, we'll still slip and fall.

Prayer is a powerful thing. I've seen what it can do year after year. I saw my parents and others praying earnestly for one particular man—a wife-beating alcoholic, who lived on our creek. And I saw that same man walk down the aisle and give his heart to Jesus. I knew God was real when I saw his life change.

Prayer has also impacted my own family. When our son, Andrew, was seven, my wife was driving with him on Interstate 81. There was a truck on the road ahead of them and she drove around it. As they passed alongside, the truck driver fired his gun down into the car and hit my son in the mouth. It was a terrible thing. But our prayers for him were answered; I saw the Lord save him from certain death. I knew the Lord was real.

Then when Andrew was 15, he had a series of dreams about a big, muscular black man. In the dream, this man would just stand there with his hands closed and watch everything that my son was doing. One day Andrew said, "Dad, this is a freaky dream. What do you think it means?" I said, "Well, I really think that the angel that the Lord has in your life is a black man."

A short time later, Andrew was involved in a really, really bad car wreck. He lost his gall bladder and spleen as a result and was lucky to have survived. About a year later, I met the paramedic that was at the scene, and what he said was unbelievable. He told me that the outcome of the wreck would have been very different "if those two guys hadn't shown up." But there were no "two guys" in the police report. "Well, I never got their names," he said. "I didn't say anything about it because they showed up and then just disappeared." I had to ask him a question, "Was one of the guys a black man?" "Yeah—a huge, big old black guy. They grabbed that door and both of them— they just pulled it open and got those kids out. And when I turned around to thank them, they were gone." So I know God is real. He sent that angel to take care of my son.

My son has been close to death's door three times. First, there was the drive-by shooting, then the car wreck, and then five years later I got a phone call. "Mr. Skaggs, you need to get here. We just don't think your son is going to live through the night." He had double pneumonia and was very sick. But I knew the power of God and that our son would live. Through our prayers, and the prayers of so many others, our son's life was spared again.

So I know God is real. He's real in my life and he's real in my children's lives. There is a joy now in my heart that has never been there before— the most unspeakable joy. Most people become Christians so they won't go to hell. That's a great thing, but Christ died for us to be so much more than that. Christianity is not like a suit of clothes that you hang in your closet all week and then put on every Sunday morning. If you're not having church in your heart the other six days, one day isn't going to help you a whole lot.

Even if I'm wrong about this thing—if I'm wrong about Jesus and about God creating the heavens and the earth, when I get to the end of my life, I've lost nothing. I've lost nothing because I've tried to live a good, honest life and do good by others. But if it's all true, then I've gained everything. And those who don't believe will have lost it all.

GOD'S ROAD MAP

The Holy Bible is a guide to help you live a happy and satisfying life. To learn more about the concepts presented in the chapter you've just read, take a look at these passages:

PRAYER

Simply defined, prayer is communication with God. The conversation needs to be real, not just trite repetition of memorized phrases. The most fundamental part of the Christian faith is that we can approach God directly. There's no need for intercessors like saints or priests to do it for us. The hardest part of prayer is remembering that it is two-way communication. So learn to be quiet and listen to what He has to say to you.

James 5:16

Therefore confess your sins to each other and pray for each other so that you may be healed. The prayer of a righteous man is powerful and effective.

First John 5:14

This is the confidence we have in approaching God: that if we ask anything according to His will, He hears us.

Second Chronicles 7:14

If My people, who are called by My name, will humble themselves and pray and seek My face and turn from their wicked ways, then will I hear from heaven and will forgive their sin and will heal their land.

Hebrews 4:16

Let us then approach the throne of grace with confidence, so that we may receive mercy and find grace to help us in our time of need.

Colossians 1:9-14

For this reason, since the day we heard about you, we have not stopped praying for you and asking God to fill you with the knowledge of His will through all spiritual wisdom and understanding. And we pray this in order that you may live a life worthy of the Lord and may please Him in every way: bearing fruit in every good work, growing in the knowledge of God, being strengthened with all power according to His glorious might so that you may have great endurance and patience, and joyfully giving thanks to the Father, who has qualified you to share in the inheritance of the saints in the kingdom of light. For He has rescued us from the dominion of darkness and brought us into the kingdom of the Son He loves, in whom we have redemption, the forgiveness of sins.

Charlotte
Smith-Taylor

WNBA Forward, Washington Mystics
(Photo, courtesy of Mitchell Layton)

Charlotte Smith-Taylor has had a lifelong passion for basketball. She was on the starting lineup all four years at her high school in Shelby, North Carolina, earning MVP four times and helping the team win two conference championships. Following graduation, this 6' forward was awarded a full scholarship to the University of North Carolina at Chapel Hill. Smith-Taylor, the most decorated player in the history of the University of North Carolina's basketball program, is the only UNC women's basketball player to have her jersey retired. She had a stellar career as a Tar Heel, culminating with a national championship win in 1994—and she was named the NCAA Final Four Most Outstanding player for her efforts. Not to be outdone by the men, Smith-Taylor became the second collegiate woman player to dunk in a game.

After graduating with a degree in Sociology, Smith-Taylor had a stint playing in an Italian league where she was once again named MVP. She was drafted by the American Basketball League's (ABL) Colorado Explosion where she spent just a year.

She also had a stint playing for San Jose. Upon formation of the WNBA, Smith-Taylor was drafted by the Charlotte Sting where she has played for six years. Her 2004 season was spectacular as she led the entire league in 3-point field-goal percentage. On July 15, 2004 Charlotte Smith-Taylor recorded her 1,000 career point.

✦·⁂·✦

Some say I hit the most famous shot in women's basketball. It was in 1994 when the University of North Carolina Tar Heels trailed Louisiana Tech 59-57 with less than a second remaining in the NCAA national championship. I remember looking at the clock thinking that with only .7 seconds on the clock, there was no way we could do anything to win this. I thought about all of the hard work we had invested in the season; it felt like it was all in vain. We'd gotten this far and now we were going to lose. In our huddle the coach said, "We're going to win this game; we're going for the win, not the tie." That meant we were going for a three-point shot instead of a two. I was wondering who was going to take the shot. She chose me, even though I was shooting only 25 percent from the 3-point line. There were players on the team who were much, much better choices than I was. It had to be divine intervention because anybody who was thinking strategically would have put their best shooter out there to take the 3. I thought she was crazy.

"God, please let me hit this shot. Please let me hit this shot." I said it over and over in my mind. I remember it so vividly. I released the shot with only about a tenth of a second on the clock, and it went in! I just immediately threw up my hands thanking God. I was in my own little world thanking and praising God while everybody else was jumping up and down in celebration. But I was just praising God.

That was the highlight of my basketball career. I mean, every player dreams of winning a national championship—that's the ultimate goal. It was like reliving my childhood. I used to be in my backyard doing the countdown, pretending to hit the game-winning shot and win the championship. Now I had done it!

I was raised in a house full of love. We didn't have a lot of material things, but I absolutely would not trade my childhood lifestyle for anything in this world. Growing up in a house of love, morals, and values is just priceless.

I started playing basketball with all the boys when I was seven years old—I was the only girl. We went to my grandmother's house and played in her backyard on a dirt basketball court. I really enjoyed the competition because a lot of the guys thought they were better just because they were boys. I was always out to prove them wrong! Basketball was the primary sport in my family so I had a real passion for the game. My uncle, Hall of Fame Inductee David Thompson, may have had something to do with that. Even though I was very young, I remember sitting around my grandmother's house watching him play professional basketball on television. He was amazing.

Basketball was my sport all through middle school and high school, and I was fortunate enough to get a full scholarship to the University of North Carolina-Chapel Hill. After I graduated, I went to a training camp to try out for the American Basketball League (ABL). I was drafted by the Colorado Explosion.

The first year I played in Colorado my family traveled out with me from North Carolina to help me get settled in. It turned out to be the worst year of my life. My mom passed away when she was out there with me. It was a total surprise; she developed double pneumonia, and we lost her. I went through a lot of guilt because the only reason she was out there was because of me. If I'd only flown to Colorado rather than having my family drive out there, she would have been fine. She didn't start having chest pains or trouble breathing until she came to Colorado. I thought maybe it was the altitude. I was really blaming myself; the guilt was incredible. Of course, now I can look at things differently.

The season started out really slow for me because of the difficult grieving process involved in losing my mother. But in the end, the season wound up being a good one for me. I had great numbers and our team won the western conference championship. It was just an awesome season. But despite all that success, I was traded. I felt so betrayed—to be traded after all I'd been through was just devastating.

I've been a Christian most of my life. A lot of times we don't understand why we go through different circumstances and different adversities, but I try not to get caught up in the "why." Instead, I focus on how the Lord is going to get me through it. In our walk we all stumble and fall; we can't do this on our own strength.

One of the ways I know God is real has been receiving the gift of the Holy Spirit, the gift of speaking in tongues. It's just an awesome thing. I remember times just being afraid of it and not really understanding it, but it's such an awesome gift to be able to speak in the heavenly language. It's only a conversation between you and God; it gives you a great sense of peace. When you are finished speaking with Him, you feel so full, so complete.

Another reason I know God is real is my WNBA career. I think when people look at my professional career and compare it to what I accomplished at the collegiate level, they probably think that I somehow lost it— that I'm not the player I used to be. But you see, when we don't know Christ we all have an identity crisis. I thank God for the position I've been in over the last six years because He's revealed so much to me. Basketball is not my identity, and it's not my foundation. God is my foundation. I just continue to trust in God and let Him lead and guide me and try not to make decisions based on what I should be accomplishing on the court. For the longest time I struggled with that. I felt like I had gotten lost, and I felt like being a starter on the team was my identity— I didn't have true worth if I wasn't a starter. Or I didn't have true worth if I wasn't an all-star. You can get lost in that. In 2003 I didn't play a whole lot. I was a cheerleader and that was the first time since I started playing competitive basketball that I was a cheerleader. It challenged my pride, and it challenged my faith; but in the process I grew. At the end of the day basketball is just a platform to share the Gospel. I am so thankful for the times of being in the valley because they helped me to realize that God is my foundation and my identity is through Him. The year 2004 was an incredible year for me professionally, maybe the best I've ever had, but I'll never forget the lessons I learned the year before.

For me, playing basketball is a great opportunity to share the Gospel. I'm able to help so many of my teammates through different life journeys, different trials, adversities, and circumstances by sharing some of the things that God has helped me overcome. He has shown Himself so powerfully during the death of my mom and broken relationships. It makes me think back to this song. The lyrics say:

> If I'd never had a rainy day,
> I'd never know you could brighten my way.
>
> If I'd never had to shed a tear,
> I'd never know you were always near.
>
> If I'd never felt loneliness,
> I'd never know of your friendliness.

Well, I know He is always nearby to brighten my way, no matter which direction the path might lead me. And I will follow His lead on the court and off.

GOD'S ROAD MAP

The Holy Bible is a guide to help you live a happy and satisfying life. To learn more about the concepts presented in the chapter you've just read, take a look at these passages:

THANKFULNESS

God does things for us all the time—some big and some small. How often do we remember to say "thank you"? It seems like the majority of our prayer life is more about asking for things. Thanksgiving is more than an American holiday; it's something we should partake in every day of the year.

First Chronicles 16:34

Give thanks to the Lord, for He is good; His love endures forever.

First Thessalonians 5:18

Give thanks in all circumstances, for this is God's will for you in Christ Jesus.

Psalm 100:4

Enter His gates with thanksgiving and His courts with praise; give thanks to Him and praise His name.

GRIEF

The loss of a loved one is probably the most painful thing in life. It has the potential to rob us of our joy for years to come. But through a relationship with Jesus Christ, we have victory over death and need not fear it.

Psalm 23

The Lord is my shepherd, I shall not be in want. He makes me lie down in green pastures, He leads me beside quiet waters, He restores my soul. He guides me in paths of righteousness for His name's sake. Even though I walk through the valley of the shadow of death, I will fear no evil, for You are with me; Your rod and Your staff, they comfort me.

You prepare a table before me in the presence of my enemies. You anoint my head with oil; my cup overflows. Surely goodness and love will follow me all the days of my life, and I will dwell in the house of the Lord forever.

Revelation 21:4

He will wipe every tear from their eyes. There will be no more death or mourning or crying or pain, for the old order of things has passed away.

Isaiah 66:13a

As a mother comforts her child, so will I comfort you.

Nancy Stafford

Actress, TV Series "Matlock" and
"St. Elsewhere"
(Photo credit: Russell Baer)

Nancy Stafford has been a familiar face around Hollywood for more than 20 years. Her reign as Miss Florida led to a highly successful modeling career with the Ford Agency. She has appeared in over 250 commercials.

Perhaps best known for her five-year role as Andy Griffith's law partner in the ABC TV series, "Matlock," Stafford's career resume also includes three years on the Emmy Award-winning series, "St. Elsewhere," the ABC series, "Sidekicks" and as a regular on the daytime drama, "The Doctors." Stafford has made appearances on dozens of programs, including "Judging Amy," "ER," "Frasier," "Quantum Leap," "Scarecrow and Mrs. King," "Magnum P.I.," "Hunter," "Remington Steele," and "Riptide."

For the past ten years, Stafford has been the host of "Main Floor," a nationally syndicated series on fashion, beauty, and lifestyle trends that airs in more than 40 countries around the world.

In addition to her impressive acting accomplishments, Stafford has also authored two books. Her first, *Beauty by the Book: Seeing Yourself as God Sees You* is in its seventh printing.

Her latest book, *The Wonder of His Love: a Journey into the Heart of God* was released in 2004.

Stafford is a popular speaker and travels extensively throughout the country sharing with students, churches, women's events, corporations, and other organizations. Together with her husband, Larry Myers, worship musician and pastor at Malibu Vineyard Christian Fellowship, they have created Rancho Monte Nido, a serene and private place for others to come for retreat and to experience God's healing and restoration. To find out more, go to www.nancystafford.com.

✦┽┠╂╂┨┾✦

When I was in first grade, I was painfully shy and terribly insecure, so Mom enrolled me in a ballet class. I loved it! This was where I could shine! I would rush into class every Saturday and dance with abandon—twirling, spinning, and leaping on my spindly legs, feeling absolutely beautiful and totally confident in my little pink tutu.

The mothers would gather in the back of the class to pick up their ballerinas, and one Saturday I glanced back and saw that they were all looking at me. *They must like my dancing!* I thought. Then I overheard the teacher say, "Oh yes, the girls are all doing so beautifully...except for that little Stafford girl. She's the clumsiest, most awkward child I've ever seen." They all laughed uproariously. I was stunned. Mortified. Tears burned in my eyes, and I buried my face in my tutu and ran across the room to bury myself in my mom's big, soft, pillowy chest. I think that was the day I realized that what I had suspected about myself was true—I wasn't worth much. I wasn't valuable. And I was ugly.

No matter what my dear family said or did to try to convince me otherwise, I didn't believe them. They were my family; they had to say that. But that big world out there told me something else, and I believed it instead. That day a lie lodged in my six-year-old heart: *"You're ugly. You're clumsy. We don't want you."* And that day I put up my first wall of protection. Through the years other walls followed, all to help ward off the pain, loneliness, and rejection of being different from others, not accepted, and not really understood.

I was raised in a church-going family in a wonderful community just outside of Fort Lauderdale, Florida. I loved going to church as a kid; it was a great place for me. I entered into a true relationship with the Lord at a very early age.

My mom and dad were remarkable parents; I've had nothing but love and acceptance from them my whole life. My dad was the most incredible, strong, and productive man I've ever known. Despite his disability (he was crippled from polio as a child), he built our house himself from the ground up. He was a quiet man with tremendous integrity.

My mom knew her little girl struggled with being shy and feeling insecure, so she did all she could to affirm me. All my life, she told me how beautiful I was, especially on the inside where it really counts.

My parents did all they could, but no matter how reassuring they were, I still had this deep-seated feeling of inferiority. As I grew into my teen years, I felt unattractive, gawky, and gangly, and I still wore bottle-thick glasses. I didn't fit in most circles. I was shy, unpopular, and didn't drink or go to parties. My nickname throughout high school was "Super Virgin." To many, I was a geek and a total dork.

I had two equally dorky friends; together we were dubbed the "tragic trio." All three of us applied to be in the very worst club in school—the absolutely lowest rung on the school's social ladder. Only a handful of people belonged to it, so we figured we had a shot.

On "rush" day, I got all dressed up, sat down by the dining room window, and waited for the honking horns that would indicate that this new inductee was in the club. Finally, I heard those horns signaling their arrival. I was excited to watch as they picked up my friend next door and my friend across the street. And then they drove away. I had been rejected.

As I entered my later years of high school, I found myself disappointed with many other Christians. I was disillusioned, and because of my immaturity, I didn't know how to talk with anyone about it. I expected everybody in church to act just like God. But of course, we don't; we're all just broken people who are saved by grace. But I didn't understand that then. I didn't understand that because Christ extends grace to us, we in turn need to extend it to each other. I judged God based on the failings of His people.

Two days after graduating from high school, I enrolled at the University of Florida. College was a whole new experience for me. Suddenly, I was 500 miles away from home and didn't have the same baggage I'd had growing up as that buck-toothed girl everybody laughed at. My braces came off and I got contact lenses. I was no longer geeky.

I had a fresh start with a new persona...and I blossomed. I very much liked the way I was perceived in this new environment; I was immediately embraced by other women, and the guys really liked me too. It was a whole new ballgame.

My faith took a backseat to my social life at the University. I didn't intentionally walk away from God, but I didn't stay in any sort of fellowship with other Christians either. Little by little, a different value system began to influence my lifestyle. I started acting more like the world and making compromises. Instead of being the pure girl I'd been growing up, I started living like the other girls of the world—partying and getting involved romantically with guys. I didn't set foot inside another church for 15 years.

Mine wasn't a fast rebellion. It's kind of like that analogy you've heard about the frog in a pot of water. If you put a frog in a pot of boiling water, it jumps out to save itself. But if you put the frog in a cool pot of water and slowly increase the temperature until it boils, the frog is cooked to death. Similarly, I gradually allowed myself to get immersed in a lifestyle I had never led before.

Though it may have looked like I was the most secure, together person, I was just camouflaging, hiding behind a mask that looked like I had it all together. Inside, I still felt inadequate and insecure. Some of those insecurities and the need for approval drove me to make some regrettable romantic decisions. I didn't date a lot of people at once, but I went from boyfriend to boyfriend. I'd date someone, but then I'd start to tire of him and would start looking around for his replacement. I'd have somebody else on the sidelines long before I got rid of the other guy. It's not something I'm proud of—but it was born out of my fear and insecurity.

Oftentimes when I was walking across campus, a photographer from the school newspaper would smile and snap my picture in a fun sort of way. One day, after a few weeks of that, I bumped into him again and he called me over. He had this big envelope full of photos of me. And they were good! He suggested I consider modeling, and soon I was doing ads for a couple of the stores that advertised in the paper. Then I was sent over to a big department store in the area, and did some ads and runway work for them.

I ended up graduating from college in only three years with a degree in journalism and public relations. After that, my plan was to go home, take a few months off, and head back to graduate school for my MBA in the fall. My folks had really sacrificed to put my brother through law school. I didn't want them to be saddled with another college bill, so I needed a scholarship.

Our next-door neighbor suggested I enter a scholarship contest—Miss Fort Lauderdale. I went to the informational meeting, and when the director brought up the swimsuit competition, I shot my hand up in the air and said, "Wait a minute. What are we doing?" He said, "Well, there's the talent part of the competition and that's 50 percent of your points. The interview is worth 25 percent, and the swimsuit competition is the other 25 percent." After the meeting, I pulled him aside and told him that it really wasn't for me. But he looked me in the eye and said, "Please don't go. I really think you'll do well."

I entered and dropped out of that pageant three times before finally making a commitment. Imagine my surprise, then, when I won and became Miss Fort Lauderdale! It never occurred to me that I might win. After all, this was my first real pageant, and most of the girls had competed many times before. I was just in it for the $500 scholarship, which would be enough money to buy my books. In my naiveté, I didn't realize that this was part of the Miss America system and that I would next go on to the Miss Florida pageant.

Only God could have orchestrated this whole experience. Never in my wildest dreams would I have ever pursued a beauty pageant. First of all, I didn't have the confidence; it wasn't something I could have ever imagined being possible. Nor was I frankly interested. I'd never been a pageant kind of girl. I would be competing with girls who had made careers out of these types of competitions. But it grew obvious that God really wanted me to do this.

Right after I was crowned Miss Fort Lauderdale, I became very ill with some sort of bronchial ailment. Before I knew it, I developed walking pneumonia and had a collapsed left lung. The doctors had to do a procedure where they punctured my chest and inflated my lung with a large hypodermic. By the time I'd recovered, I only had three weeks to prepare for the Miss Florida competition—precious little time to get it all together. I had to buy a dress, and learn how to apply real makeup, instead of the drugstore variety. Then I had to select a new piano piece that would be performed with full orchestration. I was at a whole new level.

I was totally shocked when I won the pageant and was given the title of Miss Florida. I had a really lousy attitude at first. I didn't want to spend the next eight to nine months playing pageant girl, doing ribbon cuttings, and kissing babies. But when I finally changed my attitude, I realized this was the best public relations job I could have asked for. I determined I was going to be the best Miss Florida they had ever seen and I had a blast!

After my reign, I settled down in a public relations job at a tennis and yacht club in Fort Lauderdale. Out of the blue one day, I got a phone call from an agent in Miami. The Screen Actor's Guild was on strike, so no professional actors could work. She explained to me that all the ad agencies had commercials to shoot and were looking for non-union talent. Would I come and audition?

I took a day off and headed down to Miami. After the first audition, she told me I was really good and asked me if I would stay and read for another client. In the course of one week I had five auditions and booked them all. My head was spinning!

I worked in the Miami market for about a year and then I became interested in pursuing an acting career. I headed up to New York City to attend the Stella Adler acting conservatory. I didn't go there to work—I went to study. That all changed one day when I got a phone call from Eileen Ford from Ford Models. "I've got these ad agencies and photographers calling me looking for you...who are you?" she said. I went to see

Eileen and when we met she very graciously said, "You're really old, but you're gonna make me a lot of money...I'll sign you." I was 24.

About six months later, a booker at the agency called to tell me that they had an audition coming up for a soap opera. Evidently, I was their only model with acting experience, so they were wondering if I was interested. It was strange; normally an audition like this would go through a theatrical agency, not a modeling agency, and I hadn't yet developed a relationship with a theatrical agent. So I was excited for this opportunity. It was a six-week recurring role on "One Life to Live," and I got it. It was my very first audition! Looking back, I can once again see God's plan in action.

A few weeks after that job ended, I auditioned for a soap on NBC called "The Doctors." I got the part and was on that show for about a year until it was cancelled. I was flown out to Los Angeles to screen test for a new show. There seemed to be a lot of interest in me in LA, so I moved to California.

Then I had a crisis. There was a spot on my cheek that had gotten progressively worse and worse over the years. I'd gone to a top dermatologist, but he said it was nothing to worry about. It was getting harder and harder to cover up with makeup, and it was starting to be painful...I was getting really scared. So I went to a dermatologist in Los Angeles, and he took one look at me and said, "Tomorrow you're in surgery. It's a very deep, very severe skin cancer. It's gone long undiagnosed, and I don't know what I'm going to find." Then he took my hand, looked me in the eye, and said, "You have to hear me carefully now. I cannot promise what you are going to look like after this surgery. If I were you, I'd have another career in mind."

As it turned out, they got all of the cancer without severing muscle or nerve, which is what he'd been so afraid of. He thought I'd be disfigured. This experience deeply affected me in several ways. I was devastated that my whole world, my career might come to an end. But even more importantly, I was horrified at how important my face and my body had become to me—how much of my identity and my value I'd placed on my looks. The irony didn't escape me. The very source of all my rejection and ridicule as a child—my physical appearance—had now become the source of my identity...and my income. It was a huge reality check, and I was very humbled and ashamed of how far I had strayed from any kind of spiritual core. I could still hear my mom say, "Nancy, you're beautiful on the inside, honey; that's what's important." How could I have forgotten that? I didn't feel very beautiful on the inside.

I decided to get my priorities straight. I needed something that was substantial and real; I needed a spiritual foundation again. But I didn't go right back to Christianity. I picked up a Bible and started reading it. And then I picked up a book by Edgar Cayce, and it started making sense to me. It was using enough Christian terminology and referring often enough to Jesus and the Spirit that I thought I was reading a Christian book. But I wasn't. It was grounded in new age and Eastern philosophies.

From there I studied Buddhism, Hinduism, the Bhagavad Gita, A Course in Miracles, and metaphysics—the whole new age gamut. I stayed on this spiritual quest for several years. I kept reading my Bible this whole time and mixed that in with these other religions. I figured I could make my own image of God and follow a "spirituality" that wasn't going to challenge my lifestyle.

My acting career was really starting to take off. My first audition after the surgery was for an NBC series called "St. Elsewhere," and I did that for three years. I also guest-starred on loads of different shows, including "Riptide," "Remington Steele," "Who's the Boss?" and "Hunter." The whole time I was on this eclectic spiritual search, God didn't pull the carpet out from under me when He easily could have. Instead, He continued to bless my career even though I was stumbling in the dark.

Still searching, I ordered a spiritual book that I had seen advertised on television. On my way to Hawaii to shoot an episode of "Magnum P.I.," I dropped by my mailbox and threw all of my mail into my backpack to read during the trip. When I got to Honolulu, I found out that somebody from the production team had made a big mistake and brought me in three days early. Normally, I would have loved a few days lying on the beach in Hawaii, but since I'd had skin cancer I could no longer spend time in the sun.

So I settled down in my hotel room. When I looked in my backpack, I found the book *Power for Living*, and started reading it. God had made an appointment with me...for three days I never left my room. The people in this book shared their stories and described what I was desperately searching for—a relationship with the living God. As I read it, the pain I had been covering up for so long came pouring out. I had a supernatural encounter with God.

In my own search for Him—all the miscellaneous religions—I had come up empty. It was almost too much for me to bear. It broke my heart. I didn't know what the truth was, so I felt confused. I cried out, "God, who are You? I thought I was on the right track to find You. I don't even know who You are or who I am anymore. Please, You've got to show me, You've got to help me...You've got to rescue me!"

Suddenly, I began to see my life as it really was, instead of the way everybody else saw it. At the time, I was one of the hottest actresses in town, but it was all a sham. Inside I still felt unloved, inadequate, and frightened; and I was doing anything and everything I could to fill the hole inside of me. The renowned mathematician and Christian philosopher, Blaise Pascal, once said that we have a God-sized, God-shaped hole in all of us. I was trying to fill that hole with things like money, men, houses, cars, success, and notoriety. But finally, I began to realize that those things weren't satisfying me at all. God showed me the stark reality of my life and the consequences of my sin.

I'd been avoiding God for years. I thought He would come and say something like, "See, this is why you need Me. Look at the mess you've made of things." But that wasn't it! Instead, what I sensed was His warm, loving embrace. It reminded me of when I was a little girl, singing hymns in my Baptist church. I cried when I sang those songs because I loved His presence. I was in awe as He showered me with His tender mercies and gracious presence once again.

God's love and affirmation felt like a warm blanket that melted my cold, cold heart. I let down the wall and took off my mask long enough to receive His love. I felt like a little two year old scrambling up on my daddy's lap, and let Him hold me, kiss me, and heal my brokenness. Amazingly, He wasn't there to judge and He didn't want me to clean myself up first and then come to Him. He wanted me to come just as I was. It was going to be His job to clean me up.

During those three days, He showed me three things. First, He showed me who He is—not a judgmental or harsh cosmic God who is distant and uninvolved. He is a loving, Abba Daddy who is intimate with us and wants to heal and touch us.

Secondly, He showed me who I was—that I was not unworthy and inadequate. I was His own precious daughter that He'd called by name and chosen as His own. He was going to change me into the woman He designed me to be.

And then the most powerful of all, God showed me who His Son is. Jesus isn't just a great prophet or a role model. He is the living God and He bought me with a price—His death on the cross at Calvary. Jesus is the way, the truth, and the life.

For three days, I lay with my face down on the floor of my hotel room sobbing, first in grief and repentance, and then in absolute joy and gratitude. The Lord filled me with incredible peace, and I felt sweetly whole, utterly safe and secure...and completely accepted. He began to fill my hungry heart.

I did the shoot and returned to LA with a new resolve. I prayed for two things: The first was a godly husband. The second thing I prayed for was work I could be proud of and that would honor God. And God answered those prayers.

I met my future husband at a gym. We soon discovered that we were both believers. In fact, he was a pastor! I started visiting his church and fell in love with it as I was falling in love with him. We've been happily married now for 17 years.

God also answered my prayer about finding work I could be proud of. Six weeks after I got back from Hawaii, I got a part on the ABC TV series called "Sidekicks," which was a really wholesome family show. I did that for a year until the show was cancelled. Right after that, I got a part on "Matlock" and appeared on that show with Andy Griffith for five years. Several TV movies followed, and I've hosted "Main Floor" for ten years now.

My love for the Lord has continued to grow day by day, and He continues to mold me. Our culture bombards us, particularly women, with images of physical beauty. But our true worth, value, and identity come not from what the world says, but from complete acceptance by God. In and of ourselves, we'll never be enough; we'll wear ourselves out trying. In God's eyes, once we receive His Son, *He* becomes our acceptance, identity, and security.

How do I know He's real? Because God visits us and manifests Himself to us in ways we can grasp. For those who are intellectual, He is a God of reason. For those who need His healing touch like I did, He encounters us with His tenderness and power and brings about spiritual healing. He knows us so well that He meets us in the place of our greatest need and reveals Himself to us there.

There's only one way to know for sure that He's real...just open your heart enough to let the Holy Spirit show you who God's Son really is. And see what a difference He can make in your life. I know, because God gave me the ultimate makeover.

GOD'S ROAD MAP

The Holy Bible is a guide to help you live a happy and satisfying life. To learn more about the concepts presented in the chapter you've just read, take a look at these passages:

BEAUTY

What is true beauty? It is different in every culture. Beauty comes in two forms: physical appearance (what the world sees) and inner beauty (what God sees). Inner beauty should be our goal, for it doesn't fade with time.

First Peter 3:3-4

Your beauty should not come from outward adornment, such as braided hair and the wearing of gold jewelry and fine clothes. Instead, it should be that of your inner self, the unfading beauty of a gentle and quiet spirit, which is of great worth in God's sight.

First Corinthians 15:41

The sun has one kind of splendor, the moon another and the stars another; and star differs from star in splendor.

First Samuel 16:7b

The Lord does not look at the things man looks at. Man looks at the outward appearance, but the Lord looks at the heart.

SELF-ESTEEM

To have a healthy self-esteem means to have a confidence and satisfaction about yourself. This can be particularly difficult for young women because the world sets standards that are unattainable. Yet in God's eyes, we are of tremendous value. And that's what counts.

Matthew 10:29-31

Are not two sparrows sold for a penny? Yet not one of them will fall to the ground apart from the will of your Father. And even the very hairs of your head are all numbered. So don't be afraid; you are worth more than many sparrows.

Psalm 8:3-6

When I consider Your heavens, the work of Your fingers, the moon and the stars, which You have set in place, what is man that You are mindful of him, the son of man that you care for him? You made him a little lower than the heavenly beings and crowned him with glory and honor. You made him ruler over the works of Your hands; You put everything under his feet.

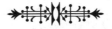

Steve Stevens, Sr.

Actor/Hollywood Agent, "Zorro,"
"Gunsmoke," and "The Roy Rogers Show"
(Photo credit: Zorro TV series, Walt Disney, 1957)

Steve Stevens broke into films at the age of 13 and has over 200 acting credits to his name. He starred in the Annette series on "The Mickey Mouse Club," and had parts in many other productions including "Walt Disney's Zorro," "Playhouse 90," "Mr. Novak," "Gunsmoke," "The Roy Rogers Show," and "That's My Mom."

Stevens spent seven years as a casting director for Screen Gems and ultimately for George C. Scott. His casting credits include "The Partridge Family," "Rage," "Oklahoma Crude," "The Savage," "How the West Was Won," "The Longest Yard," and "Enter the Dragon." Stevens has since built a highly respected agency by representing some of the industry's most famous faces, many of whom have remained loyal to him for decades: Jo Ann Worley, Frankie Avalon, Bobby Darin, Chuck Connors, Claude Akins, Slim Pickens, Amanda Blake, Doug McClure, Alan Hale, Dale Robertson, Lee Meriwether, and Forrest Tucker, to name just a few. Stevens has recently published a book, *So You Want to be in Show Business: A Hollywood Agent Shares the Secrets of Getting Ahead Without Getting Ripped Off.*

A cowboy at heart, Stevens is currently on the advisory board of Cowboys for Kids, an Arizona charity started by cowboy actor Ben Johnson, which is dedicated to helping kids who can't help themselves. In his spare time he is a coach for the Special Olympics Equestrian Athletes, training special needs children to ride horses and compete. You can find out more about Stevens on his website, www.celebhost.net/stevestevens.

★-:¦:→|:¦:|:¦:|:¦:←★

My father was brought up in a Catholic orphanage in New York and hated it. At a very young age he ran away and hopped freight trains traveling the country. He wound up in trouble with the law and on a chain gang in Louisiana. After a year and a half, he escaped and went back to New York where he met my mother. They became something of a name on the vaudeville circuit as a song and dance team.

Then my dad got involved with the gangs of New York, and we eventually had to disappear. We landed in Corpus Christi, Texas with new identities. My mother had a sister living in California who was married to the "King of the Extras" when being a movie extra was a really good profession. My aunt kept encouraging us to move out there, so in 1949 we moved to Hollywood to get into show business.

When we first moved to California, I helped support the family by selling newspapers on one of the most famous corners in the world—Hollywood and Vine. I sold papers regularly to guys like Humphrey Bogart, Slapsy "Maxie" Rosenbloom, Abbott and Costello, and Larry Fine of the Three Stooges. One afternoon it was pouring rain while I was outside trying to sell my papers. A limousine pulled up and the guy in the back rolled down his window and asked for a newspaper. He looked at me, soaking wet, and asked where I lived. When I told him, he offered to give me a ride home. It was Clark Gable. To the day she died, my mother never believed I actually got a ride home from Clark Gable.

For some reason, I seem to be the one who clicked as an actor. I got on a show called "The Lone Wolf" when I was around 13 and then on a feature called *The Big Moment* at Paramount. And bingo—I just started working. I had a lot of great roles and quickly became a familiar face in and around Hollywood.

I wasn't raised in a religious home, but my dad was very religious in his own right. He prayed every night; he prayed to his own God. My dad never forced me into anything. In fact, when I was 13 or 14 years old, he took me to a Catholic church, a Protestant church, a Baptist church, and a synagogue and said, "Here, you see what it is; here's the information. Here's the Old Testament; here's the New Testament; it's up to you, kid." That was it. But I always knew that there was some powerful being because it just seems like somebody was always looking out for me. I would pray not really knowing to whom I was praying, but I knew I was praying to someone. There's a cross that sits in the Hollywood Hills over-looking the Hollywood Freeway. It was put up there in the '50s when there weren't any houses around there. Many times I would climb up there and spend hours underneath the cross. I have no idea why.

As a kid I had to fake my way through school because it was so hard for me—especially reading. I thought it was because I wasn't very bright, but when I was 55 years old I found out I had dyslexia. And to think that I had landed in a business that was so dependent upon words is pretty amazing. Somehow I didn't just manage...I was successful! My handicap didn't stop me; God gave me the tools to cope.

When I guest starred on "The Roy Rogers Show," I got to know Roy and Dale Evans and their daughter Cheryl. It was Roy and Dale who led me to my Lord Jesus Christ. On the set of the show there was a cuss box. When you cussed, you put a quarter in the box. I bet I financed at least two of the shows personally! I was always cussing when I missed a line, and Roy decided to do something about it. He asked me if I would like to go out with him the following Saturday night. Wow! Imagine! Me and Roy Rogers out on the town together.

I got all dressed up that day and was ready to go by two in the after-noon...only five hours ahead of schedule. I had bragged about it to all the kids in the neighborhood, so when Roy picked me up that evening, they were hiding in the bushes and hanging from tree branches just to see the "King of the Cowboys" in person.

At precisely 7:00 P.M. we arrived at Bob Nolan's house, who was the leader of the Sons of the Pioneers, and I saw a lot of familiar faces there. It wasn't long before I realized this wasn't a party; it was some kind of meeting. It all started with a prayer and then someone said, "Has anyone brought any sinners tonight?" To my surprise, Roy stood up, put his hand on my shoulder and said, I would like you all to meet Steve Stevens, an actor and a sinner." Well, let me tell you, that was the most embarrassing and humiliating moment of my life...and I will always cherish it.

When I was 19, I went in a whole different direction. I would be walking down the street and people would recognize me and say things like, "Hey, you're on "The Mickey Mouse Club." I was always being asked for my autograph. And I got fan mail too. I remember one letter in particular from a man called Mr. Michael. In the letter he said that he liked the way I played bad guys. He said that he owned an ice cream parlor in Brentwood and if I was ever in the area, I should stop by and show them the letter for some free ice cream.

Months later I was on a date and like most young actors, I didn't have a whole lot of money. I had a new car and two cents in my pocket. I remembered that I had this letter in my glove compartment, so we went down to Brentwood. I'd heard of this ice cream parlor; it was quite famous. I showed the letter to a little old lady behind the counter and she told me to order whatever we wanted.

So my date and I sat at a table eating some ice cream; there must have been about two dozen people in the place. About half an hour later, the place went totally silent, and my date's eyes were as big as saucers. She said, "Oh my God, it's him." I said, "Who?" "That gangster," she said. And I turned around and there was Mickey Cohen—the John Gotti of Los Angeles in the '40s and '50s. He was a bad guy.

He came over to our table with his three bodyguards and said, "Hi, I'm Mr. Michael. I didn't know if you guys actually got those fan mail letters. You're terrific. Hey kid, do you play hearts?" "No," I said, "poker's my game." He said, "Here's my address. Come on over tomorrow night and bring the gal with you." And with that he turned around and walked away. The next two years of my life I spent with Mickey Cohen and became a runner for him. I spent three to four nights a week with him, and I saw a lot of things that were really bad, and I did a lot of things that were wrong.

It's amazing—there I was, this 19-year-old kid, and I was almost a confidante to public enemy #1. This guy was so powerful that I would see people like Frank Sinatra pay homage to him. I was in awe of the power he had. Later in life, I hung out with men like George C. Scott and Chuck Connors and many other big stars, directors, and producers on the Hollywood A list, and yet the most powerful man I ever knew in my life was Mickey Cohen. I never felt like I was really doing anything wrong by hanging out with him…I was pretty blind. Even after he went to jail, I still wanted to see him.

Even though my life was obviously going in the wrong direction, there were still so many examples of God watching out for me. I remember one time I went to pick up a package for Mickey, and a carload of thugs chased me all the way through Los Angeles and West Hollywood trying to get what I had. They were obviously going to try and kill me. I was all by myself, but because I had a hot car at that time I was able to outrun them.

There was another time when I was supposed to meet Mickey at a restaurant in Sherman Oaks. I was supposed to pick a woman up and bring her along, but she was late. On our way to the restaurant, there was something going on at the Hollywood Bowl so I got caught in traffic. I wasn't very happy about being so late.

When I finally got to the restaurant, there were sirens and cops and sheriffs—people with guns all around. If I had been there on time, I would have been sitting at Mickey's table where a man was assassinated. That's why he was brought there—to be killed. For some reason I was prevented from being there. God only knows what would have happened to me.

The first time I carried a gun I got arrested. How's that for a message from above? I got pulled over on Sunset Boulevard with my roommate, John Ashley. When I got out of the car, my gun just fell down and hit the pavement. Some waitress came out of a nightclub nearby and told the officer that I'd been in there with Mickey Cohen the night before. Well, bingo, they had me down on the ground in no time and put chains on me. The amazing thing was that I was bailed out of jail within two hours because somebody had called Mickey to tell him that one of his boys had been locked up. When I was at the front desk getting my belongings, the desk sergeant leaned over and asked me for my autograph. I can imagine the Lord upstairs shaking His head thinking, *I've got a lot of other people to look out for besides you here...get with it!*

I worked as an actor up until 1963. It was a point in my life where I didn't want to act anymore. I didn't like it, and I didn't like what I was becoming. I was pretty obnoxious and falling into that whole Hollywood trip. I was a semi-regular on a show called "Mr. Novak" with James Franciscus, and I got a call to do my own pilot. We had negotiated a deal, and I was all set to do the pilot, but the head of the studio had somebody else they wanted and I was out.

I quit show business that day; I was just so upset that it literally broke my heart. With $50 in my shoe, I headed out of LA and hitchhiked across the U.S. for a year. I hopped freights, and worked on farms to make some money. I thought a lot about my career and show business while out on the road. I decided to become an agent because I realized that an actor has no control over his own life. An actor has to rely on his agent; an agent has to rely on casting; and casting has to rely on the producer, the director, the network, and the head of the studio. As an actor, you are at the bottom of the food chain.

The vagabond lifestyle was tough. I was thrown off trains and got into fights with other drifters. Finally I realized that I wasn't a character in a movie and I'd better get my life together. So I contacted an agent friend of mine and went to work for him. I never looked back. I was an agent for a while and then had an opportunity to try being a casting director. I was in casting for seven years, four of them exclusively with George C. Scott. Working with him was the highlight of my career. Everything he directed on film I cast. Then I got married and adopted my wife Rosemary's son, and we soon had a child together. With all of that going on, my job as a casting director was no longer working out. Many of the jobs were shot outside of LA and I'd have to leave my new young family for weeks, some-times months at a time. I didn't care for that, so I went back into the agency business.

My career as an agent has been incredible. Many of my clients stuck with me for decades. Doug McClure was with me for 18 years; in fact, I held his hand when he passed away. Chuck Connors was also with me for about 18 years, and I held his hand when he passed away. What an honor and privilege that was.

But I've had another great joy in my life. I've always worked with abused, handicapped, and special children in various ways. God led me to be an equestrian coach in the Special Olympics. I teach kids with Down's syndrome how to ride horses, and working with these very special athletes is just incredible. I have terrible arthritis in my knees from all of the rodeo riding I've done over the years, and I've had a bad back for 40 years. And even though it's sometimes painful and hard to get up in the morning, all I need to do is think about my athletes and the challenges they have, and I know I can't be such a wimp.

I believe my God led me to those children so that I could better deal with my own issues. Sometimes I don't know whether I'm doing it for me or for them because I get so much out of my relationships with these kids. For some reason I get along really well with Down's syndrome children; I can really communicate with them. In the Bible, Jesus talks about how you need to be like a child to enter the Kingdom of Heaven. These people are like children forever—a great reminder to me every day that I too need to be like a child with my Father in Heaven. If I won the lottery tomorrow, I would quit working and I would spend the rest of my life and my money with children.

The last 65+ years have been like a Hollywood drama. But remarkably, I'm still here. As I look back on my life, I don't know if I would have changed anything, not even the Mickey Cohen situation. I learned a lot and I saw a lot...I grew up. I've been blessed with a great life, two great kids, and my wife who is my soul mate. I know He's real because God has always answered my prayers, one way or the other; it's the most amazing thing. My life is now 100 percent in His hands. Whatever happens, whether I feel it's good or bad, it's in His hands.

THE LIST
by Steve Stevens, Sr.

I was somewhat of a jerk,
when I was in my teens.
Nothing really bad,
just part of the scene.

I think back to my regret,
I wasn't so nice to the people I met.
So I now try to make up for,
all those I showed to the door.

Now when I do something nice,
I write it down on paper made of rice.
It stays in my pocket—that list,
sometimes I clinch it in my fist.

If I should die on my way home,
being dead I will not be alone.
At the gate with the golden mist,
I will show St. Peter my list.

"Look what I've been doing,
not what I have done then.
Add up all the good,
and let me come on in."

I know I will convince him,
I always had a way with the gab.
On the other side of the gate smiling,
arms stretched out will be my dad.

I wouldn't suggest this to anyone,
just start out right.

Then when you say your prayers,
you only need to say, "Hey, God, good night."

*If you want to read more about Steve's relationship with Mickey Cohen, check out his new book, *King of the Sunset Strip*, which will be released by Cumberland House in the spring of 2006.

GOD'S ROAD MAP

The Holy Bible is a guide to help you live a happy and satisfying life. To learn more about the concepts presented in the chapter you've just read, take a look at these passages:

PRAYER

Prayer is the way we communicate with God. It can be spoken aloud or within our hearts. But it's a two-way conversation—not just a way for us to ask for things. Our prayer life should also include times of adoration, confession, thankfulness and then making requests. God answers all earnest prayers...but perhaps not exactly the way we'd like Him to.

James 5:13-16

Is any one of you in trouble? He should pray. Is anyone happy? Let him sing songs of praise. Is any one of you sick? He should call the elders of the church to pray over him and anoint him with oil in the name of the Lord. And the prayer offered in faith will make the sick person well; the Lord will raise him up. If he has sinned, he will be forgiven. Therefore confess your sins to each other and pray for each other so that you may be healed. The prayer of a righteous man is powerful and effective.

First John 5:14-15

This is the confidence we have in approaching God: that if we ask anything according to His will, He hears us. And if we know that He hears us—whatever we ask—we know that we have what we asked of Him.

SERVING OTHERS

As Christians, our highest calling is to serve others, and to do so with a cheerful heart.

Matthew 23:11-12

The greatest among you will be your servant. For whoever exalts himself will be humbled, and whoever humbles himself will be exalted.

Matthew 20:26b-28

Whoever wants to become great among you must be your servant, and whoever wants to be first must be your slave—just as the Son of Man did not come to be served, but to serve, and to give His life as a ransom for many.

Philippians 2:3

Do nothing out of selfish ambition or vain conceit, but in humility consider others better than yourselves.

Noel Paul Stookey

"Paul" From the Trio—
Peter, Paul & Mary
(Photo credit: Sarah Farr)

Noel Paul Stookey is otherwise known as "Paul" from the celebrated musical group—Peter, Paul & Mary. PP&M is synonymous with folk music. The trio is known not only for hits like "Puff the Magic Dragon" and "This Land is Your Land" but also for their uncompromising sense of activism during a turbulent decade. The group won five Grammy awards, produced five Top 10 albums, and 37 Top 40 Hits. They also have six gold and three platinum albums to their credit.

But Noel Paul Stookey's greatest accomplishment was that evening in 1968 when he knew for sure that God was real. His discovery and ultimate thankfulness for the patience of a Creator who would be involved in his life has completely altered his motivations. His music now is from the forgiven and loved perspective that one inherits as a gift of the Holy Spirit. These days you'll find him on the campuses of Northfield Mount Hermon School, a prep school in Massachusetts where he is an artist in residence. Noel has been married since 1963 to the NMH Chaplain and sings at many of the school services. To find out more about what he's up to, check out his website: www.noelpaulstookey.com.

I met Steve backstage after a concert in Abilene, Texas in 1968. As near as I could tell, his age was late teens or early 20s. His hair was light brown, almost blonde, and his face had a worker's tan—you know, the kind with squint crinkles around his eyes, because you can't do real farm work and still wear sunglasses....

His blue eyes look up quickly to catch mine. "I want to talk to you about the Lord," he says simply. The impact of what he has said is felt immediately in my heart, and by the time we walk over to a bench to sit down, there's an urgent pounding in my chest. I get a kind of adrenaline rush that makes the outside of my skin feel 20 degrees cooler than the inside. But I'm not dizzy...it's more like I've just been "locked" into the subject material. After all, isn't this what I've been praying for?

Steve tells me about how praying the name Jesus over and over again had rescued him from this horrific "trip" and how he and his friends had devoured the Bible looking for some kind of explanation for what had happened. (After all, the reversal of a chemical effect as strong as acid is unheard of.) Even though they weren't regular churchgoers, they made contact with a minister who had explained to them in biblical terms what must have happened.

Later, we go to the motel where I am staying to talk some more. After opening the door, I do everything I can to avoid what I sense is going to be the final confrontation.

Steve says, "I think we ought to pray," and with that he and his friends fall to their knees in the motel room. I join them nervously but curiously.

"Lord," begins Steve, "I want to thank You for getting us into tonight's concert without tickets..." (I'm beginning to suspect that there's a bigger circumstance than just the four of us in this tiny motel room.) "And I want to thank You for getting me backstage without a pass to speak to Paul." (I definitely get a sense of the inevitability of this appointment.)

"...and for placing a burden on my heart to speak to him." He pauses. "And now I think he wants to talk to You."

There is no sound in the room except for the whirring of the air conditioner, and with our eyes closed in prayer there is a mutuality of humbleness that tears my heart apart.

I'm aware that for real or imagined, for now or forever, there is no denying that I am kneeling in front of my Creator and that every hair on my head is known, every minute of my life is common knowledge, and there is nothing—no information to which He is not privy. I am transparent—revealed, and in my awkwardness I realize just how long I have been "away"—just how long I have been absent from this Loving Gaze, hiding in my personal worlds invented by a combination of fame, money, and pride, and sustained by habit, ignorance, and lack of responsibility.

There is nothing I can say in defense of my life thus far. There is no excuse for any of my actions except that I have been hiding. And an apology is obviously the only thing called for.

"I'm sorry." I confess for all that is Good and Holy and Patient and Kind and Forgiving. "I'm sorry," and the tears come. "I'm sorry," and I sob more heavily; and I can feel the weight of my life apart from God run down my shoulders. "I'm sorry" and I think this moment is the fullest, the richest moment in all my life—not because of how it might change my life, but because of now. Now is here in Glory. There are no thoughts of the anxieties of the future, nor any ropes to bind me to the past....

How long I wept I can't remember, but it must have been for several minutes. Finally, when I was done, I tried to speak thanks...but there were no words. I was weightless and guiltless, and nothing like this had ever happened to me before.

The Lord has amazed me ever since. In 1969, my parents picked me up at the San Francisco airport about five days prior to the upcoming Peter, Paul, & Mary concerts in the area. I was carrying a letter that I received from some Christian group on the Berkeley campus asking me to come sing on the steps of Sproul Hall. I agreed to make a brief appearance on the way to my folks' house.

The family car pulled up in front of the information offices, and I walked up to the counter. "Hi," I said to the lady seated behind a wall of Plexiglas. "Yes, can I help you?" she blinked and looked up pleasantly. "Could you tell me what time Noel Paul Stookey is booked to sing on the steps of Sproul Hall?" "Uh, just a moment please..." She thumbed through a well-worn calendar of events. "Do you know who is sponsoring the appearance?" she asked.

"Well, uh...some Christian organization. I don't have the name off-hand," I replied. "The only event we have scheduled for today on the steps of Sproul Hall is a conservation talk sponsored by the Sierra Club," she said a little curiously.

"Oh, then...uh, thanks..." I walked away from the booth. *Oh boy!* I'm beginning to think. *I can just bag the whole thing and go play some golf.*

As the car pulled away from the curb, there was suddenly this uneasiness. And with each revolution of the wheel, I sensed this binding in my heart. "I want you to go back and sing" came this word to me. I got this sense of bringing a little light and music to a sea of conflicting spirits. And I understood that if I did nothing more than ease somebody's pain today, it would be enough. So we turned around.

I found my way to the steps of Sproul Hall and took out my guitar, tuning it briefly. Some people saw the guitar and stopped by. "What's happening?" they asked. "Uh...gonna play and sing a little..." I answered.

I started off with "John Henry Bosworth," a song about a man who underwent a life-changing experience and was encouraged by his faith. By the time I'd finished, ten or twenty more people joined my "crowd." We struck up a bit of conversation. (I didn't think anybody had really connected me with the group—Peter, Paul & Mary yet.) After a couple more tunes, I invited the audience to participate in an extended version of "Puff the Magic Dragon." By the time the last "Honoahlee" had faded away, there must have been 200 people on the steps, and I noticed that a television camera had joined us.

I talked a little about becoming a Christian, about looking in all the strange places that one looks for a real-time relationship with God, and about backstage in Texas and answers to prayer. In the background I heard what sounded like chanting off to our right about two or three hundred feet away. There must have been 300 to 400 people in our group now, so I couldn't see around them.

After the concert, someone introduced themselves as a member of the Christian group who had written me. He explained that since they had never heard back from me (...never heard back from me?), they had let the reserved time go. Wasn't it just God's way to give us a beautiful day and that nobody from the Sierra Club showed up?

A couple of days later, I headed back to Berkeley—to the municipal auditorium this time for the first concert of the PP&M weekend. It was about 4:00 in the afternoon when I walked into the cool shade of the backstage area and set my suitcase and guitar on the concrete floor. Ed Sarkesian (our production manager) and Charlie Rothschild (our road manager) walked toward me.

"Hey, congratulations, Stook," said Ed. "Yeah," concurred Charlie, "that was really terrific."

My mind was racing. During my absence, PP&M must have won some recording award or something.

"KQED has shots of them marching on the administration building, and they were talking about the confrontation that would've happened," Charlie continued. "And there you were..." Ed said shaking his head admiringly.

"KQED?!" I asked. "Yeah," said Charlie, "lots of coverage of the..."

And as Charlie went on to describe the event that they saw on television, I slowly pieced together the facts that had remained unassembled from that day. Some student organization had obviously planned a march on the administration building and was counting on support from the students in the common area to which the steps of Sproul Hall abutted. Apparently, and obviously unknowingly, I had begun a spontaneous concert 10 or 15 minutes before the march began and had stolen the interest of enough potential participants to be interpreted by the Bay area public television station as "stopping the riot."

"I had no idea," I said. "Huh?" said Charlie. "I just went there to sing on the steps of Sproul Hall. I wasn't trying to stop anything from going on...I didn't even know there was a march planned!" "Is that right, Stook?" said Ed. And then as my disclaimer settled in on the both of them, he grinned and scratched the back of his head. "Well, I'll be damned."

No, I thought. *Blessed...I've been blessed.*

MY FATHER'S HOUSE
by Noel Paul Stookey

The way to my Father's house when I was just a boy
Lay through fields of innocence
Near bubbling springs of joy
And when I'd lay me down to sleep
I'd pray the Lord my soul to keep
The road was never very steep
On the way to my Father's house

The way to my Father's house when I turned seventeen
Wandered through inviting hills
Beside a tumbling stream
Sometimes in prayer upon my knees
I would feel a distant breeze
The road was winding now through trees
On the way to my Father's house

The way to my Father's house at the age of twenty-nine
Led over a mountain that
I would seldom climb
Except in times of great despair
When I'd be looking everywhere
And then one morning He was there
On the way to my Father's house

Glory! What a refreshing story
I was so blind before He
Opened my eyes restoring me to

The way to my Father's house at the age of thirty-one
Was a ride on a rainbow;
My new life had begun
And every evening I could look
Through the pages of His book

And recognize the paths I took
On the way, on the way...

I go to my Father's house in these troubled days
The Spirit is moving in
Mysterious ways
Reminded when old doubts appear
That perfect love casts out all fear
In thanks, I tend the garden here
On the way, on the way...
On the way to my Father's house.

GOD'S ROAD MAP

The Holy Bible provides a road map to help you live a happy and satisfying life. To learn more about the concepts presented in the chapter you've just read, take a look at these passages:

WITNESSING

In the story you just read, a young man named Steve bravely approached Noel Paul Stookey to tell him about the Lord. Once we experience the joy and peace of knowing Christ, we yearn to share it with others. The Bible says that as believers, it is our obligation—and our privilege—to spread the good news.

Daniel 12:3

Those who are wise will shine like the brightness of the heavens, and those who lead many to righteousness, like the stars for ever and ever.

Luke 12:8

I tell you, whoever acknowledges Me before men, the Son of Man will also acknowledge him before the angels of God.

Matthew 18:12-14

What do you think? If a man owns a hundred sheep, and one of them wanders away, will he not leave the ninety-nine on the hills and go to look for the one that wandered off? And if he finds it, I tell you the truth, he is happier about that one sheep than about the ninety-nine that did not wander off. In the same way your Father in heaven is not willing that any of these little ones should be lost.

CONFESSION

In order to be forgiven in the eyes of the Lord, we must first admit that we are sinners. Once the slate has been wiped clean, we are open for

Him to work through us. The word confess also means to tell others about our belief in Christ. In the end, everyone will confess that Jesus Christ is Lord when He comes again. Why wait?

First John 1:9

If we confess our sins, He is faithful and just and will forgive us our sins and purify us from all unrighteousness.

Psalm 32:5

Then I acknowledged my sin to You and did not cover up my iniquity. I said, "I will confess my transgressions to the Lord"—and You forgave the guilt of my sin.

Philippians 2:10-11

That at the name of Jesus every knee should bow, in heaven and on earth and under the earth, and every tongue confess that Jesus Christ is Lord, to the glory of God the Father.

T-Bone

Dove Award-Winning, Rap Musician

(Photo credit: paradigmphoto.com)

T-Bone is undoubtedly the godfather of Christian hip-hop. A highly accomplished rapper, he delivers innovative and authentic rhymes about a troubled world—the world of inner-city chaos and gang violence. When T-Bone preaches, people listen because he has firsthand experience.

Launched in 1991, T-Bone's impressive career has spawned eight solo albums, including the newly released *Bone-a-Fide*. His work has resulted in a Grammy nomination, multiple Dove nom inations, and two Dove awards, including one for his contribution to the soundtrack for the rock opera !HERO with which he toured in 2003 and 2004. He has collaborated musically with such greats as Beyonce, The O'Jay's, Melba Moore, Michael Tait, Yolanda Adams, Audio Adrenaline, Mack 10, and KRS-One. T-bone has worked with some of the best producers in the business, includ-ing DarkChild and the multi-platinum team of Jimmy Jam and Terry Lewis.

One of the highlights of his career was his role in the box office hit, *The Fighting Temptations* in 2003. His upcoming film, *Rumble*, starring R&B queen Ciara, Adrienne Balion, and

Middleweight Women's Boxing Champ, Laila Ali will be released in early 2006.

T-Bone has had a lot of success in the world of music. But he doesn't represent hip-hop. Hip-hop didn't save him from the street; Jesus did. He uses hip-hop simply as a tool to point his homeboys to Christ.

✦•‡•┊•✕•┊•✕•┊•✦

I'll never forget hearing about my friend Ralphie twitching on the grass in a pool of his own blood. We were both freshman in high school, only 16 years old. That fateful day, a rival gang drove by in a 1964 Impala and opened fire. Ralphie was hit twice—once in the chest and once in the back. His last words weren't "I'm going to miss everyone" or "Tell my mother and father I said good-bye." He didn't even say he was scared. Instead, he said… "Just tell everyone to wear red at my funeral." You see, red was the color we were down with—our gang color.

My mother is from El Salvador and my father is from Nicaragua. They moved to San Francisco, California and raised their family in an area called the Mission District— basically the East LA of the Bay Area, a very ethnic part of town. I was raised in the inner city, living up in tall buildings and in crowded conditions. A lot of stuff comes with that urban world. Gangs are a part of life in that kind of neighborhood.

We were raised Catholic, but when I was about nine years old, my parents gave their lives to the Lord and began to seek after God. By the time I was 15, they were both pastors and started a Spanish-speaking street church to reach out to the Latino people in the community.

Eventually we moved to Sacramento, but we were still exposed to the same stuff. My sister got deep into gangs; she was dealing drugs and drinking—doing the whole gang thing. She actually had a gang that came under her, and that's when that life started to look interesting to me.

We were in the middle of a spiritual fight. On the one hand, our parents were trying to get us to go to church, but we were also trying to be in the world. One thing that kept me going to church was the music; I was being used in the music ministry playing the keyboards and the drums.

But at the same time, I was on the streets with my friends doing things that I shouldn't have been doing. I went to a continuation school, which is an alternative from your everyday high school. In the inner city, that's where you get most of the gang members, the drug dealers, and the troubled kids—not a very good breeding ground.

I started jumping people; a group of us would jump on some guy and beat him up. I'd also been helping some friends deal a little bit of weed. I began to see friends going to jail and people getting killed. My sister ran away and was living on the street. There was so much violence and so much craziness.

But I still had the conviction of a Christian in my heart because I was raised in the Word of God. When I heard about my friend Ralphie bleeding to death that day, I said, "You know what, man, there's got to be more to life than this."

One Sunday, shortly after that, I went to my father's church. The speaker that day was a friend of his from Nicaragua. He seemed to know exactly everything that was going on in my life. It was kind of like I could see my whole life flash before my eyes. This guy was painting a remarkably accurate picture of what I was doing...and it wasn't pretty. As I listened, I closed my eyes and prayed, "God, if You're real, I want to give You a try and give You my life 100 percent." I walked up to the altar and surrendered everything. I made a choice that day, a decision to move into Christianity and serve God. I became what I called my first record, a *Redeemed Hoodlum*.

When you have a life-changing experience like that, the most natural thing in the world is to want all your friends to change too. So I went out into the streets and did a lot of street evangelism. I'd been rapping since I was about seven years old—doing it at house parties and little clubs around town. But once I became a Christian, I couldn't find any music to listen to, let alone perform. If a guy from the streets who loves hip-hop gets saved, what does he listen to then?

I began writing some Urban Inspirational hip-hop in hopes of making a difference. One of my friends invited me to perform at his church. I was hesitant to go, because I didn't think my style of music would be accepted. But at his urgings I went and did my music, and then an evangelist came out and preached. The first thing that hit me was that I was seeing people in church who would never normally come. I saw gang members come up to the altar and give their lives to the Lord. I discovered that God could use hip-hop to speak to people.

That first church concert was great, but as I began to do them more and more, I saw that there were a lot of closed-minded people who were stuck in tradition. I was kicked out of many churches. They would stop me in the middle of my show and say, "Get out of our church. This isn't from God. We don't believe in this; this is from satan."

I'm one of the pioneers of gospel hip-hop, and I've been doing it professionally now for over 15 years. It wasn't easy. But I knew that God could use this music to reach people, so one day I said, "You know what, God. I'm leaving everything and am going to dedicate everything to You. I'm going to go out and make music. And one day I'm going to make it, and I'm going to give You glory and preach the Word throughout the nations."

And that's exactly what I did. At the age of 16 I left home and moved down to Fresno. Sometimes I ate out of garbage cans because I had no money, but my faith was always there. I knew that God was going to show up.

One day I was discovered by a manager who'd seen me rapping. I cut a demo with one of his other groups, and they were amazed at what I was doing. At the same time the Gospel Music Awards were sponsoring a New Artist Showcase. Any artist from the world of country, black gospel, southern gospel, rock, ska, hip-hop—any genre—could enter the competition. I reluctantly sent in three songs, but I knew I would never hear from them...they wouldn't want anything to do with my kind of music.

To my surprise, about a month later I got a letter that said I'd been selected as one of the finalists. I was astonished! Now you have to remember, there were only three finalists out of over a thousand entries. Even today, I'd say the chances of a rap artist making it were very slim, probably less than one percent. I figured they would pick more mainstream gospel or rock groups.

At the finale, I performed in front of artists I'd listened to for years. The audience was filled with big executives from different labels. It was a huge deal. I performed a song, doing what we call tongue twisting, which is what you do when you talk real fast. They'd never heard anything like that before. At the end of the night there was a standing ovation. I still remember the platinum-selling group, DC Talk, walking up to the front and getting on their knees saying, "We're not worthy, we're not worthy."

After the show I was approached by all kinds of records label reps shoving record deals in my face. And the rest is really history. Since then I've made eight albums, been nominated for a Grammy, won two Dove awards, been on platinum and gold-selling albums, and even had the opportunity to make a number–one hit movie. God made a way out of no way. That's how I know for sure that God is real—I was a 16-year-old kid who left everything to make it. I starved, and I slept on people's sofas because I had no way of paying rent. But I knew this was what God had called me to do. I was going to do whatever it took. It just shows you, if you put your faith in God and you trust in Him, He will show you that He is real. As it says in Philippians 1:6—He's faithful to complete what He started. God will never leave you hanging.

Rap is the language of the street, and God is the language of love. When you put the two together, you see amazing results take place. Too many people think that they can only relate to God in a traditional way. But you can just talk to Him the same way you'd talk to a friend—because that's what He is. "What's crackin' God? How You doing? I'm going through these things, man; I'm struggling right now. God, You feel me?" If God can listen to people speaking languages all over the world like Chinese and Vietnamese and I can pray to Him in Spanish, He can sure understand street talk. Our God is a God who relates to everyone. If He could use a donkey to speak to Balaam in the Bible, He can definitely use T-Bone to speak to this generation.

My career has been incredible. One of the highlights was working on the film, *The Fighting Temptations* starring Beyonce and Cuba Gooding, Jr. back in 2003. I got that part only through the intervention of God.

I had just finished working with Yolanda Adams on her new album, which was produced by the biggest record producers in the world, Jimmy Jam and Terry Lewis. I got to be great friends with them. A few months later Jimmy and Terry were overseeing the music on this new movie.

There was a character in the movie who was a God-fearing, rapping convict. The part was originally written for Nelly, but they had some contractual differences they couldn't work out. After that, they auditioned Method Man, Petey Pablo, Redman, Keith Murray, LL Cool J, and Busta Rhymes—all kinds of huge artists. None of them seemed to work out. Busta Rhymes had actually flown down from New York to audition. This was shortly after September 11th, so security at Paramount was real high. When he arrived at the studio, he'd forgotten his ID. Even though they knew who he was, at the end of the day they wouldn't let him in without identification, and he never even got to audition.

After going through all those people, the film was still without a rapper. Jimmy Jam and Terry Lewis said, "You know what—we know a guy and this part is his life. He's been to jail; he does gospel rap for a living; this is who he is. This part is basically his life story." I went down to Hollywood to audition and then continued on to the Rock the Desert festival where I was scheduled to perform. When I landed at the airport in Texas, I got a call from my manager. She told me to pack my bags and clear my schedule because I was off to Atlanta to shoot the movie for at least two months!

When I arrived in Atlanta, I was picked up by a limo. I was all excited, telling the driver that I got a part in the movie. But he said, "Just because you're here doesn't mean you got the part. I drive people every single day to meet the producers, and I drive them back to go home the next day." I didn't understand; I thought I had the part. Now I was nervous.

That night I met the director and the producers and went through another script reading. When I was done they said, "T-Bone, we'll let you know in the morning what we think. If we like you, the part is yours. If not, then we'll be sending you back home tomorrow morning. The next morning came and I got a phone call, "You need to be up and ready. They loved you and you have the part. Welcome to the family."

I know that God intervened for me. They'd gone through names ten times bigger than me and still, I got the part. It just proves, when God wants you to have something, it doesn't matter what people try to do, God's gonna give it to you.

Being a conscious rapper hasn't been easy. I'm a living martyr—I'm ready to die for what I believe in. I don't fear gang members or drug lords. I don't fear anything because I serve a powerful God. When you're out there preaching the Word, the enemy is definitely going to attack you. So, if you're not being persecuted, you should examine your life. Because if you are a threat to the devil, he is going to try to take you out. I am, on the other hand, a big threat to the devil, and there have been many times when he has tried to put me out of business.

One of the biggest events that happened to me was in Compton, California. Compton has long been notorious for having the highest crime rate in the country; it is infested with gangs. One night my friend and I were sitting in a BMW at a gas station making a phone call. A group of gang members came up to us and one guy said, "What's crackin', 'cuz?" When he said " 'cuz," that meant he was a Crip. I was from the Bay Area where a lot of the slang is from the Bloods' gang, where the color is red. I was wearing red in the form of a 49ers jacket that night. I was already raved; I wasn't thinking about what I was saying when I answered, "What's up, blood?" That triggered something in him; he was obviously upset and left.

Next thing you know, he came back with a bunch of other guys. They looked like bandits with blue bandanas across their faces. They came up to the window and stuck a gun to my boy's head and told him to get on the ground. Then they came up to me and said, "We're going to murder you, Blood." They made us both get on the ground, and we knew they were going to kill us.

But the power of God came on me and God said, "Stand up. You're not a gang member, and you're not going to die like one." I became fearless. I got on my knees, turned around, and faced them with their guns pointing at me and I said, "I'm not a gang member, so I'm not going to die like one. God has set me free." I turned around and lifted up my hands and said, "God, I thank You that today is my graduation day. I thank You that today I will be in paradise with You."

The Bible says that demons flee when they hear the name of Jesus. And as I began to worship God that night, all of those gang members put down their guns and took off running.

Even more amazing than that…at the exact same time this was happening, my parents were in Compton preaching at a church service. In the middle of my father's sermon and in front of the entire congregation, my mother stood up and said, "Honey, stop preaching. We need to pray for our son right this second, because something terrible is happening." So the whole church prayed for me and I was saved. Coincidence? I don't think so. If that doesn't show you God is real, I can't tell you what else will.

I could give you a hundred reasons how I know Christ is real. About eight years ago, 15 gang members broke into my home in Fresno, California at 3:00 in the morning. They came into my bedroom and stuck guns to my head and pistol whipped me. They threw me through the glass of my bathtub, and beat me with pipes, weights, and bats to the point where blood was coming out both of my ears. They were ready to kill me, and I thought I was going to die. I had gotten thrown down to the ground, and I picked up my Bible and said, "What are you doing? I'm a minister of the Gospel." But they didn't care. Even still, I knew God was going to allow me to survive. I knew He wasn't done with me yet.

They dragged me outside and a bunch of guys rolled up in a van. It was a frightening thing to realize these guys wanted to murder me. By some supernatural force I hit one of the guys and took off running. To me, it was a miracle that all of these guys couldn't catch me and kill me. I know it was because God was with me.

The Bible says that everything that the devil means for evil, God will turn around for good. This was a time when God opened up my eyes, and He said, "Son, you need to go out and have an urgency when you preach tomorrow. Because even though you are a Christian and you are saved, tomorrow isn't promised to you either. You need to make sure you're right with Me every day." Yeah, God has shown up in my life so many times.

Let me give you one more, quick story. I was doing a concert, and right in the middle of the music I stopped and started preaching about God's love. I didn't know it at the time, but there were several gang members in the auditorium who were not there for my concert. They were there to kill someone. As I began to preach the Word and these guys heard my testimony, God touched them in a miraculous way. The gang leader walked up to the front and put his gun down at the altar. His whole gang followed him and put down their guns and their colored rags as well. Then they went up to the guy they were going to murder and hugged him and asked for forgiveness! It was unbelievable.

These events still seem mind-boggling to me when I look back. When you are 100 percent sold-out for God, you're fearless. It doesn't matter how many guns are pulled out on you, and it doesn't matter if gang members come into your home and try to murder you. God protects His children. I'm not afraid. And if I die...oh well...because you know what? In Philippians 1:21, Paul said, "...to live is Christ and to die is gain." When I die, it just gets better. I would count it an honor to be taken out for His name.

Every day when I wake up and look at my home, the things I have, the places I've traveled in the world and my wife, I say, "You know what, man, I don't deserve any of this." I'm a sinner and I mess up every single day. And even though I don't deserve it, God still gives it to me. That is so humbling. No matter how much I fall, and no matter how much I mess up, God still loves me and continues to bless me, even me—a redeemed hoodlum.

GOD'S ROAD MAP

The Holy Bible provides a road map to help you live a happy and satisfying life. To learn more about the concepts presented in the chapter you've just read, take a look at these passages:

PERSECUTION

To be taken out for Christ's sake would be an honor for T-Bone. That is something all Christians should be willing to do.

Galatians 5:11

Brothers, if I am still preaching circumcision, why am I still being persecuted? In that case the offense of the cross has been abolished.

Philippians 1:28-30

Without being frightened in any way by those who oppose you. This is a sign to them that they will be destroyed, but that you will be saved—and that by God. For it has been granted to you on behalf of Christ not only to believe on Him, but also to suffer for Him, since you are going through the same struggle you saw I had, and now hear that I still have.

Matthew 5:11

Blessed are you when people insult you, persecute you and falsely say all kinds of evil against you because of Me.

First Peter 4:13-14

But rejoice that you participate in the sufferings of Christ, so that you may be overjoyed when His glory is revealed. If you are insulted because of the name of Christ, you are blessed, for the Spirit of glory and of God rests on you.

Luke 6:27-28

But I tell you who hear Me: Love your enenmies, do good to those who hate you, bless those who curse you, pray for those who mistreat you.

David Wheaton

Professional Tennis Player
(Photo credit: Springfield News Leader)

In the 1990s, David Wheaton was one of the top tennis players in the world. This Minnesota native with the powerful serve and backhand, competed regularly against tennis greats like Pete Sampras, Andre Agassi, Jim Courier, Michael Chang, Ivan Lendl, and Boris Becker. During his tenure on the professional tour, he won the largest prize money event in tennis—the Grand Slam Cup in Munich in 1991. That year, Wheaton attained a world ranking of #12 and in 2004 he claimed the Wimbledon Over-35 Doubles Championship.

While he officially retired from professional tennis in 2001, Wheaton is still involved in the game. He currently serves on the Board of Directors of the United States Tennis Association and competes occasionally.

Wheaton is the host of "The David Wheaton Show," a Minneapolis-based radio program that offers a Christian perspective on current events, culture, and faith. He is also an inspirational speaker and the author of *University of Destruction—Your Game Plan for Spiritual Victory on Campus*. For more information, go to www.davidwheaton.com.

Tennis is a ruggedly individualistic sport that teaches you to rely on yourself. That's the opposite of the Christian way of life. I had to learn the hard way to shift my focus to where it belongs—solidly at the foot of the cross.

I come from the ice hockey state of Minnesota, hardly a famous breeding ground for professional tennis players. In the land of 10,000 lakes, we have nine months of winter and three months of tough sledding. Unless you have indoor courts, tennis is definitely not a year-round sport. Despite the climactic challenges, I developed into one of the top tennis players in the world. I credit two things for that: God-given ability and family dedication.

My grandfather, John Hessey, was always involved in fitness and sports. He liked to swim, speed skate, road bike and downhill ski. As a matter of fact, he was the country's oldest active member of the National Ski Patrol when he was in his 80s. His weight-lifting regimen continued until he passed away at age 101.

Gramps was particularly interested in tennis and golf. He became a professional tennis instructor in his 70s and taught my mom and siblings how to play the game. After I was born, we spent a great deal of family time on the tennis court.

My mother tossed me my first tennis balls when I was just four years old. In those days, I only wanted to hit backhands. Well before I ever hit a tennis ball, I had started perfecting my left-handed hockey slap shot. That slap shot was to become the foundation for my best shot in tennis— my backhand.

When I was eight, I played my first tennis tournament. I made it all the way to the finals, but lost the eight-game pro-set match to a 12 year old, and refused to shake his hand afterward until my best friend talked me into it! By the very next year, I had become my section's best U12 player and went to the U.S. Nationals. From the time I was 11 until I finished my junior career at 18, I was consistently ranked nationally in the top 10. By the time I was 18, I was ranked number one in the country.

As a 9th grader in 1984, I went on to become the youngest winner of the Minnesota State High School Singles Tournament. By this point, finding good competition in the state was becoming a problem. Halfway through my sophomore year in high school, a famous tennis coach named Nick Bollettieri, invited me down to his tennis academy in Florida to help me develop as a player.

It worked. I finished my junior career winning the prestigious U.S. Open Junior Championships in 1987. I was not only the number-one ranked American junior, but also one of the top players in the world. I could have turned pro then, but my parents stressed the importance of education and encouraged me to attend college instead.

At Stanford University, I worked my way up the lineup to eventually play number one singles and doubles and help lead them to the NCAA national team championship in 1988. I finished my year there as an All American and was awarded the Block S award for the school's most out-standing freshman athlete. I had a great year; in July of 1988 I officially turned pro.

My first summer on the tour was disappointing, and I found myself ranked 865 in the world by the fall of 1988. I would have to start at the bottom and work my way up. Six months later I pushed my ranking up to 125, a level where I could get directly in the main tour events.

By the spring of 1990, I won my first ATP Tour title at the U.S. Clay Courts in South Carolina. I also made it to the men's singles quarterfinals at the U.S. Open. The most memorable moment in my career came on the grass courts of Wimbledon in 1991. After negotiating my way through difficult early round matches, I took on Andre Agassi in an epic five-set match in the quarterfinals on Centre Court. I fought back from being down two sets to one to achieve a five-set victory. But I was edged out by Boris Becker in the singles semi-final.

My dream year concluded as I beat Michael Chang in the final at the Grand Slam Cup in Munich. In Germany I experienced an overdose of fame, fortune, and success. I had just pocketed the largest prize money in tennis history—two million dollars—and my success was being broadcast all over the world—pretty heady stuff for a 22-year-old kid from Minnesota.

But 15 minutes after the trophy was awarded, all 12,000 fans filed right out of the stadium. I vividly remember experiencing an incredible letdown and thinking how quickly it had all come to an end. I'd spent my whole life practicing tennis and had worked so hard to reach this level of accomplishment. For the first time in my life, the brevity of earthly success hit me hard.

That victory in 1991 changed my life. But I didn't become a happier person as a result of my big win; it was just the opposite. I may have appeared outwardly successful, but I was inwardly conflicted. Deep down, I was unhappy and unsettled.

I was raised in a close-knit Christian family and was clearly taught the Bible and Christian values by my parents. I made a profession of faith when I was five years old in a very simple way. But when I got into my teens and early 20s, I definitely got away from that profession. I may have thought I was a Christian, but my life didn't line up with the way I was raised.

I wouldn't say I was the worst kid around, but no matter where I was on the scale of extremes, I was not living the Christian life. If you would have seen me outwardly, you'd have thought I was a good kid. But inwardly, I was not living the life God would intend for a believer. And that's because my heart wasn't right. I believed in Christ, but that was it.

I felt like I was missing out on what the world had to offer once I got into high school and college. I thought the temptations of the world looked more fun. You've heard that the Gospel is the "good news," right? Well, that implies that there's some bad news as well. And the bad news is that we're all sinners and separated from God until we come to that point of humbling ourselves and repenting. I found myself at that point when I was 24.

In 1993, my parents encouraged me to go to a Christian seminar called the Institute in Basic Life Principles. In the seminar they explained God's way of life, comparing how we live to the Ten Commandments. It brought out things like self-acceptance of God's design for us, being under authority, and being morally pure. These were definitely not the characteristics of my life. The seminar showed me that I might think I was a Christian, but I wasn't living like one. It confirmed and finalized in my own mind, something I'd been thinking about for some time. I knew I was sinner, but I was rationalizing my behavior. I had alienated myself from God through my sin. I was dishonoring my parents, and I was in the wrong kind of dating relationships. Most importantly, my motivations for why I was living were totally self-directed, rather than God-directed.

The teachings in that seminar convicted me and brought me to the end of myself by the end of 1993. I decided to stay home from the Australian Open due to a minor injury. I probably could have played, but I couldn't go on anymore with the inward conflict I was feeling. I was home for two months and during that time I went through the workbook from the seminar and starting reading, studying, and memorizing key passages from the Bible every day. Those two months were a huge period of spiritual transformation. God changed my heart, and I repented of my sins with a purpose to go a new direction. For the first time, I really understood what it meant to trust in Christ as my Savior and follow Him as Lord. I had been a professing Christian, but not a possessor of the faith. He needed to be in control.

It wasn't like life got easy, or that all of a sudden I was this sinless guy. There was plenty of temptation to go back. I was just trying to put one more day between my new life and my old life.

The difference in my life was like a 180-degree turn. Suddenly, I started having victory over some of the previous sinful tendencies in my life. When you become a "possessor" of a saving faith, you learn to draw on the Holy Spirit's prompting and power to give you that victory. God helped to change me in so many ways. My perspective on my career changed; instead of playing tennis for personal reasons, I started seeing it as an ability that God had given me. And along with that gift came a responsibility to compete for His honor and glory and not my own. My relationship with my parents also improved, and I began to honor them and take their counsel on things in my life. When I listened, a lot of things got much, much better for me. I was also able to get away from a dating relationship that wasn't right before God. Before Christ, that had been too difficult to overcome.

But one of the biggest changes was that I developed a strong desire to read the Word of God. It really came alive! Before my transformation, the

Bible didn't mean anything to me. Now His Word renewed my mind. Overall, I wanted to do what was right. I wanted to be able to put my head on my pillow at night knowing I was in a right relationship with the God of this universe. I wanted a clear conscience.

How do you know He's real? Look around you. When you look at the universe and consider the way things are designed, built, and ordered, that's great evidence of God. It's astounding—the universe is so gigantic, and yet only in this thin little realm of the earth is there intelligent life. It seems to me that it takes much more faith to believe there is no God than to believe there is.

Evolution and the big bang theory contradict many of the scientific laws too. Something can't come from nothing; that's a scientific law. Things don't tend toward order; they tend toward disorder. That's another scientific law. If we really did evolve from amoeba, there should be all these millions and millions of in-between fossil species, and we don't see that. I see very unconvincing evidence for those theories and much more convincing evidence for creation. The Bible says in Genesis 1:1, "In the beginning God created the heavens and the earth."

Yet personally, the evidence of my transformed life is the biggest reason I know He's real. Christ transformed my life from one that was susceptible to sin, and gave me the ability to overcome temptation and sin. When you focus too much on yourself, you're never satisfied. You're only truly satisfied when you serve God and others. Ephesians 2:1 perfectly describes the before and after picture of my life, "And you He made alive, who were dead in trespasses and sins." He has made me alive.

Being a committed believer in Jesus Christ has given me the most important thing in life—something fame, fortune, success, and the pleasures of sin could never offer—a sense of joy and contentment which comes from being in a right relationship with the God of this universe. And that is truly priceless.

GOD'S ROAD MAP

The Holy Bible is a guide to help you live a happy and satisfying life. To learn more about the concepts presented in the chapter you've just read, take a look at these passages:

SELF-RELIANCE

The life of a Christian requires dependence upon God. We live in a very "me" oriented culture, based on personal strength and achievement. But to be truly successful in the eyes of the Lord, we must lean on Him for everything. Not only should we rely on God, but also on other believers, our brothers and sisters in Christ.

Second Corinthians 1:8-10

We do not want you to be uninformed, brothers, about the hardships we suffered in the province of Asia. We were under great pressure, far beyond our ability to endure, so that we despaired even of life. Indeed, in our hearts we felt the sentence of death. But this happened that we might not rely on ourselves but on God, who raises the dead. He has delivered us from such a deadly peril, and He will deliver us. On Him we have set our hope that He will continue to deliver us

Psalm 10:2-6

In his arrogance the wicked man hunts down the weak, who are caught in the schemes he devises. He boasts of the cravings of his heart; he blesses the greedy and reviles the Lord.

In his pride the wicked does not seek Him; in all his thoughts there is no room for God. His ways are always prosperous; he is haughty and Your laws are far from him; he sneers at all his enemies. He says to himself, "Nothing will shake me; I'll always be happy and never have trouble."

OBEDIENCE

Nobody likes being bossed around. It begins as children when we say things like, "You're not the boss of me!" Yet our daily lives revolve around submitting to authority—to our spouse, our parents, our boss, and our government. As we submit our will to the Lord, He won't always make sense. But remember that through obedience comes a tremendous sense of peace.

Jeremiah 7:23

But I gave them this command: Obey Me, and I will be your God and you will be My people. Walk in all the ways I command you, that it may go well with you.

Ephesians 6:1-3

Children, obey your parents in the Lord, for this is right. "Honor your father and mother"—which is the first commandment with a promise—"that it may go well with you and that you may enjoy long life on the earth."

Jacklyn Zeman

Actress, Daytime Drama,
"General Hospital"
(photo credit: Charles William Bush)

Jackie Zeman is one of the most recognized and well-liked actresses on television today. Well-known to die-hard soap opera fans as nurse Bobbie Spencer, on ABC's daytime drama, "General Hospital," Zeman is now in her 29th season, with more than 4,000 episodes to her credit.

Zeman graduated from high school in New Jersey at age 15 and went off to study dance on a scholarship at New York University. She did numerous television commercials before landing her first daytime TV role on "One Life to Life."

Zeman has guest starred on several series including "Chicago Hope," "Mike Hammer," and "Love, American Style." She has been a frequent guest on talk and game shows including: "Good Morning America," "Oprah," "Live With Regis and Kathie Lee," "Donahue," "Hollywood Squares," and "Wheel of Fortune." Her achievements have included four Daytime Emmy nominations, a Soap Opera Digest Award, and the Hollywood International Favorite Actress Award.

Honored to share her time and resources with others, Zeman is a devoted philanthropist. She is a board member of the Leukemia Society and received their Charlotte M. Meyers Volunteer Recognition Award. As a spokesperson for the American Heart Association, Zeman received the Les Etoiles de Coeur Award. In June 2000, Zeman received the Gabriel Project's Distinguished Achievement Award for her continued support of children in need of life-saving heart surgery. Find out more about this charity at www.thegabrielproject.com.

I'm grateful to still be working in television on a fabulous show after all these years. It's truly amazing to me. God brings us opportunities all the time, and we can choose to hear Him and follow, or choose to say "no" and go the other way. Most of my life I've decided to listen, and it's been an incredible journey.

I feel really blessed, because I had a wonderful childhood. We lived in New Jersey in a lovely suburban, middle-class neighborhood. It was me, my mom and dad, my two sisters, a dog, and a cat. My mom didn't work outside the home, and she used to cook and clean and make all of our clothes. Mom and dad were both deacons, and my mom taught Sunday school at the Old South Presbyterian Church. It was a real "Father Knows Best" kind of life.

My mom spent a lot of time behind the wheel driving me to dancing school. And it really paid off. When we were about 13, my friend Phyllis and I opened a dance studio in her basement. Her dad put in a ballet bar, mirrors, and a dance floor; and we taught ballet, jazz, and tap to the kids in the neighborhood. We'd put on shows and get all the kids involved. We had so much fun teaching those kids…and made a lot of money doing it too.

After I graduated high school, I got a scholarship to dance at New York University. My first job as a professional was a TV commercial for Hunts Ketchup. I was dressed as a tomato with just my legs sticking out wearing green tights and tap shoes. In the middle of the floor was a big bottle of ketchup and it was my job to tap-dance around it. As a result of doing that commercial, I got my Screen Actors Guild card. I was on my way!

I'd been living in New York City for a while. One weekend, I went home to New Jersey to celebrate my 17th birthday with my family. In the middle of the night, when we were all sound asleep, our beagle, Gretel came running down the hall barking like crazy. When we woke up, the house was totally engulfed in flames. I ran into the bathroom, wet a towel, and threw it over the dog as I ran down the hall to head out of the house. I remember holding her in one arm and grabbing some beloved family photos off the wall with the other, as I ran out the door.

Less than a minute after we all made it safely to the sidewalk, the house exploded and blew off the roof. The fire department gave our dog a medal for saving our lives. If it were not for Gretel, we all would have passed away in that house. I truly believe that God made sure that we survived by working through our beagle.

I learned early on in life to seek God's guidance when making big decisions and in everyday life. And I've been rewarded by having things fall into place just perfectly. Very early in my career, I was invited to audition for a big movie that was being cast. But when the scenes came out that I would have to do the test for, there was so much bad language that I said there was no way I could do it. My conscience wouldn't let me do it—and my mom and dad wouldn't have liked it either.

So I turned down the audition for the movie, which turned out to be the box office hit, *Saturday Night Fever* starring John Travolta. But I didn't regret the decision not to audition. I don't believe God meant for me to be in that movie.

Following my heart really paid off. The same day that I was supposed to have auditioned for the movie, I got called in to read for a soap opera in New York. The audition took place in the executive producer's office, and the scene was a long, sad monologue where I had to cry. It was going very well, and I burst into tears right on cue when the phone rang on the producer's desk. To my horror, he answered the phone right at that critical moment! I was mortified and embarrassed. I was so young and inexperienced; this was one of the first auditions I'd ever had. Consequently, I thought I must have been so boring that he had to talk on the phone.

When I was done reading, I went out on the street to find a payphone so I could call my agent. I told her, "It didn't go very well. I thought I was doing fine and then the phone rang and he answered it." What my agent said next really surprised me. "Oh, they just called. You got the part! He answered the phone because he already knew that they wanted you; He didn't need to hear anymore." I was floored and so grateful.

The show was "Ryan's Hope." Ironically, two hours later, my agency got a phone call with an offer for me on another show, an ABC show called "One Life to Live." My agent told me I could take whichever one I wanted, but "One Life to Live" would pay more money. I went for the money, of course.

Around this same time, I got called in to audition for a Jergen's Soap commercial. When I walked into the office, the waiting room was full of these tall, thin, gorgeous models who all looked like cover girls. I looked at the casting director and said, "What am I doing here? I don't belong in this room. I don't look like any of these women. They're going to laugh at me!"

In those days, when you auditioned for a commercial, you actually went into a room where all the clients were sitting around a table. There would be between 12-20 men who would watch and then decide who to pick. So, once I saw the models in that waiting room, I figured I was sunk. But the casting director gave me the copy and said, "Jackie, those girls are all really pretty. But they're models and they need an actress—you can get this. It's just 30 seconds of copy. Go into the ladies' room and don't come out until you have it memorized. They're going to look at those girls, but they won't have the copy down; they'll be reading it."

So I went into the bathroom and learned the copy. I practiced a few times in front of the mirror and then walked into the conference room. I hopped up on the table and sat there like I was sitting in a bathtub and delivered my lines. And you know what? I got that job. As it turned out, I only got paid scale for that commercial, which was about $200. But there were residuals when the commercial ran... and that Jergen's commercial ran for two years. I made $25,000 the first year alone for just one day's work.

So all of a sudden, I was a working actress. I had my ketchup commercial, my Jergen's soap commercial, and two offers from soap operas in the same day. I felt like my life was soaring; I was just so happy and so lucky. But it wasn't luck. By asking for guidance and being open to what God wanted for me, I was following the path He laid out for me. I guess turning down the audition for *Saturday Night Fever* wasn't such a bad idea after all.

When I first started on "One Life to Live," the producer called me into her office and said, "I'm not really supposed to tell actors this, but I want you to know because you're young and this is your first contract. We sign everyone to three-year contracts; that's just what we do. But your part isn't going to last that long; the storyline is going to last only four to six months. When I call you back into this office in three to four months to tell you your time is up, I don't want you to feel like it has anything to do with the quality of your work. It just is what it is. Please keep this under your hat and respect me by not repeating it to anyone." Although the news was disappointing, I thought it was very kind of her to tell me. Nowadays most producers wouldn't do that.

Six months later, she called me back in to the office and said, "Remember when I told you this was only going to last …" My heart was beating really fast. And I was thinking, *She told me it was coming; I'm going to get canned.* But she continued, "Well, it was supposed to last for four to six months. But the response has been so good from the audience and the writers really like what they're seeing on the show. So you're in; we have no plans to kill off your character at this point."

What started off to be a four to six-month opportunity lasted two and one-half years. The day they finally killed off my character on "One Life to Live," I got a phone call from the head of Daytime at ABC Television. She asked me if I would come to California to do a part on "General Hospital." I literally shot the end of my part on "One Life to Live" and the very next day got on a plane and flew out to California to start "General Hospital." And I've been there for 29 years.

I had a really tough year after I moved out to California. I was just 24 years old and all of a sudden several of the people in my life were gravely ill. My father had leukemia, and I was back and forth on a plane to visit him. At the same time, my husband was diagnosed with cancer as was my father-in-law. That year was full of stress for me. I'd gotten a new job, moved across the country, and my father and my father-in-law died. My husband was on chemotherapy and gravely ill. Ultimately, he didn't survive either. My whole world changed in the space of just 12 months.

During that time I was very, very aware of the presence of the Lord in my life. I was clinging to Him, and that's what got me through. I truly believe that we are spirits having a human experience on this earth, and that made it a little easier for me. It's times like this when you have to find your faith; you have no other choice.

I learned something important during this experience of loss. The Lord was there for me when I needed Him...when I needed to know that everything would be okay. I knew I needed Him to guide me and things would get better. As I've gotten older and gained more wisdom, I understand that it's more than just asking God for help when you need Him. When I want to be connected to the Lord and talk to Him, I always try and say "thank you" before I ask for something. It's so natural to say things like, "Oh, please, God, do this" or "Don't let this happen." But I really try to catch myself and be grateful first for what I do have. Because only when we appreciate what we have, are we really in a position to ask that we be given more.

As I was driving home from the studio one evening, I got a call from my good friend, Kac. She told me that they were starting a special program on Wednesday nights at her church on the topic of prosperity. She wanted to know if I would be willing to speak one evening. It's not that I didn't want to do it, but I was thinking, *What qualifies me to speak on prosperity?* I hadn't written a book on it or anything, so I certainly was no expert. But she said, "You've been married for 17 years; you have your girls; you're a working mom; you've got a dog, a cat, and a house. You have the kind of life that a lot of people would like to have. And in the 20 years I've known you, I've never seen you complain. I think people would be interested in hearing how you balance and put that all together."

Before I knew what I was saying, the word "okay" popped right out of my mouth. But I was second-guessing myself right away. After all, what was I going to say for an hour and a half on the topic of prosperity? And this was at a church, so I had to be profound!

That evening, as I sat quietly before the Lord, I prayed, "Okay, Lord, help guide me so that I do a good job when I get up to speak to those people. If I'm meant to do this, I want to deliver something of value to the world. Please help me make it be a productive time."

As I concluded my prayer, He answered me. On the window of the French doors in my bedroom there was a flash of light...it kind of twinkled. It my heart, it was as if a head nodded, but it wasn't a head; it was a round globe of light. It was only there for a moment, then it was gone. In my soul, I knew that God answered me, and I knew my speech was going to be just fine.

I've learned that if you ask the question, you will get the answer if you are truly open to hearing it. When you are having trouble making a decision or are at a crossroads in your life and are confused about which path to take, cry out to God and ask for His guidance. If you ask Him to show you, He will. When you work in synch together with God, it is amazing what you can accomplish.

I'm still learning what being a Christian is all about. I do know that the Lord is always there right beside us; He is ever-present. I think the more aware we are of that, and the more we take advantage of and really embrace that, the more we will be blessed. I've gone through periods when I didn't make time for God. I wasn't doing a Bible study, and I'd strayed from going to church regularly. And my life didn't run as smoothly. When I'm more open to prayer and spending quiet time with the Lord, my heart is happy and my spirit lifts up. I know I'm a better wife, mother, friend, and business woman in every way. Spending time with God isn't a luxury; it is a necessity.

As I move into the next chapter of my life, I'm beginning to realize how wonderful it is to have an opportunity to give something back to the world. Each day we have a choice—it can be a great day, or a not-so great day. That power of decision is your most valuable asset, because the decisions you make are the life that you will lead. So choose wisely, and let God lead the way.

GOD'S ROAD MAP

The Holy Bible provides a road map to help you live a happy and satisfying life. To learn more about concepts presented in the chapter you've just read, read these passages:

GUIDANCE

Life is a series of opportunities—both taken and missed. As we become more and more in tune with the will of God, the opportunities He places before us become more recognizable. God will guide us, but we must first invite Him to be with us—and in control.

Psalm 32:8

> *I will instruct you and teach you in the way you should go; I will counsel you and watch over you.*

Proverbs 3:6

> *In all your ways acknowledge Him, and He will make your paths straight.*

Jeremiah 29:11

> *"For I know the plans I have for you," declares the Lord, "plans to prosper you and not to harm you, plans to give you hope and a future."*

ATTITUDE

You have a choice each morning. You can decide that it is going to be a good day or a not-so good day. Life's a lot more rewarding when you keep a positive attitude.

Proverbs 15:13,15

> *A happy heart makes the face cheerful, but heartache crushes the spirit....All the days of the oppressed are wretched, but the cheerful heart has a continual feast.*

Philippians 2:5

Your attitude should be the same as that of Christ Jesus.

Ephesians 5:15-17

Be very careful, then, how you live—not as unwise but as wise, making the most of every opportunity, because the days are evil. Therefore do not be foolish, but understand what the Lord's will is.

Zoro

R&B Drummer with Lenny Kravitz,
Bobby Brown, and Frankie Valli

Legendary drummer, Zoro, has toured and recorded with such prominent artists as Lenny Kravitz, Bobby Brown, Frankie Valli and the Four Seasons, The New Edition, Jody Watley, Sean Lennon, and Lisa Marie Presley. He has been voted "#1 R&B Drummer" in the *Modern Drummer Magazine* readers' poll four times. He has also received "Best Funk Drummer" honors in *Drum! And Rhythm* magazine in the United Kingdom.

Zoro's best-selling book, video and DVD series, *The Commandments of R&B Drumming: A Comprehensive Guide to Soul, Funk & Hip Hop* were awarded the "#1 Best Educational Products Title" in the *Modern Drummer & Rhythm Magazine* readers' polls. You can see his latest performance on a double DVD called, *The Modern Drummer Festival–2005 (Hudson Music/Modern Drummer Magazine)*.

Dubbed "The Communicator," Zoro inspires and entertains audiences around the world as a player, educator, motivator, and Christian speaker. He also speaks at churches on the strategies and biblical principles needed for success and godly living. To find out more, visit www.zorothedrummer.com.

I grew up in an environment of poverty and hardship. Still, I look back at my childhood with fond memories because I had a wonderful mother who loved me and taught me about the Lord. And for that I will be eternally grateful.

There were seven kids in my family, and our mother raised us all by herself. She was from Mexico City originally, so we didn't have any extended family—no grandparents, uncles, or aunts. They were all still in Mexico. She was all alone taking care of us.

We were very poor. My mother had some significant health issues, including debilitating arthritis, which made it impossible for her to hold down a job. Consequently, we were a welfare family, getting food stamps and barely getting by. And we were always moving. We moved about 30 times by the time I was in the fourth grade. Sometimes those moves would just be a mile or two down the street to a different home. In those days, there was a limit on how many kids could live in an apartment. My mother would have to lie and say there were only four or five of us so that the landlord would rent to us. But eventually, we'd be found out and have to find a new place.

I can still keenly remember those moving days. Because it wasn't far enough to use a U-Haul truck (we couldn't have afforded it anyway), we had to move things by hand. My youngest brother, Robert, and I would physically move things like beds and dressers on our little red Radio Flyer wagon. We had a lot of hardship and heartache in our lives, but there was always a sense of adventure with our mother.

To me, growing up without a father was a difficult thing. I had always wished I had a dad—always wished for that special male figure to mentor me. But just having a father isn't the answer. Having a great one would have been the answer. I actually met my father for the first time when I was 18. I understood then, that if my true father had been in my life, I would have turned out to be a completely different guy. As it was, I had only my mother's influence, which was one of total love and passion. She had a tenderness about her that I now give to my own children. If my father had been in the mix, it would have changed that...he didn't have those tools. God protected me—something meant to be bad really turned out to be a blessing. A father was the very thing I was looking for but never found. But the Lord showed me that I was to become that which I was looking for—someone to mentor and motivate others.

I received the Lord as a young boy of eight or nine at one of those vacation Bible school church camps. I remember walking up to the altar crying while they were singing a song called, "Lamb of God." That was the beginning of a journey.

My love for music started in childhood. We didn't have much money, but my mother always had albums. She'd play her music and dance and sing with me. I used to put two Folger's coffee cans together and just bang them with my hands like I was banging on the drums. The gift of rhythm was in me from the beginning. Then one Christmas my mother bought me a Mickey Mouse drum set out of the Sears catalog. But the drum skins were made of paper, so it lasted all of Christmas Day before I destroyed it. That was that.

In 1977 Elvis died. I was a big fan as a kid, and for some reason his death was like a spark for me; all of a sudden I wanted to play music. I tried playing the guitar; I tried singing but those weren't my natural gifts. Eventually, I got around to the drums. When I was 16, I bought a used set from a kid at school for $80. From the second I picked up the sticks I knew that's what I wanted to do. I began diligently studying, practicing, and dreaming. In order to join bands and start making some money with my music, I needed a new drum set and a set of wheels. After school I worked as a janitor at the high school. That was a very humbling experience. As soon as the bell would ring at the end of the day, my classmates could see me vacuuming the library. They'd make fun of me, but I was doing it for the money. That summer I worked two jobs, a total of 16 hours a day, so that I could save up enough money. For eight hours I worked as a cook/cleaner at a whitewater rafting business. Then in the evening I worked another eight hours as a janitor and groundskeeper at a community college.

I was busting my behind, but at the end of the summer my goals were achieved. I had my new car and my new set of drums and I was able to join local bands and develop as a young player. I also joined all the school bands—the stage band, the jazz band, and the marching band.

Two years later I graduated from high school and moved down to Los Angeles with a family band that was trying to score a gig at Disneyland. The band never went anywhere, but because of them I did end up in LA, the music capital. I know now that God was directing my path to where there was more opportunity. Had I not hooked up with the Robell Brothers, I don't know how I would have ever gotten out of Oregon.

I had the good fortune of having a sister who lived in Beverly Hills. It was even more fortunate that she was a model and spent more time traveling the world for photo shoots than she did at her place. But since she was paying rent anyway, she asked me if I wanted to move in.

I was only 17 or 18 and was starved to meet other musicians my own age. Even though I had already graduated high school, I started hanging out at Beverly Hills High to see if I could meet some new people. I had a plan...I dressed up real slick, took a huge boom box, a pair of drumsticks, and a practice pad, and sat out on the lawn playing along with the music...just waiting for somebody to come up and talk to me.

That's how I met Lenny Kravitz. He was going to school there and came up to me one day. I met him and a few other musicians, including Kenny Gordy, the son of Berry Gordy, the founder of Motown Records— my favorite record label. Some of the people I met at Beverly Hills High have proved to be lifelong friends.

When I moved down to LA at 17 my heart started on fire for God. I started tuning into some church programming and really liked the way this old guy was talking. Soon I was sending away for his books and really got into them. Around that time there was a big event called "Jesus at the Roxy." It was a Christian concert with several great soul and R&B artists headlining it. One of the groups was Earth, Wind and Fire, which was my all-time favorite group. I went to the concert with the intention of meeting them to further my music career. And I wasn't disappointed. I met Philip Bailey, the lead singer, and Ralph Johnson the drummer.

I spent quite a bit of time talking with Ralph. When I told him about the TV evangelist I was into, he told me that it was a cult. I remember being so discouraged after I heard that. I was trying with all my heart to find the truth and I was lead astray by this guy. The whole experience got me offtrack spiritually. Instead I focused on the drums.

In 1983 I got a break. Philip Bailey needed a drummer to substitute for Ralph. For me, it was a dream come true. There I was, this young kid playing with all these experienced pros. It gave me so much confidence.

After that, Lenny set up an audition for me with a band called The New Edition. Before the final stage of the audition, I sat in my car and prayed, "Lord, if this is Your will, then give me Your favor to get this gig. Let me go in there and play with the confidence and the zeal that You know I have in me. If it's not Your will, then close the door down. "

I got the job, and that put me on the big stage in a worldwide tour. It was an incredible experience. From there I joined Bobby Brown and toured with him in his heyday—the "My Prerogative" era. While this was happening to me, Lenny's career was just starting. I joined him on his first two albums and tours, Let Love Rule and Mama Said (1989-1992).

But let's go back for a moment. During the Bobby Brown days, I got married. He was even the best man at our wedding. I was 26, and my wife was only 19. God was still in my heart at this time, but He wasn't in charge. If He had been, I never would have married this person; I would have at least consulted God first.

I was still seeking God though and along came Mrs. Affifi, the most incredible Christian woman. Her son, Osama, was a very close friend of mine from the Beverly Hills High days. Every time I went over to his house his mother would ask me, "When are you going to get right with the Lord? When are you going to go to church?"

Well, a couple of years into my marriage I was at Mrs. Affifi's house and she was still asking those questions. When some of her friends dropped by, we started talking and I shared some things that were going on in my life. They all ended up praying for me. It was such a powerful moment; I had never experienced anything like this before. It was probably the biggest spiritual turning point in my life. I didn't leave Mrs. Affifi's house for a week, and I went home a changed man. I made a commitment from that point on to pursue the Lord with all my heart.

My wife wasn't too excited about my commitment, and we started to grow apart. I got a job with a French superstar named Vanessa Paradis (now married to Johnny Depp) and was on tour with her in Europe for about six months. When I came back from the tour, my wife told me that she was having an affair and wanted to be separated. It rocked my world.

Looking back, I can see we didn't have a very healthy relationship, but I didn't really know any better. My mother had never had a husband the whole time I was growing up so I didn't know what a good marriage was supposed to look like. I tried to reconcile. I was willing to forgive and start all over again, but she was unwilling and wanted a divorce. My heart was completely, absolutely, 100-percent broken.

During the time I'd been on tour I was sending money home. I believed strongly in tithing 10 percent of our earnings to the church, and together we'd made a commitment to doing that. But when I got home from France, I looked in the checking account and asked if she'd been doing the tithing. "No, I blew all that stuff off. Who cares?" I remember getting very upset.

After doing the math, I found out that the amount of money that was left in the bank was almost exactly what I owed for my tithe. I made a cold, hard, calculated decision to tithe the money anyway. That left me with practically nothing to operate on and no promise of any future gig in sight. I was really in dire straights.

We had a house together in Seattle and a small, modular home in Los Angeles. I told her to take the house in Seattle and I'd take the place in LA because that's where I rehearsed and was closer to the action. Not long after we broke up, there was a big earthquake in LA. My place was devastated and I lost everything. I literally had to move in with a little old lady from Pasadena. There I was, going from these hot gigs, being on MTV and thinking I had everything going on, to renting a room from a 90-year-old lady from my church. I was broke; I even had a yard sale and sold my lawn mower, my stage clothes, everything that was of any value.

I still owned the house after the earthquake and I didn't know how I was going to make the payments. I knew I was going to lose my house and my credit. But my landlord, Lorraine, said, "In the name of Jesus, you are not going to lose your house and you're not going to lose your credit. God is going to make a way."

And He did. It turns out the insurance adjuster was a Christian and the company paid my claim. I wasn't expecting anything at all, but God blessed me and I got everything back. When the money came in, I paid all the back payments and saved the place. And after the repairs were completed, the house was actually nicer than it had been before. I believe that God blessed me because I honored my commitment to tithe. Proverbs 3:9-10 says, "Honor the Lord with your wealth and with the best part of everything your land produces. Then He will fill your barns with grain, and your vats will overflow with the finest wine."

Just when I needed it most, God blessed me with an audition for Jodi Watley who was really big at the time. The problem was that I hadn't even been practicing; I wasn't in shape musically because I was so depressed. But somehow I found the strength to go to the audition. Again I prayed, "Lord, if it's Your will, please give me favor to get this job. If not, close the door down." I did get the job and that sparked my hope and confidence. When I got in my car afterward, I cried tears of joy. God was so faithful; He never let me down. I was right down to the wire again and He came through.

After the gig with Jody Watley, I found myself working for Frankie Valli and the Four Seasons. We often played in Las Vegas, and one day, God made a divine appointment for me with an unlikely character named Frank Dimatto. Little did I know that Frank was about to change my life forever.

I was at a watch outlet store outside of town shopping for a sports watch. When I walked into the store, I saw this big, buff guy with long hair—the biker type. He had earrings in both ears, and he really looked like a mean pirate. For some reason I caught his eye as I walked in the door and we got to talking. He was really into working out and was a fired-up Christian. We made a connection right away. I'd never met anybody like this cat. He was the first guy who made faith real to me. My whole life I'd gone to church and I believed I had faith, but I'd never seen this kind of faith operate. I was at the end of my rope, and he was like my lifeline. He started powering me up, started filling me with the spirit and praying for me.

By this time I was divorced and I'd made a deal with God to not sleep with anybody until the day I got married. And this time, I was going to let Him select the wife. I'd done it once my way and it blew up in my face. I told Frank my story and what I'd been through and one night he asked me, "So, you want to get married, dude? Because when Frank Dimatto prays, people get married. Everybody I've ever prayed for who wanted to be married was married within a year." I didn't even know anybody to marry, so I thought, *Why not?*

Frank had a friend named Dennis Tinerino, who was Mr. Universe at one time. Dennis and his wife, Anita, were going to this little church in North Hills, California called Overcomers. About a week after I'd met the Tinerino's and told them my story, Anita was in church and the pastor was talking about celibacy. Anita was sitting behind a girl named Renee who happened to be the pastor's daughter. Renee was 28 and single and had been waiting on the Lord for a husband for almost eight years.

After the service Anita called me up and said, "Zoro, I found your wife." Anita played cupid and set us up on a date. Now, I'd been on blind dates before that had been pretty awkward, but when Renee answered the door there was a connection between us right away. Anita, Renee, and I went to church together that night and then a few days later Renee and I went on another date—this time alone.

The next weekend I went to her church and during the service I looked over at Renee and I just felt the Lord saying, "This is who I have for you." It was crazy—I'd only known her for a week! I met her mom and dad that day and two weeks later I asked Renee to marry me. I found out later that Renee had told her friend about me after we'd first met. She said I was the man she was going to marry. So her parents met me only once, and there I was asking for her hand in marriage. But they felt totally at peace about me; they felt like I was the man God brought for her. Within four months to the day of us meeting, we were married. Remember Frank Demotte telling me that when he prayed for anyone to be married, they were married within a year? Well, you can add me to that list! After 11 years of marriage, Renee and I recently renewed our vows. We have two beautiful children, Jarod (7) and Jordan (4).

Since the time I married Renee, everything I have laid my hands to has prospered—my walk with God, my profile, my career, my finances, and my ministry. God honored two of the right choices I made—not that I didn't make a lot of wrong ones along the way, or that I was perfect. But I did make two commitments. One was to stay celibate until my wedding night. Both of us honored that. The other commitment was that I wrote that tithe check and continued to tithe.

I'm still reaping the rewards of those two decisions. And it's only getting better and better. In the fall of 2003 I had a dream about Lenny Kravitz. It was a very vivid dream where we were back together again on stage, just like the old days. We were young and having a great time. It was especially weird because Lenny and I had been busy doing our own thing, and I hadn't heard from him at all in over four years.

The next day he called. Yeah—out of the blue I had a dream about him and the next day he called. I told him about the dream and he got goose bumps, "That's crazy, Z. Last night was the first time I ever opened your instructional drum videos in the four years since you gave them to me. I was watching your videos while you were having the dream about me." Obviously, God connected us again.

In December I told my wife that I felt like something was around the corner. I didn't know what it was, but I felt like God was going to bring me something great. A couple of weeks later Lenny called and asked me to join his band again.

The year 2004 was an incredible year. We played on a gazillion television shows; we played a concert for over 100,000 people in Hyde Park in London; and Lenny and I were on the covers of loads of magazines. We even played at the opening night of Monday Night Football! It was the best year of my life.

Many people talk about the Lord and know a lot about the Bible, but there aren't too many people that fully believe Him and trust in Him. But I'm learning to. Too many of us trust Him with only certain things...but not the big ones. Instead we like to carry the weight on our own shoulders. Well, I'm learning to go to sleep at night without a single worry or concern. I just give it all back to Him and leave it at the throne. I've seen the power of God move in my life...and it is moving rapidly!

God brought me through an underprivileged childhood and helped me accomplish some pretty amazing things through His faithfulness. I always felt rejected because I didn't have a father. But after 43 years, God has healed my broken heart. I thought I needed to earn God's love, but I know there's nothing I need to do for Him to love me unconditionally. That's what grace is all about.

I may have grown up without an earthly father, but I'll always have a heavenly Father to show me the way.

GOD'S ROAD MAP

The Holy Bible is a guide to help you live a happy and satisfying life. To learn more about the concepts presented in the chapter you've just read, take a look at these passages:

GIVING

Everything we have comes from God. We may earn it, but ultimately He's the one who gave us our jobs in the first place. We are merely stewards of His property, and to give some of it back to further His Kingdom and help those less fortunate should not be a hardship; it should be an honor. God particularly blesses those who tithe at least 10 percent of their earnings.

Malachi 3:10

"Bring the whole tithe into the storehouse, that there may be food in My house. Test Me in this," says the Lord Almighty, "and see if I will not throw open the floodgates of heaven and pour out so much blessing that you will not have room enough for it."

First Chronicles 29:14

But who am I, and who are my people, that we should be able to give as generously as this? Everything comes from You, and we have given You only what comes from Your hand.

Second Corinthians 9:7

Each man should give what he has decided in his heart to give, not reluctantly or under compulsion, for God loves a cheerful giver.

EMOTIONAL HEALING

It's a complicated world full of pain and brokenness. Zoro felt the sting of poverty and the bitterness of growing up without a father. But through his faith in Christ, he was able to overcome his trials and be fully healed.

Psalm 147:3

He heals the brokenhearted and binds up their wounds.

Isaiah 40:31

But those who hope in the Lord will renew their strength. They will soar on wings like eagles; they will run and not grow weary, they will walk and not be faint.

Second Corinthians 1:3-4

Praise be to the God and Father of our Lord Jesus Christ, the Father of compassion and the God of all comfort, who comforts us in all our troubles, so that we can comfort those in any trouble with the comfort we ourselves have received from God.

Epilogue

You've just read all kinds of reasons why Jesus Christ is real. Maybe you're thinking a little bit about your own salvation and life situation. What most of these stories have in common is that these miracles and wonderful things happened *after* the subjects submitted their lives to Jesus. His impact on their lives is unmistakable.

The best way to know He's real is to find out for yourself. Just over ten years ago, I gave my life to the Lord. In my wildest dreams I couldn't have imagined what He had in store for me. Perhaps this is the perfect moment for your rebirth as well. Whether you are already a follower of Christ or have just met Him for the first time, you can be assured of where you will spend eternity. If you don't know Him, understand that Jesus has been waiting for you your whole life, standing patiently right beside you. The Holy Spirit might be knocking on your door right now— go ahead and open it.

Today you have an opportunity to secure your salvation and know the peace of having Christ in your life. All you need to do is say this simple prayer and allow Jesus Christ to move into the driver's seat.

Heavenly Father,

I come to You asking for the forgiveness of my sins, sins that have separated me from You. I believe that Jesus is Your Son, and that He died on the cross at Calvary, was resurrected, and is alive again so I might be forgiven and have eternal life with You in Heaven. I ask You right now to come into my life and be my personal Lord and Savior from this day forward. Because of the promises in Your Word, I am a new creation, born again and cleansed by the blood of Jesus Christ. In the holy name of Jesus I pray, Amen.

If you have said this prayer for the first time, share your decision with a trusted Christian friend or pastor, or send me an email. I'd love to hear from you—amy@hesreal.com.

If you have a story of how God has been real in your life, you can submit it at www.hesreal.com for possible inclusion in a future edition of *How Do You Know He's Real?*.

Additional copies of this book and other
book titles from DESTINY IMAGE are
available at your local bookstore.

Call toll free: 1-800-722-6774.

Send a request for a catalog to:

Destiny Image₍ᵣ₎ Publishers, Inc.
P.O. Box 310
Shippensburg, PA 17257-0310

"Speaking to the Purposes of God for This
Generation and for the Generations to Come"

For a complete list of our titles,
visit us at www.destinyimage.com